THE "IT" GIRLS

Also by Meredith Etherington-Smith

JEAN PATOU

THE "IT" GIRLS

Lucy, Lady Duff Gordon, the Couturière "Lucile,"
and Elinor Glyn, Romantic Novelist

Meredith Etherington-Smith
and
Jeremy Pilcher

HARCOURT BRACE JOVANOVICH, PUBLISHERS
San Diego   New York   London

Copyright © 1986 by Meredith Etherington-Smith and
Jeremy Pilcher

Library of Congress Cataloging-in-Publication Data
Etherington-Smith, Meredith.
    The "it" girls.
    Bibliography: p.
    Includes index.
    1. Duff Gordon, Lucy, Lady. 2. Glyn, Elinor,
1864-1943. 3. Sisters—Great Britain—Biography.
4. Women—Great Britain—Biography. 5. Great Britain—
Biography.   I. Pilcher, Jeremy.   II. Title.
CT3320.E83 1986   823'.912'09 [B]   86-33511
ISBN 0-15-145774-3

Printed in the United States of America

First United States edition

A B C D E

For Diana and Maria

CONTENTS

List of Illustrations

Acknowledgements

Our thanks must, above all, go to Christopher Davson, Elinor Glyn's grandson. Without his help, and that of his wife Kate, this book would never have been written. His interest in, and his sympathy with, his grandmother, his patience in the face of a barrage of questions, and his generosity in letting us have the results of his own meticulous research into his grandmother's life were of inestimable help in building up this portrait of her. We owe a debt of gratitude to Sir Anthony Glyn too, for access to *Romantic Adventure*, his excellent biography of his grandmother which was the foundation on which much of our research rests. Our thanks also to Elspeth Chowdary Best, Elinor's granddaughter and literary executor, for her help and in particular for letting us use Lord Milner's letters to Elinor. Guy L. Saunders generously provided valuable information and photographs on the early years in Canada and on family background.

On Lucy's side, our thanks and grateful appreciation to her grandson, the Earl of Halsbury, for all his help and encouragement and to Lady Flavia Anderson for her reminiscences of her grandmother's later years. Sir Islay Campbell was kind enough to unravel the Saunders and Sutherland family trees. We are also extremely grateful to Lady Campbell, Lucy's great-granddaughter, for her enthusiasm and help, and in particular for permission to use some of the exquisite fashion watercolours from her grandmother's record-book. To Lady Caroline Blois, another of Lucy's great-granddaughters, our thanks for encouraging us in the first instance, and for her help in introducing us to the It Girls' descendants.

Many other people have given us their time, help and encouragement and we would particularly like to thank Jane, Lady Abdy, Susan Mayor of Christie's, Valerie Mendes of the Victoria and Albert Museum, Nicholas Mosley, Lady Alexandra Metcalfe, Paul Tanqueray, Hugo Vickers and Rosie Wynne Finch.

Our research assistant, Julian Bremner-Leitao, deserves plaudits for her enthusiasm and curiosity. Our thanks also to Gillon Aitken and to our editor, Penelope Hoare, for her encouragement and her editorial pencil.

We thank Elinor's publishers, Gerald Duckworth & Co, for their kind permission to quote from Elinor's novels and essays, and from Dorothy Parker's *Constant Reader* for which, in each case, they hold the copyright. Permission to quote from Elinor Glyn's letters to R. D. Blumenfeld, to Harpers Magazine and to Thomas Waldo Story kindly given by the Harry Ransom Humanities Research Center, the University of Texas at Austin. *My Autobiography* by Charles Chaplin quoted by permission of The Bodley Head. *Nancy Cunard* by Anne Chisholm quoted by permission of Sidgwick & Jackson. *Silver and Gold* by Norman Hartnell quoted by permission of Bell & Hyman. *Edwardians in Love* by Anita Leslie quoted by permission of Century Hutchinson Ltd. *Studies in Sublime Failure* by Shane Leslie quoted by permission of Ernest Benn. Quotations from *A Girl Like I* by Anita Loos are copyright 1966 by Anita Loos and are quoted by permission from The Anita Loos Trusts, The Viking Press Inc. and Hamish Hamilton. *Swanson on Swanson* by Gloria Swanson quoted by permission of Michael Joseph. The extract from *Traffics and Discoveries* by Rudyard Kipling quoted by permission of The National Trust and Macmillan London Ltd. An extract from his column in *The Times* quoted by permission of Bernard Levin. All extracts from *Vogue* quoted by kind permission of Condé Nast, all of which extracts are copyright Condé Nast.

Foreword

'Elinor Glyn? Isn't there something about sinning on a tiger-skin? Didn't she write a scandalous novel?' Of such half-remembered fragments are legends born.

The purpose of this biography is to reveal the truth behind Elinor Glyn's self-constructed legend and to contrast it – as she was contrasted in life – with the less durable reputation of her equally formidable sister Lucy Lady Duff Gordon, better known as the couturière Lucile. Legends endure, but reputations are more fragile and 'Lucile' has been largely forgotten by fashion historians.

Both women were remarkable. Typical children of mid-Victorian middle class notions of 'polite' up-bringing, they were repressed and lonely when young. But through circumstance and force of personality, they were unwittingly instrumental in announcing a more liberated age for women. Elinor wrote about female sensuality, illicit passion and a relationship between an older, dominant woman and a younger, dominated man. Her sister gave these attitudes outward form in the shape of feathery trailing chiffon tea-dresses, worn sans corset over rose-pink chiffon underwear.

They came into their own in the extravagant hey-day of Edwardian England, a period which prized maturity and savoir-faire in a woman, and they were typical of the age in their over-heated excessiveness and in their extravagance. They dealt in mystery; in love-letters; in emeralds worn with clouds of purple chiffon; in secret passion. Silk roses festooned their drawing rooms and boudoirs, which were among the first to be decorated in a manner inspired by the last years of the eighteenth century. They surrounded themselves with sensation: the smell of gardenias and tuberoses; the adoration of young men; the romance of escaping to foreign lands.

To their contemporaries they were fascinating because they embodied an entirely individual sense of heightened reality, whether in the way they dressed, in the way they decorated their surroundings, or in what they said, wrote or designed.

The success they achieved in their chosen metiers would have been outstanding in any age; considering the restrictive mood of the late Victorian age, when they both began their careers, it was little less than miraculous. So was the fact that – though each earned her own living (and supported her husband and children) – they were accepted by society in an era when to be in trade or to write risqué novels was virtually a sentence of social suicide for a 'lady'. That they were both 'ladies' was never questioned by their contemporaries, although their antecedents were far less grand than they persuaded their peers to believe.

These antecedents, and the sisters' escape from them, played a vital part in shaping these very diverse women. So did a shadowy figure who is as much a subject of this biography as Elinor and Lucy – their mother. Had it not been for Mrs. Kennedy's determination and her support of her two daughters, they would never have succeeded as they did. Mrs. Kennedy was the centre of their lives: their prop and their critic, the one person they could never deceive. They were competitive, one with another, and never more so than in the tom-tiddler's game they played to come first in her affections. She never failed them and she inspired them to survive and to triumph over defeat.

Lucy and Elinor were temperamentally so different that they could never really get on with each other. Lucy was the Red Queen, Elinor the White. Lucy loved dramas and arguments. Elinor loved solitude, peace and good manners. Nonetheless their lives were inextricably entwined and have a curious interior relationship.

Lucy's frail cobweb creations are now in museums. Elinor's novels are primarily of interest to students of the early years of the century. But the sisters' sense of adventure and daring, their courage and their wonderful follies, cannot be gainsaid. They were the first of a new self-determined breed of woman who came into her own after the First World War.

PROLOGUE

(1830–1880)

'But so much of life is like a rushing torrent tearing along making a course for itself, without power to choose through what country it will pass, until it meets the ocean and is swallowed up and lost.'

Three Weeks

i *Saunders and Sutherlands*

Lucy and Elinor Sutherland were, though sisters, completely different personalities. Only the qualities of generosity and stubbornness united them. In almost every other respect it was as if they were descended from different stock. Lucy had a fiery temper with a short fuse. She was direct and headstrong from an early age. Elinor was more conventional and always more self-conscious and careful of her dignity. They were both very tenacious in adverse circumstances; but this fortitude was probably derived more from their early up-bringing than from their common ancestry.

Their antecedents go a long way towards explaining the differences between them, inheriting as they did a heterogeneous mixture of English, Irish and Scottish genes, the Irish and Scottish traits predominating. Lucy demonstrated the liveliness, almost impudence, and the slightly feckless charm of her Irish forebears, while Elinor, who once described her sister as 'much more human and gay' than herself, was a battleground of contradictions – romantic with an almost mystic streak of fantasy inherited from her Scottish forebears, with a cynicism and world-weary outlook on life derived from her maternal grandmother's passion for the attitudes of eighteenth century France.

Lucy's and Elinor's father, Douglas Sutherland, was of Scots descent. Born in Nova Scotia in 1838, he had a very distant claim to the extinct Earldom of Duffus. He was extremely proud of his ancestry.

Their mother (confusingly also Elinor by name) was born of almost equally respectable lineage. The Saunders were a pioneering Canadian family, somewhat come down in the world, but remarkable both for their fortitude and their talent for survival under the most primitive of circumstances. They never forgot that the family had originally owned substantial estates in Buckinghamshire.

Their maternal grandfather, Colonel Thomas Saunders, was partly brought up in France. (His father, a discharged bankrupt, ended his days as British Consul in St. Valery sur Somme.) Thomas Saunders married Lucy Anne Willcocks, daughter of Sir Richard Willcocks, J.P. and Police Magistrate of Dublin. Their first daughter was born

in India, their second in France. By 1833 the family had moved to
Guelph, Ontario, Canada.

There they lived a live of pioneering hardship. Thomas Saunders
corresponded with two of his uncles in London, often asking for
financial help. In a letter dated March 1836, two years after their
arrival, he tells them that 'the early part of this winter we were nearly
burnt out of our wigwam. The logs about the chimney caught fire,
and we have been nearly frozen since. . . . You have no idea of the
sufferings of new settlers in this country. No negro in the West Indies
works harder.' Later that same year, he tells his uncles that his crops
were destroyed by frost on the 4th and 5th of August. He must, he
advises them, advertise for a mortgage to buy supplies to last the
winter and get clothes, the usual from St. Valery not having been
received.

The 'usual' from St. Valery was a huge barrel called 'le tonneau
bienvenu' which arrived every year. It contained everything that
Thomas's parents thought their pioneer son and his family might
need: corsets, silk stockings, the latest Paris dresses, even expensive
gloves and wigs.

What supported the Saunders through their early, almost unendur-
able years in Canada was the conviction that they were aristocrats
and that this placed them in a position above their neighbours, at
the same time demanding of them certain standards of behaviour,
however difficult these might be to maintain. Even when they were
working virtually as farm labourers during the day, they changed
into the latest fashions from Paris for dinner every night. They sat,
by the fire in their log cabin, reading improving books. Lucy Saunders
was the stuff of which pioneering women were made. She had lived
through troubles in Ireland when very young and – even though she
slept on a straw bed, made her own candles and soap, and wore
cast-off clothes – she never forgot her gentility. Her greatest grief
was when her last pair of silk stockings went into holes. Appearances
were everything.

Lucy Saunders possessed strength of mind and character, but her
concepts of aristocratic behaviour were, even then, out of date. She
was isolated from European society. The nineteenth century – with
its new democracy and industrialisation and its consequent re-
arranging of class structure – had little meaning for her. In the
backwoods of Canada, she maintained social and moral standards
which derived from life at Versailles in the eighteenth century.

In her rigid behaviour and her worship of the aristocratic ideal,
Lucy Saunders set a pattern of reactions in her granddaughters. Elinor
would always look at life through the distorting mirror of idealised

eighteenth-century attitudes, and Lucy would spend a great deal of time rebelling against them.

By 1840, Colonel Saunders' fortunes had risen. He became Clerk of the Peace for the Wellington District and he built a comfortable house. He and Lucy eventually produced eight daughters and one son. By 1860 they had prospered to the point at which they were able to live on a small country estate, just outside Guelph, called Summer Hill.

Eight sisters ensured a lively social life at Summer Hill; the young men of the neighbourhood were welcomed for picnics, croquet, small dances.

Elinor, the seventh daughter, was sixteen and Douglas Sutherland twenty, when they first met. He had paid a visit to the Saunders' home during one of his first jobs as an engineer on the Grand Trunk railway, then being constructed. It was love at first sight, but they were young and penniless and three years went by during which Douglas was allowed to visit frequently. He entertained Elinor with musical pieces of his own composition. He drew, he painted, and he was a very successful engineer. Elinor was more down-to-earth. 'My mother was the practical one of the family,' Lucy later maintained, 'for she had a shrewd brain and a lot of commonsense locked away in her adorably pretty head.'

Elinor and Douglas married in 1861 and set up home near the Saunders in Guelph. No sooner had she unpacked her trousseau and her wedding presents, than their wooden house caught fire and burnt to the ground. But Douglas was shortly offered an excellent job in America, necessitating a move to New York where, for the first time, Elinor tasted the pleasures of high society to which she believed her birth had entitled her.

The Civil War found the young Sutherlands' sympathies torn between North and South. The energetic Douglas moved to Brazil, where he had obtained a job as second engineer in the construction of a railway into the interior. Elinor went with him – she was not her mother's daughter for nothing. Her most cherished possession, a white silk wedding shawl, was eaten by rats. When she returned from the interior to the Legation in Rio, she found that her sister Fanny had sent her a miniature tissue-paper pattern of the new gored skirts which had just arrived in the 'tonneau bienvenu' from Paris. To Elinor, who was always fascinated by clothes, this was an exciting innovation after the endless yards of crinoline that had, until then, been the fashion.

His contract in Brazil having been successfully concluded, Douglas Sutherland found employment on the building of the Mont Cenis tunnel. He took his wife to London, en route to Italy, and he left her at 64 Albany Street, near Regent's Park, presumably lodgings. It was in London, in St. John's Wood, that Lucy Christiana was born in 1862. She was named after her two grandmothers. Sixteen months later, on October 17, 1864, Elinor was born in Jersey, where Mrs. Sutherland had gone to stay with her aunt who had married a Frenchman.

Barely five months after Elinor's birth, Douglas Sutherland fell ill with typhoid which he had contracted in Turin. Leaving her children in the care of her aunt, Mrs. Sutherland went to Italy to nurse her husband back to health. Finding him to be very ill indeed, and worsening daily, she decided on one last desperate move – to bring him back to London, where there was no language problem, and where she thought she could obtain better medical help.

Travel conditions in the early 1860s were rugged, even for the healthy, and they proved too much for Douglas. He survived the journey only to die, aged just twenty-eight, in the lodgings in Albany Street where they had stayed in happier times. Mrs. Sutherland never again spoke of her terrible rush across Europe in unheated trains, through customs and then on to the steamer, with her young husband dying as she watched him.

Before he died, Douglas laid what the Victorians would have called a sacred charge on his young wife. He 'enjoined her to make every effort to bring up her children in England, and that they should be taught to remember their illustrious Scottish ancestors and never to allow themselves to act unworthily of this noble blood'. This dying request, and its constant repetition, assumed the status of a myth.

Elinor (or Nelly as her family always called her) could not have remembered anything of this terrible time, but Lucy, who was aged two, said that one of her first vague memories was of seeing her mother in mourning, weeping bitterly as she sorted out some papers that had belonged to her husband. 'It made a deep impression on me,' Lucy wrote, 'and to this day I can recall the consternation which came over me.'

Because she was widowed so early, Elinor Sutherland became dependent on her two daughters, and they on her. Douglas Sutherland was buried in Kensal Green cemetery. Mrs. Sutherland, left with hardly any money, returned to Canada and the shelter of her family home, taking the little girls with her.

It was at Summer Hill, ruled by their strong-willed grandmother, that Lucy's and Elinor's first impressions were formed. Their mother faded into a background of unmarried aunts and re-assumed the status of youngest-but-one daughter, and the formidable Mrs. Saunders, who still regarded herself as an aristocrat in unfortunate exile in the wilds, became the formative influence on their development.

'She was a very terrifying old lady in her stiff, black silk dresses and snowy lace caps with their pink velvet ribbons and her severe rules of etiquette which must never be infringed,' Lucy remembered.

Lucy soon developed tomboyish high spirits and flashes of rebellion. She earned disapproval by climbing trees; she got into trouble by shifting restlessly during Bible readings and prayers, always an important part of life at Summer Hill. Her charm, high spirits and energy were interpreted by her grandmother, not as a natural outpouring of energy and intelligence, but as wilful rebellion, to be discouraged at all costs. And the cost was great, as Mrs. Sutherland began to realise.

Elinor responded very differently. Her character liked discipline and order; she would always subscribe to the correct way of doing things and to historical precedent. She liked to know where she stood. 'My sister, who was a natural rebel, hated Grandmamma and her rules and teachings,' Elinor wrote in her autobiography *Romantic Adventure*. 'I loved her and must have been in tune with her ideas for they never irked me. My dramatic instinct responded to her demand for elaborate manners, aloofness, strict discipline and righteous pride.'

The moulds were hardening. By the time she was five, Lucy had already developed an antipathy for anything that hinted at authority, and instinctively rejected the 'done thing' which, under her grandmother's regime at Summer Hill, meant ancestor worship. Later she would extend this early antipathy to include the whole of polite society and all its shibboleths. Elinor would herself develop ancestor worship and the exaggerated idea of 'noblesse oblige' to lengths so ridiculous that they became the butt of her sister's jokes. 'Aunt Nelly does love a duke,' Lucy remarked to her nieces in later life. Elinor, on the other hand, referred to her sister's rather bohemian friends as 'your aunt's third rate set'.

But both girls were fascinated by Versailles, which came to symbolise beauty, peace and order from which they were, through an accident of time, exiled. Their grandmother's stories of court life became an ideal to which they both returned again and again for reassurance and for comfort.

One aspect of life at Summer Hill did excite Lucy into temporary good behaviour and that was the arrival of the 'tonneau bienvenu' from her grandfather's relatives in France. From an early age she was fascinated by the clothes it contained. It was after she had been at the local school for a year or two that she discovered not only that she could make clothes, but that she loved doing so. Later, she remembered that she tried her first creative inspirations out on her dolls, dressing them in frocks and underclothes made from every bit of scrap material she could find. In discovering the pleasure of dress at a very early age, she was following the invariable pattern of any 'born' fashion designer, developing, without encouragement, an early aptitude for colour combinations and an interest in line and texture.

Meanwhile Elinor's analytical mind was irritated by the local clergyman who made occasional visits to Summer Hill to drill the girls in their catechism. His tactlessness and didacticism led the sisters to dislike him intensely, and this led to their rejection of everything he tried to teach them. Elinor tried to discuss his ideas with him, but the more she did so, the more dogmatic he became. For the rest of her life, she tried to find the answers. Although she believed in a God, a deity, she rejected the orthodox Christian dogma in favour of other, heterodox beliefs. In early life, she was much influenced by stories of the Greek gods. In middle life, she was a ready subject for the New Thought and, later, she dabbled with spiritualism.

As they grew older, their grandmother's severity became more irksome to the sisters, while Mrs. Sutherland remained aloof, still grieving over the loss of her husband and brooding on how she was going to fulfil his dying request. But, finally, relations between Lucy and her grandmother became so difficult that even the distant Mrs. Sutherland began to notice and to worry, and this may have decided her to make a hard and unhappy decision: to marry David Kennedy, the one man in Guelph who might be persuaded to take them back to England.

ii *A New Life*

David Kennedy was born in 1807, the second son of a prominent Scottish family, the Kennedys of Knocknawlin. He joined the East India Company.

In 1853 he retired at the age of forty-six, probably for health reasons, with savings amounting to just under £5,000. Eventually he settled in Guelph, which he thought would increase in value once the Grand Trunk railroad (the same that had employed the young Douglas Sutherland) reached the Pacific. The long hard winters gave his chest a great deal of bother, and his diaries are full of the details. He was not a great diarist. A typical entry reads: 'Very hot. Cabbage all eaten up. Colonel Saunders bezique. Rats in wall.' Being thus a neighbour and one of social parity, he would have known Elinor Saunders from girlhood. When she returned to Guelph as Mrs. Sutherland he was sixty-three and set in his ways. And yet this dour, rather cranky, late middle-aged Scot began to pay particular attention to the disconsolate widow.

By June 12, 1871, he was noting in his diary the expenditure of £2.50 (not an inconsiderable sum) for Lucy's eighth birthday. On August 31, he wrote: 'Cloudy. Raining. No hay. Talked E. Glum.' This must have been a proposal, for on September 4, she wrote:

> I think it better to tell you at once that it is quite impossible for me to change my mind, at the same time I thank you for your kind intentions. I will not speak of this to anyone and I would rather the subject was not mentioned again. Hoping we shall still be friends.

This polite rejection, written on black-edged paper appropriate to Mrs. Sutherland's widowed status, obviously cut deep, for David Kennedy kept it in his wallet until he died.

He was not to be deflected, however, noting: 'Mr. Meredith 3 times married 3rd time after 13 years.' And: 'After dinner walk. Billiard room. Always E.' He enlisted the help of heavy guns: 'Called Saunders, told Mrs. S. re E.' By October 12, Mrs. Sutherland had reconsidered: 'Exhibition 11 till 12. Note to E. Wait reply. Yes. To bed as usual.' The next day he noted that they went for a drive and

talked about going to England with the children. On October 16, he
told her that England would not do. Next day it was: 'Nelly birthday
7. Must make up mind to remain here, no chance of England. Will
that do for her?' On November 9, there is a cryptic entry: 'Dined S
[Saunders] joke all off and going to England.' Mrs. Sutherland had
won the first round.

Her obsessive desire to take her children to England must have
overcome Mrs. Sutherland's natural reluctance to marry Kennedy.
In doing so, she (who will from this point on be referred to as Mrs.
Kennedy) exchanged a domineering mother for an equally difficult,
soon to be tyrannical, husband, who would eventually isolate Lucy
and Elinor from human companionship for the rest of their childhood.

They were married on November 14 and spent their honeymoon
in the United States. After an uneventful year in Guelph, they set sail
for England on the *Circassian*.

Kennedy let the house and farm in Guelph. He would have trouble
for the rest of his life in getting the rent, his only source of income,
paid regularly.

The voyage was rough. Lucy had brought her family of dolls and,
being a gregarious child, spent a great deal of time in the saloon,
building up a reputation as a pianist by playing *The Fairy Queen
Waltz*. It was full of runs and trills, which sounded very difficult,
and Lucy enjoyed the admiration of the passengers. Elinor, on the
other hand, spent most of her time with her mother who read to her
while watching the sea and the sky alternately appear and disappear
outside the porthole. *Alice in Wonderland* was not a popular choice,
for Elinor did not like the Red and the White Queen being made fun
of. She was far more impressed by George Macdonald's *Princess and
the Goblin*; it appealed to her growing imagination and also provided
a set of principles with which to fill the vacuum left by the failure of
the didactic clergyman to instill Christian principles in the mind of
this small, interested girl. Elinor's idealism, and her belief that women
should inspire men to great causes, she subsequently traced back to
this book, read to her when she was seven years old. It made another,
rather more sinister, impression on her: her imagination was so vivid
that the dark mine in the story became terrifying to her and she
would suffer from claustrophobia for the rest of her life.

Meanwhile, the charming elderly admirer, protective of mother
and daughters, was no more. Mr. Kennedy revealed himself en
voyage as a mean, domineering and cruel in the manner of a particularly heavy Victorian paterfamilias. Not only were children to be

seen and not heard; his wife, too, was included in the interdiction. Mrs. Kennedy had never managed to stand up to her own mother and faced with a tyrannical husband she soon slipped back into her accustomed role of submission. She went to great lengths to keep the peace, even at the expense of her children's happiness.

To Lucy and Elinor he must have seemed as restrictive and as old as their grandmother. His obsession with his health and with the problem of his dwindling assets soon turned him into what his stepdaughter Elinor later described as a 'crotchety, cranky, invalid'. By the time the *Circassian* reached Londonderry, Lucy made no secret of the fact that she loathed him and Elinor, refusing to deal with the problem at all, had withdrawn into an easier world – populated with fairies, goblins and mystical guests. She consoled herself for the unpleasant present with dreams of London, a city she was sure had streets paved with gold and stately palaces containing beautiful ethereal women and men like the knights of old.

Reality soon intruded on Elinor's fantasy life. Londonderry streets were in many cases cart tracks, inches deep in mud. Their hotel had bugs and peeling marbled wallpaper. The normally irrepressible Lucy was also soon depressed by the drabness of the streets and the grey fog. Even at that age, her appreciation of colour and atmosphere made her dread lest her home was to be in such an 'ugly country'.

The day after they arrived at Londonderry they set out for Balgregan Castle in the Mull of Galloway, which belonged to David Kennedy's elder brother, Peter. The castle was fertile territory for Elinor's imagination. After their arrival in the dark, they were shown by grand-looking footmen into a room filled with ladies and gentlemen in full evening dress. Peter Kennedy welcomed them and Elinor recalled that he wore a brown evening coat and a high stock collar, which would have been old-fashioned male attire for the beginning of the 1870s but, with its faint air of the eighteenth century, must have looked perfectly natural to Elinor.

What Elinor could not have realised was that their welcome was formal, rather than whole-hearted, for the Kennedy family had been surprised at the marriage of the elderly bachelor to the unknown colonial widow with two children. But Lucy was old enough to sense her mother's anxiety. Her awareness of the atmosphere fostered a child's natural contrariness in Lucy, and an unfavourable impression was created.

Elinor, on the other hand, typically maintained later that the family were immediately impressed by the beautiful sad widow and her two prettily behaved children, already endowed with naturally aristocratic manners.

For once, however, both children were at one in being lonely in this strange shadowy house. Conforming to the customs of the day, Mrs. Kennedy left them in the charge of unknown nurses, one of whom locked them in a cold billiard room for most of the day while she pursued a romance with a young game-keeper. Other visiting children made fun of their colonial clothes and the odd expressions they had picked up from the men on their grandfather's estate in Guelph, in spite of their grandmother's strictness over their speech. They were outsiders in the charmed aristocratic circle for which their mother had sacrificed so much in order to gain them entrée. Being sensitive children in their different ways, they were aware of it. Elinor in particular never forgot it.

Children, deprived of warm parental love, either began to live in a fantasy world, as did the Brontës, or become vociferously rebellious in protest. Elinor and Lucy were no exception but, being intelligent and perceptive, they began to realise that they could not rely on their mother for protection and must look after themselves, and each other. Such self-reliance, forced on them at the early ages of nine and seven, would stand them in good stead during the course of their remarkably eventful lives. For, even then, they both possessed an intrinsic toughness that enabled them to have sufficient strength of character never to acquiesce in what must have seemed a frightening and inexplicable change in their circumstances.

Leaving Balgregan after a lengthy stay, the Kennedys went on to relatives in Yorkshire, where Mr. Kennedy was taken ill with bronchitis. He was advised to spend the rest of the winter in a milder climate, and the family set off for Jersey, passing through London on the way.

Another disillusionment was in store for Elinor. Where was the fairy city of which she had dreamed? Their route from King's Cross to Waterloo Station led through some of the worst slums in Europe; the rookeries of St. Giles and Seven Dials had shocked even Dickens, hardened as he was to poverty. To the young Elinor, passing through them twenty years later, they came as a profound shock. They changed her entire outlook.

'There was no room for poverty in my fairy world, and least of all within the precincts of the celestial city which I had imagined London to represent,' she wrote in her memoirs. 'The gulf which lies between the romantic and the sordid was never more clearly visible to me than on that day.' Visible, yes; unforgettable, yes. But admissible – never. Elinor never reconciled the aristocratic ideals of her grandmother with contemporary reality. When she tried to write about poverty or the lower classes, she made a poor job of it.

Having spent the winter of 1871 in Jersey, Mr. Kennedy found it congenial to stay on. It was cheap, he had the entrée to the Government House set, and the mild weather suited his weak chest. A pattern had been established. Mr. Kennedy, his tyrannical nature exacerbated by his chronic lack of money and his wife's meekness, seemed determined to crush the spirits of his two unwanted step-daughters. The whole house revolved around him and his every want. Mrs. Kennedy, a refugee long in retreat from a reality too difficult to struggle against, still mourning her first husband, silent and cowed, was the perfect victim. Lucy was not. Now a sullen and resentful nine-year-old, she exploded into ungovernable tempers which infuriated Mr. Kennedy even further. Elinor developed into a quiet child, totally out of touch with the real world, living in an imaginative territory peopled by aristocratic shadows.

iii   *The Diary of Miss Nellie Sutherland*

Their arrival in Jersey coincided with the celebrations for the wedding that morning of the Dean of Jersey's beautiful daughter Lily le Breton to the wealthy Mr. Langtry. The harbour was decorated with flags, and garlands of flowers were festooned from all the windows. Elinor and Lucy were told that Lily had 'gone away to London to be a great lady'. Both, in their future lives, would become friends with this most famous of all Victorian beauties.

Jersey in the 1870s was a sleepy society, composed of two separate groups. On the one hand were the middle and upper middle class English expatriates who had settled on the island, as had Mr. Kennedy, because of the mild winters and the low cost of living. They came, as did Mr. Kennedy, from the ranks of retired servants of the Empire: Colonial administrators, ex-Army and ex-Naval officers, living on small pensions or half pay. The other society was indigenous: descended from the original Norman French inhabitants, it still had its own, separate class structure. At the top were the seven seigneurial families, at the bottom were the farm labourers. All still spoke a local patois, as Elinor later described, 'Combien est ce nice cabbauge?' being one example she quoted. Shrewd, earthy, they were regarded by the English settlers as little better than aborigines.

The island was ruled by a Lieutenant-Governor supported by a regiment. In this almost colonial atmosphere, the social niceties were observed very strictly indeed. To be part of the Government House set was extremely important. It was a narrow, self-satisfied little world – with which Jane Austen would have been familiar. Mr. and Mrs. Kennedy felt very much at home. They rented a house called Richelieu in an area known as Bagot, which lies outside St. Helier on the road to St. Clements.

Richelieu was, by all accounts, a happy choice. The owner, a Mrs. Coombe, was a woman of taste and education, and had furnished her house accordingly. She must have been attractive, as well as an intelligent woman, for she had married four husbands in the same regiment, promoting herself with each marital engagement from private to the last incumbent, a captain. The house contained good family pictures, among which were a Lawrence of her last husband's grandmother and an immense Gainsborough of a man on a rearing horse. A silks-and-satins lady by Lely hung in the drawing room. Both Lucy and Elinor had a keen sense of the visual, and childhood in such an environment encouraged their taste. Lucy, in particular, absorbed much detail from the Lely and similar paintings; many years later, the fruit of her observation would appear in the details of her clothes.

Elinor found much to encourage her in the library, where her unsupervised reading was the foundation of her wide, if patchy, knowledge. She was given Kingsley's *Heroes*, and this awakened a passionate interest in Greek mythology and an admiration for Greek ideals; the goddess Pallas Athene was a particular favourite and later she would often play a 'Pallas Athene' role in inspiring young men to acquit themselves nobly in life. Fifty years later, Elinor still read *Heroes* regularly. The library contained translations of the Greek classics, too, and before long Elinor was poring over fragments of Epicurus and Thucydides with the same eagerness with which she had read *The Princess and the Goblin*. But there were no library steps and, with the peculiar blindness that the Kennedys – together with most parents of that generation – had towards developing the tastes and education of their children, none were provided. The eight-year-old Elinor had to be content to read books that were within her grasp physically, if not mentally. They were a strange mixture, ranging from an early unexpurgated Pepys' *Diary*, through *Don Quixote* in eighteenth-century French, to the novels of Scott and Lady Blessington and the works of Byron. Agnes Strickland's quarto volume series, *The Queens of England*, was a particular favourite; Elinor was ever after to remember with shame having coloured in some of the engravings.

Kings and queens (and dukes too) were to remain an enthusiasm. On one occasion, she remembered that her mother had reprimanded her for altering the spelling of her name from Elinor to Eleanor, after Eleanor of Castile. Elinor was furious, as she believed she wasn't acting from snobbishness but merely from her justifiable love of romance. This sentiment, amounting to infatuation, never left Elinor and for the rest of her life titles, royal or not, held a fascination for her which acquaintance with some of their least romantic holders failed to shake. Lucy on the other hand could scarcely have cared less. Elinor's royalist propensities were at first focused on the Stuarts, through careful study of Pepys' *Diary* and no doubt strengthened by Mrs. Kennedy's stories of the Sutherland family and its connection to the Old Pretender. Charles II was a particular favourite, Elinor writing 'Dear Good King' under his portrait in a child's illustrated

History of England, and 'Nasty Old Beast' under the portrait of Cromwell. Later, she developed her fascination with the French royal family and with Versailles.

Mrs. Kennedy became even more withdrawn and submissive, dependent as she was on her husband for all the expenses involved in educating, feeding and clothing her two girls. With an exiguous annuity of about £10 a year, she was forced by Kennedy to beg him for money to pay even the smallest housekeeping bills.

Governesses came and went rapidly. They were unable to deal with Lucy's headstrong contrariness and Elinor's opinionated outlook. Both girls were by now virtually ungovernable and matters were made worse by their mother's behaviour toward them, a mixture of nagging about their manners and neglect of them in favour of keeping Mr. Kennedy happy. Both girls were united in their resistance to any form of organised learning. Elinor thought every governess too stupid to merit attention – probably with reason, for Kennedy would never have paid for really good teachers. Lucy was more interested in painting and drawing and making dresses for her dolls copied from old masters such as the Lely.

Only one teacher earned Elinor's respect, and this was the French master. Smelling of patchouli and stale tobacco, wearing rather grubby linen, Monsieur Cappe was able to transmit ideas convincingly and encouraged Elinor in her literary adventuring. Stimulated by this encouragement, she wrote lengthy essays for him in English and French, although, as she was the first to admit later, he never succeeded in teaching her any grammar.

In after years, Elinor took a somewhat perverse pride in the spelling mistakes in her manuscripts, which her publisher, Gerald Duckworth, could not have appreciated when he came to decipher them. She never learned to spell and all her letters quoted in this book have been edited accordingly.

It is useless to speculate whether Elinor would have developed into a better writer if her education had proceeded along regular lines, or whether the early lessons absorbed from her grandmother had already helped form her unique combination of high romance, worldly cynicism and diverse if patchy knowledge of a vast number of subjects. There are passages in many of her books when her pose is dropped and she concentrates on straight descriptions of people, society, decoration and clothes; and these are always fresh, apposite and extremely well observed, set forth in uncharacteristically economic language. Elinor was always successful when describing scenes which she had herself experienced, and which were not blurred by an aura of personal romance.

Socially, Lucy and Elinor were only allowed to 'know' children of the Government House set and their main outlet for high spirits and childish energy was to be allowed to play with Ada Norcott, the daughter of the Governor, Lieutenant-General Sir William Norcott. Several afternoons a week were spent either at Government House or at Richelieu, acting in plays or making elaborate paper dolls. Ada Norcott cut them out; Elinor, who had discovered a natural talent for pen and ink drawing, painted their faces; and Lucy dressed them in the latest fashions.

A brief moment of freedom from their dull routine came when Mr. and Mrs. Kennedy went to England for a visit and the girls stayed at Government House, where they spent much time putting on charades and little musical pieces. Elinor was mortified, for she was always given comic parts in which she had to wear false noses and padding. She was, by the convention of the time, considered ugly, for she had red hair, and her mother's friends used to pity her. Lucy conformed much more to the contemporary ideal of beauty, having golden-brown hair. Ada Norcott had the ne plus ultra of waving golden hair.

Insensitive adults had given Elinor the idea that in some way she herself was to blame for her looks. The only dissenter was the Governor himself who told the little girl that she might grow up to be a beauty as she did have dark eyelashes. Elinor never forgot this kindness. To be told at an early age that one is ugly is to be left with a pronounced complex on the subject, and Elinor proved no exception. She became obsessed with her appearance and even in old age was still concerned to be told that she was beautiful. Her disciplined efforts to preserve her beauty, ranging from scrubbing her face with the hardest nailbrush she could find to having one of the earliest face lifts – a process so painful she had to have her arms strapped to her sides for ten days after – could be said to originate in this early trauma.

During Lucy's and Elinor's stay at Government House, Lily Langtry came back to the island. The accredited beauty of her age, the chére amie of Edward VII, the subject of hissed conversations among the virtuous Cranfordish wives of Jersey, she was then about to make a move that would effectively banish her from all but the raciest society. She was going to go on the stage.

She became an object of fascination to the two little girls. In her memoirs, Mrs. Langtry wrote:

After our first experience of London life, we paid a visit to the Island in the yacht Hildegarde and incidentally dined at Government House. As I deposited my cloak and took a last survey of myself in the glass, I observed the two pretty red-headed girls named above peeping from under the muslin-covered dressing table. How they got there I don't know, but someone contrived this ambush to satisfy their curiosity.

Elinor remembered too, describing Lily Langtry at the height of her beauty as wearing:

A white corded silk dress, with a tight bodice and a puffed-up bustle at the back. The low neck was square cut, with a stitched pleating round the edge, and her elbow-sleeves had lace frills. Her golden-brown hair was worn in a curled fringe in front like the Du Maurier drawings and was tied at the back with a bright scarlet ribbon bow 'en catogan' [a term for a pony-tail turned under on itself, somewhat as men wore in the eighteenth century]. She was the first grown-up person we had ever seen who did not wear a chignon. . . .

Soon Lucy's and Elinor's busy, social days at Government House came to an end with the return of their mother and stepfather. Back at Richelieu, circumstances became more straitened than ever as Mr. Kennedy's health declined as he grew old. He now spent much of his time in bed, with Mrs. Kennedy in attendance. Money was tight, as the Guelph rents came in later and later, and Mr. Kennedy became more morose and more parsimonious. Lucy and her stepfather were now on such bad terms that, at barely sixteen, she insisted she must leave Jersey and was allowed to go and stay with English and Scottish friends and relations on a series of extended visits that lasted for two years. The Norcotts left the island too, and Elinor was now alone.

As part of his retrenchment, Mr. Kennedy also dismissed the last in the long series of governesses. Elinor was just fourteen and her formal education would never be resumed. She was thrown entirely on her own resources, her only companion being her collie dog, Roy. From this time dates her periodic habit of shutting herself away to write or think – sometimes for weeks on end. Elinor had acquired the habit of solitude.

The lease on Richelieu having fallen in at around the time Lucy left Jersey, the Kennedys moved to a new house in St. Helier itself at Number 55 Colomberie. There was no library here to console Elinor but Mr. Kennedy sent for his books from Scotland. These were dumped, still in their packing cases, in a small ground floor room at the back of the house, and Elinor spent the next two years immersed in Dickens, Thackeray, the *Memoirs* of the Duc de

Saint-Simon, Gibbon's *Decline and Fall*, Sterne's *Sentimental Journey*, Voltaire's *Zadig*, Chesterfield's *Letters to My Son* and La Rochefoucauld's *Maxims*. The last two of these books became Elinor's constant companions throughout her life, and she could (and often did) quote from them readily. Of them all, the *Memoirs* of the Duc de Saint-Simon probably made the greatest impression on her. Her grandmother had, as it were, prepared the ground and, to the lonely Elinor, the court at Versailles became more real than her own existence.

It was now that Elinor first demonstrated her tenacity and her hunger for knowledge. She was quite intelligent enough to realise that she must try and continue her education by her own efforts. Through reading Gibbon's *Decline and Fall* she became as well versed in Roman as she was in Greek history. Whenever she wanted another book, or further information on a particular subject, she walked to the St. Helier public library. Thus she became remarkably well-informed about anything that interested her; if a subject had not captured her imagination, she abandoned it. The minutiae of eighteenth-century aristocratic life in France developed into a life-long interest and she knew an enormous amount about its literature, customs, furniture, clothes, art, architecture and history. The Italian Renaissance was another enthusiasm, developed through reading John Addington Symonds. But between these poles lay darkness.

At about the age of fifteen, Elinor started to write stories – not juvenilia, such as the Brontës' mythical kingdom, but youthful versions of her later romances, born out of her loneliness and isolation. The brief fragments that survive in carefully copied versions in penny notebooks reveal much about how she regarded herself at the time. *A Gawky Schoolgirl*, written in 1878, shows how deeply she felt about being told she was ugly.

> I am very pretty with straight features, big grey eyes and curly golden hair. I am seventeen and have – or will have on my eighteenth birthday, five thousand a year. I dare say, dear reader, you are saying to yourself, how vain. But I am not. I have been pretty ever since I was born and have known it ever since I could understand what the word 'pretty' meant so I have given up all vanity on the subject. I am possessed of abundant spirits and a hot temper and my name is Kate Brandon.

She then re-wrote this in a characteristically cynical manner.

> I believe I am rather pretty with straight features, big grey eyes and curly bright golden hair. I am seventeen and have – or will

have on my eighteenth birthday – five thousand a year. Perhaps that accounts for people thinking me pretty.

The next year, 1879, she began a diary, which she called at first *The Diary of Miss Nellie Sutherland*. She kept it, more or less regularly, for the rest of her life, and in later years told her grandchildren that it was her legacy to them. Sadly, only very early entries have survived. At first she used penny notebooks, but later she wrote in thick volumes bound in purple velvet, kept in canvas bags fastened with Bramah locks. The diaries – some thirty of them – existed until the Second World war when they were, apparently, destroyed by fire.

The surviving early entries give an impression of how dull this bright girl found her life in Jersey. A sample: 'Morning sewed. Afternoon called at Government House but saw no one. Evening can't remember.'

But Elinor's life began to quicken its pace. At sixteen, she could attend small dances, at which she began to find that she was, in spite of her red hair, attractive to the opposite sex. As this extract shows, her long days of isolation were beginning to come to an end:

Friday 3rd September 1879
Morning go to Mac's to clear their floor, make it up with Duncan, have great fun. Floss comes to dinner. Afternoon do my dress. Evening Duncan brings me flowers for tonight. Evening the Mac's dance, have splended fun, dance five times with Herbert and sit out four. . . . In nice, nicer, nicest dances dance seven times with Duncan. They have a scrimmage for the end dance and I give it to Percy. Great fun altogether.

Her childhood was almost over, and for the time being long hours spent poring over books would be abandoned in favour of frivolity, flirtation and fun.

POVERTY

(1880–1890)

'Damn it all. A man is not obliged to marry every woman
he kisses.'

Three Weeks

i *Mrs. Wallace*

The years passed pleasantly enough for Elinor. There were tea parties, lunches, picnics and croquet and, as she grew older, constant mutual speculation among her girlfriends as to whether they would or would not 'take' one or another of the plentiful suitors on the island.

A fragment of a diary written in 1888, when she was about to leave Jersey for ever, gives a picture of how she passed the time.

> No one would ever think to see the smart worldly society 'Miss Sutherland' that she was once a little Donkey with a heart and kept old ball programmes and dead flowers. To think I am only 22 [she was actually 24] and have not one illusion left – at all events tonight. I wonder if there are a great many women who have had as many lovers between 14 & 22 as I have. I really began at fourteen. I think B.C. was the first. How glad I am that I have always had sense and never listened to them. Miss Buchanan said today that anyone's impression of me is that I am a worldly heartless society coquette ah, well, they don't know. It is a sad world. Sometimes I wish I were asleep.

When Elinor was nearly seventeen life began to offer more in the way of excitement, for Lucy returned to Jersey – and Lucy was now officially 'out'.

The tomboy had grown up into a pretty, vivacious young woman. She was not a great beauty in the accepted sense for that time. She was not fair and she did not have classical regularity of feature, but she had a piquant, mobile face with a rather naughty expression and a mass of light brown hair with red lights in it.

She was still extremely self-willed and would admit no interference, but her abounding energy had found an outlet in the pursuit of love. No sooner had she arrived back on the island than she started breaking the hearts of the various young officers stationed in Jersey whom she met at parties and picnics. It was not long before she achieved the singular and rather scandalous feat of becoming engaged three times in as many months and then, with equal facility, breaking each engagement as lightly as she had entered into it.

Mr. Kennedy's straitened circumstances virtually ruled out the services of even a local dressmaker. As a measure of economy, he had cut the dress allowances of Mrs. Kennedy and her daughters even further than the tiny amount he had previously allocated them. Lucy now graduated from making clothes for her dolls to designing and sewing clothes for herself, her mother and her sister. It was during the hours she spent stitching in the little, high-ceilinged boudoir at 55 Colomberie that she developed, not only her superlative proficiency with the needle, but also the idea of making dresses for the personality of the wearer, rather than merely following the lead of current fashion to be seen in such periodicals as Godey's *Ladies Journal*.

In a sense she was a century before her time, for the notion that it is desirable to be stylish and exhibit individual taste has only recently superseded the dictates of the leaders of group fashion. This eighteen-year-old provincial debutante, living in the small backwater of Jersey society, had already instinctively developed the idea that, in order to stand out, she must dress to suit her own personality, rather than follow established standards.

'I studied my own type with as much care as I used to study, many years later, the types of women who came to consult me from all over the world,' she wrote in her memoirs, *Discretions and Indiscretions*. 'I found out exactly what suited me, and I decided to adopt an original style of dress, taking my inspiration from the old masters.'

She pored over books and made detailed studies of a lace collar or cuff in eighteenth-century portraits, copying ribbons, bows, silk flowers, as best she might. While Elinor was educating herself by reading, Lucy was laying the foundations of her future profession by a species of visual education.

'I had one dress of which I was especially fond,' she remembered. 'It was in black velvet which fell in soft folds to the feet, and there was a little tight bodice, which was finished with a deep belt. It could easily be worn today [1932] which shows how little clothes change in their essentials from one generation to another.'

Perhaps she remembered this particular dress so vividly over fifty years later because she was wearing it when she fell seriously in love for the first time. 'Before that I had only been loved, and it was a new and wonderful experience. He was a young Captain, not one of the usual group of officers who used to be in and out of our house every day, but a newcomer to Jersey, and I met him for the first time at a dance where I wore this black frock.'

Eager, as was every Victorian mother, to get both her daughters 'off' respectably, Mrs. Kennedy began to entertain great hopes for the Captain was eminently eligible.

But Lucy's tempestuous nature – until now exercised in violent quarrels with her stepfather – asserted itself and she fell out with her suitor. Her pride and her fiery temper prevented an early reconciliation. Lucy was no milk-and-water miss and, to Mrs. Kennedy's dismay, Lucy packed her bags and left Jersey immediately. She went to stay in a friend's house at King's Walden in Hertfordshire. And it was there that her impetuosity led her into a fateful decision.

'I used to suffer agonies of grief in silence, for I was very proud and would hide my wounds at all costs,' she wrote. 'I decided that there was only one thing to be done. I must let him [the Captain] see that I did not care. So to this end I married the next man who asked me, and he happened to be James Stuart Wallace.'

Anyone less suitable could scarcely be imagined, even by her distraught mother, now used to the blows of fate. James Wallace was a wine merchant with a fondness for drink and for pretty women. He was well-connected and popular, a typical late-Victorian man-about-town with a reputation for loose-living in a fast town-and-country set. A week after meeting during the King's Walden houseparty he proposed and, in a spirit of defiance, was accepted. Not for the last time in her life Lucy exhibited the extreme stubbornness that would not only be a contributing factor in her subsequent professional success but would also lead her into her other disasters. Never willing to listen to advice, her resolution would always stiffen at the slightest hint of opposition and no-one would be able to do anything to change her mind.

Lucy Sutherland and James Wallace were married in London on September 15, 1884, in spite of Mrs. Kennedy's protestations. Lucy was, as she admitted, still in love with the Captain. 'I cannot pretend that anything but pique would have made me listen to him [Wallace], for we were hopelessly unsuited to one another in every way, and he was more than twenty years older than I was. Still, anything was better than eating out my heart for the man who had gone from me, and Jim was good-looking and successful enough to please any woman.'

Perhaps she hoped that, in the manner of romantic tales, her former suitor would repent and fly to her rescue, but he didn't; and the night before her wedding Lucy cried herself to sleep over the old love and made up her mind to be a really good wife to Wallace.

At first, in spite of what Lucy wrote later, things went on reasonably satisfactorily, or so it would appear from a mention in Elinor's 1888 diary. 'Lucy's wedding day 4 years ago. Ah. Now I remember with what sickening sensations I awoke that morning. What a nightmare it all was – however, things have turned out better than we hoped.'

This ill-assorted couple – the experienced man of the world and his schoolgirl wife – lived outside London in a rented cottage in Cranford Park, Hounslow, a large estate belonging to Lord and Lady Fitzhardinge, an odd, unconventional but delightful couple who were friends of James Wallace's father.

Lord Fitzhardinge had a curious history: his father, the then Lord Berkeley, had tried to prove that he had married his wife some considerable time before the true date of the wedding, in order thus to legitimise his eldest son. He went so far as to swear to an earlier marriage date in court. But Counsel asked him again, 'Lord Berkeley, you have sworn that you married Lady Berkeley on this date?' 'Yes,' was the reply. 'Will you,' said Counsel, who obviously knew his man, 'give the Court your word of honour as a gentleman that this early marriage took place?' Bibles were one thing, the honour of a gentleman quite another, and Lord Berkeley refused to swear, thus losing his case. His eldest son forfeited his right to the title and to the considerable entailed estates that went with it. But the eldest legitimate son, guarding his mother's honour, always refused to take his brother's place. Lord Berkeley's power in the West of England being considerable, the dispossessed son was made a peer in his own right and the entail cut so as to enable him to succeed to Berkeley Castle. The only loser in this neat arrangement was the unfortunate Lady Berkeley who was ostracised by society for the rest of her life, to the point where her daughter, Lady Caroline Maxse, had to be brought out by an aunt.

Lord Fitzhardinge was a very small man and in the somewhat ponderous humour of the time was naturally called 'The Giant'. He was an eccentric, who invariably sported a tall hat with hedgehog quills sticking out of the crown. At the time of Lucy's marriage, Fitzhardinge was in late middle age and he and his wife, a statuesque if not corpulent lady, were very kind to the little bride, extending their interest to her younger sister, who came on visits. Elinor later painted a funny portrait of Lady Fitzhardinge in *The Visits of Elizabeth*: '. . . You might have prepared me for what Lady Theodosia looked like. . . . I found her lying on a sofa covered with dogs and cats . . . she had evidently been asleep, and it looked like a mountain having an earthquake when she got up, and animals rolled off her in all directions.'

Cranford Park was a cheerful place, with frequent houseparties composed of leading members of the faster elements in society such as the then Duke of Beaufort and his two sons. Lord Fitzhardinge had been in the Blues and liked to keep open house for the young officers from the cavalry barracks at nearby Windsor, which livened things up a great deal. One of the attractions was the cooking of François, who was held to be the best chef in England. A fractious individual whose speciality was 'Poulet Celestial', François finally had to go, for he couldn't manage on less than two thousand eggs a week.

The Cranford Park menage must have seemed the ultimate in sophistication to Lucy, so lately accustomed to Jersey or to rather dowdy relatives in the provinces. It was perhaps not as 'nice' as the sticklers in late Victorian society would have liked, in their notions of who would 'do' and who would not. Although the Fitzhardinges were very popular, they could not, by reason of their rather shocking antecedents, expect to move in the highest circles, and so they substituted a mixture of racing friends and young officers and their girlfriends (who tended to be girls of fairly dubious virtue). The newly-married Lucy and the infinitely more experienced Wallace became members of an almost continuous party. Looking back, Lucy admitted she had been lonely because she didn't subscribe to the fairly lax morals of the society in which she now moved. 'I could have had, had I wished, a dozen lovers to console me, but although I liked the companionship of men, as I have liked it all my life, I would not listen to them.'

The Wallaces now began to lead what Lucy described as a 'sort of Micawber existence'. When Wallace had money he was generous to a fault, and because he was – at least in the early days – proud of his young wife's vivacity and appeal to the opposite sex, she always had money for beautiful clothes, although she insisted on making them herself.

Two months after her marriage, Lucy realised that she was going to have a child. She was dismayed, for she knew that she was not in love with her husband, and their finances were then at a very low ebb. But, typical of her positive attitude to almost anything life could throw at her, she decided to make the best of it.

She wanted her child to be both musical and beautiful; being a believer in the new, popular theory of pre-natal influence, she set out to make sure this would happen. Devoting the early months of her pregnancy to making herself a wardrobe to compensate for what she described as her temporary loss of beauty, she then toiled round picture galleries and played the piano for hours a day. The unborn child's musical education was augmented by one of Lucy's admirers at that time, the well-known violinist Tivardar Nachez, who used to come to her cottage and play to her nearly every evening during her pregnancy.

On August 25, 1885, Lucy had a daughter, whom she christened Esmé. The baby hated music during her early childhood, especially violin music. But she was beautiful, and Lucy became a devoted mother, growing to love her little daughter dearly as the only compensation for her unwise marriage, which had started badly, and was soon to get worse. Lucy was one of those rare mothers who prefer very young children. She treated Esmé like one of the army of elegant dolls she had left behind with her childhood in Jersey. Hours were spent making exquisite clothes for her and dressing her up to be admired by the Cranford Park visitors. Lucy was not happy but life – between her admirers and her beautiful child – did have some compensations for the increasing waywardness of Wallace.

ii *Le Chat Nellie*

In the spring of 1880 Elinor's romantic nature was awakened by her first visit to Paris and her first experience of adult passion.

She had been invited for a week's visit by a Mademoiselle Duret, whom she had met in Jersey. Elinor's distant cousins, the Fouquet le Maîtres, were away from Paris and at first life in her elderly friend's flat in the Boulevard Malesherbes seemed dull (and, it might be suspected, too bourgeois for Elinor's already developing taste). Poor Mademoiselle Duret took Elinor to see Sarah Bernhardt in *Theodora* in an effort to entertain her. It was an over-heated romance unsuitable for a young 'miss', but Mademoiselle Duret believed that Elinor was too young to understand the passionate aspects of the play. She was wrong. Elinor later wrote in her diary:

> It made an immense effect on me . . . as she [Bernhardt] moved and undulated over her lover. Strange thrills rushed through me. Although I analysed nothing in those days I know now I had suddenly found my group – the group of the Sirens, the weird fierce passionate caressing and cruel group. I remember long sentences of her love words to Andreas. I used to say them to myself and act the scene before the dim glass in the little back room in the rue de la Borde. I had no idea of anything sensual – it was merely a sudden flint touching steel which had ignited the tinder. I remember letting down my hair as a cloak and covering this imaginary lover with its copper waves. He had no personality – he was not Andreas. He was something for the rousing of the soul of me. . . . I remember trembling in my bed the whole night through. This was a sudden awakening to the possibilities of life.

Reality in the shape of a good-looking young Frenchman, armed with a letter of introduction from the Culzean Kennedys, was to prove a great deal more exciting than the mythical Andreas.

He managed to spend three days in Elinor's company. She was, of course, carefully chaperoned the whole time. However, he soon discovered that Mademoiselle Duret's English was not good enough for her to understand when he made passionate declarations of love to her charge. He took the two ladies to visit the Jardin des Plantes, and here Elinor saw her first tiger. No doubt 'G' (as she referred to him) pointed out the similarity of colouring between her red hair and the tiger's, and he certainly started her off on the pursuit of a life-long obsession with cats big and little by whispering 'belle tigresse' in her ear. 'Le Chat Nellie' was the title Jacques-Emile Blanche gave to the painting of her as a marmalade Persian cat, which he painted in 1894 in Dieppe.

Elinor had been given that most valuable of gifts to one unsure of her own beauty – a strong and unique self-image which she could elaborate at will.

The clandestine romance took what might have been a dangerous turn when 'G' asked Elinor to elope with him, but she was not the product of her grandmother's teachings for nothing and she returned to Jersey a few days later with a souvenir of her first experience in the form of a new copy of the *Maxims* of la Rochefoucauld. But this was not the last she heard of 'G' as she admitted in her 1888 diary: 'I tear up all the Paris letters from G,' she wrote. 'What fools men are. . . . G was so good looking. However, he has grown stout now. I am glad I did not take him – it is a queer world.'

Three years later, Elinor, now aged nineteen, had not found a husband in Jersey and Mrs. Kennedy felt it was time for her to be launched in a wider social milieu. There was no question of bringing her out at a London Drawing Room; the Kennedys were neither rich enough, nor had the entrée into Court circles. Mrs. Kennedy did the best she could, regularly packing her off on a series of visits to any friends or relations in England or in France who would have her. For the next nine years, Elinor stayed in other people's houses more or less as a poor relation.

Both girls were devoted to their mother, treating her like an elder sister. This devotion was in sharp contrast to Mr. Kennedy's treatment of her as a nurse-companion. The atmosphere at 55 Colomberie had been conspiratorial, and the three women had spent many hours making clothes and planning wardrobes for visits. When she was on a round of such visits, Elinor wrote to her mother very frequently and, for the time, very frankly as this letter of May 8, 1883 shows:

Well darling Mammy I have arrived here all safe. . . . from what I have seen of this house I shall be bored to tears. . . . Oh. When you send my blue dress send my velvet body with the cream lace, the one laced down the front. . . . though I may not want it in this benighted place. I may if something better turns up. Have you written to Mrs. Wilson? Do you think she will ask me – I don't believe I could stand more than a week of this.

In the same letter Elinor writes about her effect on their old acquaintance, the former Lieutenant-Governor of Jersey, Sir William Norcott:

.... I verily believe Lady N was so jealous (because of the time when I went to lunch he – Sir W – insisted upon me coming into his little room .... she came in too & fussed about but he held the door open for her & then said 'Now at last I have time to kiss you my pretty child.') that she never told him I was coming. .... I met him on the Parade & when I told him I had been to tea at their house he was furious. .... I expect they caught it at dinner ...

Two days later, she writes again, describing the reaction to her new dress:

Fancy what these idiots said when I went down and showed it to them. Mrs. S. .... looked up 'Oh. An evening dress I suppose?' I said 'certainly not.' 'You are surely not going to wear it *in the street*?' I said 'Of course I was, it was for the park' and then she sniffed. 'Hem, silver is a great deal too gaudy for the daytime, I think'. I was so furious that I nearly told her she was a fool, but just restrained myself & was most polite. They are such idiots.

After Lucy's marriage, Elinor frequently stayed with her sister and lost no time in becoming a particular favourite of Lady Fitzhardinge who, kind-hearted as she was, asked Elinor to stay at Cranford Park itself and on occasion took her to London for parties. She brought her out, in effect, and introduced her to part of the world of polite society – the racier part.

From this time dates Elinor's need to entertain, to sing for her supper as it were. A minor talent now came into useful play. She had always drawn little caricatures of her friends to amuse herself and now she discovered that she could in some measure repay hospitality by amusing other people with them too, compensating in a small way for her lack of means and high birth. The genial Fitzhardinges were diverted by this and took her to Kempton and Sandown so that she could see 'yet more people and be able to make pictures of them from memory. I did a great many sketches and it was Lord Fitzhardinge's joy to show them to the guests who came down to Cranford.'

During the years of country house visits and occasional sorties to London Elinor was developing another, more important, talent – for writing. She kept fragmentary diaries and chronicles of particular incidents (such as a visit with her mother to the annual fair at Neuilly) in penny notebooks, largely for her own amusement and frequently illustrated with little drawings. Many of the incidents she described in these notebooks and in letters to her mother are used in their entirety in her first and funniest book *The Visits of Elizabeth*, which contains recognisable portraits of many of the people she met during this period of her life.

But the notion of writing books was far from Elinor's mind, in her twenties. Her preoccupation was marriage. For without marriage she had little status and no independent existence outside the stifling world of Jersey and visiting. She soon realised that her own particular Prince Charming wasn't going to be easy to find. Thanks to her reading, she was cynical enough to realise that it wasn't going to be enough for her to marry for love. If she wasn't to end up penny-pinching like her mother, she must marry for money as well.

Although she was by now attractive to the opposite sex, she would have no dowry and, however she might play on the history of her noble ancestors, the fact remained that she was generally regarded as a colonial nobody, albeit a very pretty and amusing one. She resented this deeply for the rest of her life.

Elinor wanted romance, and she wanted security, which explains why, in her first two seasons at Cranford, in 1885 and 1886, she refused three proposals. Her suitors had money and influence, but they were elderly and physically unattractive. Princes, yes. Charming, no. The most important of these suitors was the Duke of Newcastle. One side of Elinor's nature, the cynical, worldly side, would have dearly loved to have been a Duchess. But the other side, the 'Chat Nellie' of passionate romance, could not reconcile itself to an elderly Duke, as she later explained:

> He was absorbingly interested in the details of ecclesiastical apparel . . . . my French cousins used to tease me, saying that 'Les Yeux bleus vont aux cieux, mais les yeux verts vont à l'enfer'. . . . and I can only imagine that my peculiar looks attracted him like forbidden fruit.

She sometimes wondered what would have happened to her if she had accepted: 'Should I have written books at all? How would I have got through life?'

She used this ducal proposal in 1934 in *Did She*:

> The Duke. . . . was awfully kind and sympathetic and then he asked me to marry him. He said he knew that I was not like any

modern girl, but he had ideas about the family, and a sense of duty and dignity and right. He knew I could not love him, he said, but although he was sixty four, he knew he would grow to love me . . . . and a Duchess's coronet would not be unbecoming to my queenly brow.

James Wallace favoured another suitor, a millionaire. But Elinor, judging him by her grandmother's standards, realised that he would not have been allowed into Summer Hill under any circumstances; the snobbish side of her nature rose up and she refused him. Wallace was so furious that he sent her back to Jersey in the autumn of 1887, where she had to remain until the following April.

As part of her social round before being sent back to Jersey that year, Elinor had been invited to visit Hillersdon in Devon, owned by W. J. Grant, known as Billy. A bachelor in his mid-forties at the time, he was amusing and had been, among other things, an Arctic explorer. He became a devoted friend and more than twenty years later, when she again went to Hillersdon, she tried in her diary to describe her feelings on that first visit. Elinor could be romantic, snobbish and mondaine; she could also be self-pitying and morose:

Twenty years ago since I first floated on this lake. I remember I was unhappy even in those days. Always some sword of Damocles hanging over me. First a cantankerous stepfather. Then an unspeakable brother-in-law making home impossible. There were long visits to French relations, rich and prosperous, and returning laden with exquisite clothes flung at me as a parting gift, galling always. Then there were those visits for the autumn balls and the women hated me. Why, I wonder. My old friend [Billy Grant] said because I was so white and slim and red-haired and could dance and speak French and had not red arms and carried my head very highly and wore Doucet ball dresses, and when one has not connections, even in England, surely these were causes enough in all conscience. An upstart half-foreign person. Who dared to sail into the sacred precincts and cause havoc among the young country squires and especially ensnare the heart of the great catch of the neighbourhood [the Duke] and then not marry him.

A girl with such an appearance must be bad. Red hair and black eyelashes and green eyes. . . . No really nice woman creature could have colouring like that. She must be stoned.

But I had my triumphs in those days. Now that I look back upon it all, there was something a little pitiful about it. A poor little lonely girl hiding many troubles under a haughtily set head, longing to be protected and loved. Timid really and very tender-hearted and antagonistically treated by women for no fault except nature's bizarre choice of red, white and green. Always the centre of the passionate love of men, always proud, always alone. Ah me. How I remember when I decided to marry. I thought I would choose some good Englishman who would be kind to me, where I could shelter from the turmoil and have some domestic happiness and peace – and above all a home. Ah me.

When she wrote this memoir, Elinor was unhappy and depressed. Her years of visiting may well have seemed gloomy and hopeless. However, the fact remains that, under the circumstances, she had had a reasonably good time, even though she obviously felt slighted on many occasions. It is hardly surprising, bearing in mind her attitude to women such as Lady Norcott, that she was more popular with men. She herself always preferred masculine company and, in an era when an unmarried woman was not expected to have friend-ships with the opposite sex, Elinor managed to make many platonic male friends.

The winter of 1887 passed slowly in the depressing atmosphere of 55 Colomberie but in April 1888 Elinor's French cousins, the Fouquet le Maître family, prodded, no doubt, by Mrs. Kennedy, asked her to spend the first of what were to become many seasons in France.

Elinor was now twenty-four, and showing no signs of marrying. She could not go back to Cranford Park until James Wallace had forgiven her for rejecting her millionaire suitor. Fresh fields seemed to be indicated, and the Fouquet le Maîtres, although distant connec-tions, were willing to acknowledge their kinship with their poor but extremely attractive guest, and to take her about in the Faubourg society to which they belonged. They were aristocratic, affluent and rather old-fashioned. Their fortunes having survived the French Revolution virtually intact, they owned a château, la Valasse, near Bolbec and an Hôtel Particulier at 131 Champs Elysees. Mrs. Ken-nedy must have congratulated herself on her stratagem, for Elinor would now be launched afresh, in the best French society.

From the château in Normandy, Elinor wrote to her mother:

Darling Mammy, it is too lovely here. Such a sweet house, all done in the Louis Quinze style. It is really old & of that period. The salons are white wood with Watteau panels let in, so quaint and pretty. The gardens are lovely.

We are going to Paris tomorrow and on Tuesday next, we go
with the Comte and Comtesse de Ségur in their yacht for a trip on
the Seine. We shall be travelling till Saturday. We are to stay at the
hotels at night and yacht in the day time. There are to be ten of
us, won't it be lovely fun? These de Ségurs are very gay people.
Jeanne comes on Saturday for the day, and this afternoon we are
going to drive and call at the de Ségurs. I *wish* Lucy was here.
Bernard is so sweet. Do not write to me from Tuesday to Friday.
My clothes are not much crushed. I am going to try and buy a
journal book tomorrow to write in. . . .

Elinor later used her journal entries on this visit to France in *The
Visits of Elizabeth*, describing with relish the havoc she caused among
the young men of the party and painting a very unflattering portrait
of the female Fouquet le Maître cousin nearest her in age, describing
her as 'A big dump with a shiny complexion, and such a very small
mouth . . .'

'Le Chat Nellie' had started to show her claws.

iii *Divorce*

In the autumn of 1888, Mr. Kennedy decided to leave Jersey and take a house in London in order to be nearer his chest specialist. He was now eighty-one, but his temper had not improved, nor had the atmosphere at 55 Colomberie. Leaving Jersey after nearly twenty years was an upset for him and he was, as Elinor remembered, 'even crabbier than ever'.

Stimulated by change, Elinor decided to start a journal once more; this one lasted for about a week. But the few entries she did make convey her pleasure in leaving the stifling atmosphere of the island. The move, and the consequent sorting out of her possessions, aroused in her a powerful nostalgia – a sentiment which would be so regular a feature of her subsequent work and life.

> . . . . I came upon an old Diary written by me in 1880 when I was young and foolish. . . . it made me sad, so many things have happened since then, illusions vanished tastes changed. . . . Lucy Jim and Esmé left this morning. To think there was no Esmé & no Jim – eight years ago. How I wonder what our new life will be in London. I don't think many people will regret us in Jersey. They have not loved us much. Or we them.

Four years after Lucy's marriage, the rift with Mr. Kennedy had been healed to the point where Elinor thought it worthwhile to note in her diary 'Monsieur [the nickname the sisters had given to Kennedy] actually goes to Lucy's house.'

Lucy and James Wallace had left the cottage in Cranford Park that summer and had taken a house in London. Lucy had been responsible for finding and taking a temporary lease on a furnished house at 58 Drayton Gardens for Mr. and Mrs. Kennedy, Elinor, accompanied by Roy, the collie dog, and two servants they brought with them from Jersey. The reconciliation appeared to be complete.

But whatever Elinor, or indeed their mother, may have thought about Lucy's marriage, things must have been even worse than they had been at the beginning. In her discreetly worded autobiography, Lucy is, as always, deliberately vague about detail:

When my little daughter was about five years old, the wretchedness of my married life was suddenly ended. My husband left me and went away with a girl who was dancing in pantomime.

This was probably a euphemism on Lucy's part to describe one of the girls who danced in 'ballet' at one of the popular music halls such as the Alhambra, a favourite haunt of the late-Victorian man-about-town – where he could be sure of a warm if not strictly conventional welcome from the ladies on the stage or from those who walked the promenade.

Elinor advanced another reason for Lucy's problems: 'My poor mother . . . was now faced with a new trouble, being greatly distressed over my sister's unhappiness with her husband, whose failing for drink had by now reached a ghastly stage.'

The intimate details of Lucy's life with the alcoholic Wallace are lost. But it is safe to suppose that her existence tied to a man whom she had never loved – a man who drank and who had a very bad temper – must have been horrific. So much so that Lucy decided on a move that might banish her from polite society for the rest of her life. She sued Wallace for divorce. In her autobiography she says that she did this against the advice of all her friends; but she had been to see a famous palmist, Cheiro, who had advised her on this bold step.

It is not surprising that her friends counselled her against this plan, even though she would appear as the innocent party, for in late Victorian times divorce was unthinkable for a woman. As Elinor put it: 'Divorce was extremely rare. If the woman was the culprit it spelt the end of her social career and no return was possible. Husbands, however erring, were seldom got rid of, for the position of divorced wives, even though quite innocent, was invidious and in Queen Victoria's day they were not allowed to go to court.' Many society ladies would not let a divorced person in their house, under any circumstances.

At about the same time that James Wallace ran off with his pantomime girl, Mr. Kennedy died. Mrs. Kennedy finally found herself free from his constant demands on her attention and her time. He left her his estate, which would have been sufficient for her own needs, had she not decided to support Lucy's wish for a divorce and had she not paid for it. Divorce was an extremely expensive process in those days, and Mrs. Kennedy used a large part of the money she had been left to pay the costs. There was a little left invested to provide an income which would support Mrs. Kennedy, the penniless Lucy and Esmé. Mrs. Kennedy moved to a little house at 25 Davies Street and Lucy and Esmé went to live with her.

James Wallace had left a bitter legacy. Lucy was left with what one can only suspect was a distaste for men. For the rest of her life, she was much happier in the company of women, or of unthreatening boys who were much younger than she was and often homosexuals. She tended to distrust men, and later this led to extreme complications in her dealings with businessmen.

Her divorce had another long-reaching effect – it did indeed exclude her from polite society. Elinor's daughter Margot summed up this attitude years later to her son. 'Of course poor Lucy didn't have the entrée to those circles,' she told him. 'She had to be content with café society . . . oh, all those awful people.'

Lucy's entrée to café society, in reality the haute bohemia of the 1890s, came through Ellen Terry. During a run of *Faust* Lucy was invited to a Colonial reception on stage, was introduced to her, and was asked to call on her. They became firm friends immediately, with perhaps a touch of schwärmerei on Lucy's part, as she unwittingly revealed in her memoirs:

> Although I went to her house many times, I rarely saw Ellen Terry without her little circle of girls. . . . I never knew any woman who possessed in such a degree the art of inspiring affection in her own sex. she was not a young woman then, but she was the friend and confidante of dozens of girls who adored her and loved to serve her in all sorts of little ways. . . . soon I became one of the group and was admitted to her house at all hours.

This friendship with a powerful woman conformed to a pattern that would repeat itself over and over again during the course of Lucy's life. Her most intimate friends were women like herself – financially independent through their own efforts, surrounded by a circle of dominated men and younger women who played the roles of acolytes. In these early days, Lucy was the acolyte, later she would collect devotees of her own; legions of faithful secretaries and assistants prepared to serve her in much the same hero-worshipping manner as she had originally devoted herself to Ellen Terry. The company of women posed no threats and in a sense it was a repetition of the early and close relationship she had had with her mother and her sister, to the exclusion of the cantankerous Mr. Kennedy.

That is not to say that the newly-divorced Lucy did not have male admirers, or enjoy such admiration. One, in particular, the noted laryngologist Sir Morell Mackenzie, introduced her to some of the most notable figures of the artistic world of that time. Lucy attended his Thursday Evenings which were 'famous for their gatherings of celebrities. At one of them I met Oscar Wilde. I thought him the oddest creature I had ever seen, with his long golden hair, his black velvet knee-breeches and the sunflower in his buttonhole.' Lucy found Mrs. Wilde 'even stranger. . . . dressed with a total disregard to taste. . . .'

It was now that Lucy's courage, optimism and will to succeed came to her aid. Money had to be found from somewhere. Lucy decided she must set to work. But to do what? She realised that, although she could play the piano well, her skill was not great enough to lead to a career on the concert platform. She toyed with the idea of going on the stage, which horrified her mother. And business was not possible as she had no training in secretarial work. Barely educated as she was, Lucy could only sew.

'Looking back on it all,' she wrote, 'it seems strange that the step which was to lead me to the greatest happiness I have ever known in my life should have been taken in a moment of intense sorrow. One morning, when I was making a little dress for Esmé, I had a flash of inspiration. Whatever I could or could not do, I could make clothes. I would be a dressmaker. My mother was not wildly enthusiastic about it. It would need capital, she told me, and there would be a lot of competition to fear.' Mrs. Kennedy was probably also chary of the idea of her daughter going into 'trade' and thus becoming irredeemably déclassée.

But Lucy would not be discouraged. Telling her mother that the outlay would be practically nothing as she would do everything herself, she agreed that she would not take expensive premises, but would make clothes at home in Davies Street. And as for clients, Lucy was confident that she would find them among the friends who had often admired her clothes.

And so it was. The first of these friends to be dressed by Lucy was a minor but elegant member of society, the Hon. Mrs. Arthur Brand, who, paying a morning call a few days after Lucy had evolved her plan, mentioned that she had had an invitation to stay with a Mrs. Panmuir Gordon, whose houseparties were famous. Mrs. Brand wanted a new tea-gown to take with her, but was afraid there would not be time to fit it.

The tea-gown was one of the most important weapons in the sartorial armoury of the late Victorian and Edwardian society lady. It filled the gap between shooting tweeds, which were worn when the ladies went out to have lunch with the guns, and the final change of the day into formal evening dress. The ladies would come down to tea – usually served at numbers of small tables – and flirt with their chosen attachments. It was a point d'honneur to be dressed in an exquisite and rather sexy 'teagie', as contemporary slang termed these pretty nonsenses. The tea-gown originated from the peignoir. At the time that Lucy started to make clothes, it had developed into a filmy garment, still with overtones of the boudoir, but respectable enough to be worn in public without corsets.

In the sexually adventurous world of late Victorian and Edwardian society, a gown that needed no corsets had its uses. Gentlemen called on their mistresses in London at tea-time and, in the complicated yet necessarily discreet saraband of extra-marital affairs indulged in by the Marlborough House set and the many who emulated them, the tea-gown played an important part. For the advantages of a pretty gown that needed no indiscreet ladies' maid to unlace and then lace up corsets could not be over estimated. By her tea-gowns was a lady judged fashionable or frump, and dressmakers created exquisite examples of their art. The tea-gown was the personification of the informal side of the Edwardian social scene, just as the cloche hat came to symbolise the flapper society of the 1920s.

Lucy saw in the unwitting Mrs. Brand an opportunity to essay a design for a woman who moved in just the circles she wanted to dress. And Mrs. Brand needed little persuasion, for she had always wanted Lucy to design a gown for her, having admired Lucy's own clothes but, feeling it would be insulting, had never liked to ask.

Lucy immediately set to work on the dining room table at Davies Street, taking her inspiration as she later admitted from a 'tea gown I had seen Letty Lind wear on the stage. It was accordian pleated and I sewed every stitch of it myself, working at night to get it finished on time.'

Fifty years later, Lucy still possessed a photograph of that first dress. It had successively hung in salons in London, Paris and New York and she was very superstitious about it, regarding it as a mascot, for it brought her the luck and the entrée she needed.

A few days after its appearance at Mrs. Panmuir Gordon's house-party, every woman who had seen it had given Lucy an order for something similar. Lucy had found her métier.

Now it was that Lucy revived the ideas she had developed in Jersey in designing clothes that were not rigid copies of Paris fashion, but rather individual exercises in style. In christening her designs 'Personality' dresses, Lucy showed a facility for a catchy label that she was to develop into a fine art as the years went by.

It was not long before more and more members of the tea-gown set fluttered to the new dressmaker. They were intrigued and flattered by the idea of having something designed especially to suit their personalities and, moreover, something unique.

Lucy had started designing at a perfect time. Rigid Victorian society was beginning to relax both its rules for entry and its behaviour. The old landed aristocracy was in the process of losing its power, and 'new money' was being let in, encouraged by the Prince of Wales. Rich Americans were coming to London to marry off their Dollar Princess daughters to Titles. The curtain was rising on the luxurious, lavish Edwardian era. Clothes were extremely important to these new society women; they were not grand enough to look dowdy, they had to be dressed to perfection. The smartly-dressed woman could and did go to Paris to be dressed by Worth or by the new star, Jacques Doucet, if she was rich enough. But there was no guarantee that, on her return to Mayfair, she would not see the same model on one of her friends. If she was not rich enough to go to Paris twice a year for her clothes, then the society woman had to fall back on the needle of one of the 'little dressmakers' who abounded at that time and who were expert in copying the fashion plates in such publications as *Art, Goût, Beauté*. To have a tea-gown or morning dress or ballgown designed for her was a delightful idea indeed, and quickly caught on in a society ever hungry for novelty.

'Everyone who had heard of me wanted to have one of my "personal dresses",' Lucy said, 'and I bought an order book. Soon its pages were half-filled. I could not afford an assistant, so I not only designed the dresses myself, but cut them out and sewed them, working far into the night. And when they were finished, I used to wrap them up and deliver them myself.'

Looking back, Lucy admitted she often laughed to remember how the entire staff of the famous dressmaking house (which employed at its zenith hundreds of workpeople) once consisted of one young woman who used to cut out her models on the dining room floor, with a watchful eye on the sticky fingers of her baby daughter.

This solo operation, carried on with a little help from Mrs. Kennedy when she could spare the time from looking after Esmé, lasted for about six months, after which Lucy had made enough money to launch out and take on four girl assistants. One of them was an expert fitter, which left Lucy free to create new models in the form of coloured sketches, from which her clients could make their choice. At this early stage in her career, she never repeated a design, unlike the Paris couturiers, but later, of course, she started making 'editions' designed not so much with an individual in mind but rather a mood.

One of Lucy's earliest clients was Lady Angela Forbes, 'Daisy' Warwick's half-sister, who was astonished to find that Lucy made

'the most lovely frocks for £8. . . . I really think she did a great deal
to revolutionize dress in London. All her frocks in those days even,
were recognizeable by her finishing touches, which generally consisted of minute buttons and little frills of lace and ribbon. She had
a wonderful collection of old embroidered collars which she used to
adapt, and she gave me a lovely one which she put on my going-away
coat.'

One of the reasons for Lucy's success was a unique design hand-
writing. A dress designed by her is unmistakable. It has a delicacy
and intricacy, coupled with a harmony in colour combination, that
stands out. Her dresses always had a multitude of minute details. It
was almost certainly from portraits, such as Boucher's exquisite
rendering of Madame de Pompadour, that Lucy first got the idea of
making intricate silk flowers that could be placed at the waist, or on
a shoulder, or knotted into a sash, and then be removed and used in
a different way.

Some of her flowers have survived and they are miracles of observation and of intricate design. They are wired and their stems wound
round and round with shaded green silks. As well as being exquisite
examples of handiwork they also demonstrate Lucy's other superb
talent – for colour. She was never afraid to use strong colours
together. Her surviving hand-painted designs from the early 1890s,
with their fabrics swatched down the side of each drawing, show
that she was using brilliant combinations of scarlet, viridian, tyrian
purple and jade, twenty years before these striking colours ('Like a
blow to the head' as Poiret would describe them) became the rage in
Paris, inspired by Bakst's designs from the Ballet Russe.

But, daringly ahead of her time as she then was, Lucy could also
produce clothes in typical Edwardian sweet-pea shades, lavishly
trimmed with antique laces and sprinkled with sequins. How pretty
her society clients must have looked in these ravishing drifts of
colour.

Her designs were, at their best, impressionistic; they were never
really strong on line or cut. Their merits lay in decoration. Without
initially realising it, Lucy had returned to the fundamental principles
of eighteenth-century court fashion, in which the actual shape of the
dress did not change quickly, but rather evolved slowly over the
years, while the constant change that is the essence of fashion was
effected by a faster evolution in decorative trimmings, which could
be removed at the end of a season.

One season, flowers would be all the rage at Versailles, for instance;
the next, knots of striped ribbon, called coquelicot; the next, puffs
and swags of lace. This was the principle Lucy would follow in

creating tea-gowns or balldresses of antique lace glittering with artfully placed flowers and sequins. Even her walking dresses would be trimmed with knots of soutache or Brandenburg braiding.

It became apparent to Mrs. Kennedy that Lucy's success was going to continue and that her headstrong elder daughter really could survive on her talent. This success did not happen overnight; Mrs. Kennedy had to support Lucy and Esmé until about 1893, after which her investment in her daughter started to pay increasingly gratifying dividends.

But equally important was the fact that Lucy herself was contented and busy.

SOCIETY

(1890–1909)

'No man is an impossible husband if he is a duke
at least no duchess ought to find him so,
and if he were that is not the slightest excuse.'

Points of View

i Elinor Glyn – or The Reluctant Virgin

Elinor was still looking for a husband in 1890. She had been 'out' for over seven years in England and France, and to the despairing Mrs. Kennedy seemed no nearer being settled.

During these years she had become an extremely accomplished and very successful flirt. Dressed beautifully by her sister, or in fragile lace Doucet gowns given to her by her Paris cousins, she looked infinitely more mondaine than most of her contemporaries. But they married, one by one, and she did not. She had acquired a reputation for capriciousness amounting to foolhardiness, for however many men proposed to her, and many did, none of them was quite right.

Elinor thoroughly enjoyed admiration and had developed the habit of leading men on and then rejecting them. She enjoyed the chase, and always would, rather more, one suspects, than the consummation.

But Elinor began to get edgy, for she knew that every passing season lessened her chances. Although she enjoyed Paris, she knew time spent there was wasted, for no Frenchman she felt worthy of her would ask for her hand because of her lack of 'dot'. A fragment in one of her penny journals written at this time shows just how bitter and disillusioned she felt underneath her red, green and white exterior. She called her short story *No Luck or The Vicissitudes of a Poor Young Virgin*.

They began early in life. . . . & now after years of hard work she is still on our hands. I have questioned her very closely but she is unable to give any exact details of the first one, so we had better jump over the schoolroom experiences and begin at about 17. This was a one-legged man – he came, they got on – he was comfortably off, & our hearts beat with hope, when unfortunately he took it into his head to get a wooden leg. . . . this put her off, she said she knew the unscrewing noise at night would get on her nerves & she'd hate to feel anything so hard if she happened to be sitting next to him. So this little affair ended.

The unnamed heroine rejects or is rejected by several more suitors and Elinor concludes the story on a gloomy note:

She is still our virgin & if after reading these cruel vicissitudes some kind reader's thoughts aren't touched he had better look at the following picture & if that does not fix him, I am afraid she will be doomed for an old maid.

The picture is still stuck into the marbled notebook. It is, of course, of Elinor.

Money was an ever-recurring worry. Mrs. Kennedy's slim resources were needed to support Lucy's dressmaking venture. For, having realised that this was not a momentary divertissement but might develop into the means of supporting all four of them, Mrs. Kennedy was sinking her small capital into 'Mrs. James Wallace' as and when it was needed to purchase materials and pay staff.

Elinor's wardrobe and travelling expenses assumed a low priority. Mrs. Kennedy impressed upon her on many occasions that she must be more careful than ever and bring herself to accept someone, even if he did not live up to what must have appeared impossibly high standards.

Lack of money notwithstanding, Elinor visited the Fouquet le Maîtres again in 1889 and in 1890. She enjoyed the sensation she caused riding (rather badly, for she was afraid of horses) in the Bois, dressed in a tall shako hat and a form-hugging riding habit of rather daring design. Attending a cotillion at the British Embassy in the summer of 1890, she danced opposite the American heiress, Mary Leiter, who would become the first Lady Curzon. She also made a firm friend of Sir Coudie Stephen, First Secretary at the British Embassy, who fell a little in love with her and remained so until the end of his life. Elinor had fun but, as she remarked in her memoirs, 'Mademoiselle Jeanne de Fougère and I seemed to be the only girls who ever had a good time, perhaps because, as we had no dowry, we were not considered marriageable.'

In the winter of 1891 she was asked to stay at Hillersdon once more by her friend Billy Grant. The occasion was a coming-of-age dance during which Elinor was obviously up to her old flirtatious tricks. After the ball, four men in the houseparty quarrelled over her and jumped into a nearby lake in their evening clothes and then, according to her, came back to Hillersdon and bathed in their host's best champagne.

Even allowing for high-jinks normal at country houseparties at the time, this sounds suspiciously as if it might have been imaginative embroidery on Elinor's part. But something happened and, in the small world of society, word soon got out about the exploit. The word clearly reached Essex where the Chisenhale-Marshes, old friends of Elinor who had a large house near Epping Forest, told a neighbour of theirs, Clayton Glyn.

Essex mamas had despaired of Clayton Glyn, for he showed no signs of marrying. Now in his late thirties, he lived near Harlow in a house on an inherited estate where he bred pedigree Jersey cows and led the sporting life when not on lengthy trips abroad.

Whatever the truth of the Hillersdon story – and it probably lost nothing in the telling – it captured Glyn's imagination and he became curious to meet the girl who could have provoked such happenings. 'A woman who could induce solid old A.B. —— and B.C. —— to jump into a lake at three o'clock on a winter morning must be worth looking at,' he remarked to the Chisenhale-Marsh family, who promptly arranged that Elinor should be asked for a weekend visit to meet him.

He was obviously not disappointed in the elegant sophisticated redhead with the polished fingernails and the 'Parisian' clothes. But whether, as Elinor always maintained, he lost no time in making it clear to her that he wanted to marry her is moot. He detested fuss or any show of sentiment and always hid his real feelings behind a mask of cheerful good humour. This was not exactly the stuff of high-flying romance, but Elinor knew that he was probably her last chance of a respectable 'parti', and she decided to take him.

Clayton Glyn had an established position in society, the manner of a grand seigneur and what Elinor airily assumed were sufficient funds to keep such a position up. 'I believe one of the reasons I was so attracted to him,' Elinor wrote, 'was because I was unconsciously reminded of the illustrations in my books of Cinderella's fairy Prince, for his thick silver hair was like the powdered wigs of the eighteenth century, to which the story of Cinderella always seems to belong.'

In her autobiography, Elinor gives the impression that an engagement, or rather, a wordless understanding, followed her first meeting with Glyn. But in reality it took just over a year for Elinor to capture her Prince Charming. In February 1892, she retreated to Monte Carlo, chaperoned by her mother (whose shrewd idea this probably was), in order to bring Clayton up to 'scratch'. The ruse succeeded: he followed her and presented her with a large diamond engagement ring from Cartier. Mrs. Kennedy and Elinor lost no time in setting the wedding date for April 27 of that year but, as soon as this had been agreed, Clayton departed for England once more to 'see to the young pheasants'. Elinor was naturally rather surprised and hurt by this, and she 'saw little more of him before the wedding. But for the ring I should have imagined that I had dreamt the whole incident, for he seldom wrote.'

Clayton had not gone back to see to the young pheasants. He had gone back to raise £2,500 against his already encumbered expectations, in order to do up Sheering, the house in which he lived, for Durrington, the principal house on the estate, had already been let on the death of his father, some five years previously.

Far from being well off, as Elinor thought, Clayton Glyn lived in a morass of debt, a state of affairs going back to his great grandmother, Henrietta Glyn. This redoubtable lady had spent twenty years virtually squatting at Durrington, from about 1820 to 1840, periodically being evicted by court order, for she was only a co-tenant of the house and had no right to live in it. Late in 1844, she had finally got possession by offering £15,000 to the co-tenants. She had borrowed the sum, and this started the pyramid of Glyn borrowings, which continued through the following two generations.

Clayton Glyn's father was an exception to the profligate Glyn tendency. He had married well and lived at Durrington in thrifty style on his wife's money from about 1862 until his death in 1887. During this time, he attempted to develop the Homerston Estate, as his land was called, as a vast building project, in order to re-establish the Glyn finances on a sound footing.

Clayton had been born at Durrington, a charming Georgian house, and had wished to go into the Army, but instead was sent to Oxford to read law. While there, he overspent his allowance in common with many another aristocrat of the time, and fell into the hands of moneylenders always ready to lend to a young man with expectations. Clayton had inherited the spendthrift tendency.

Although he qualified as a barrister, Clayton never practised, but helped his father with his building project until, in 1887, Clayton senior died. When, in the following year, his mother was run over and killed in the drive at Durrington, Clayton let the house, and was never to return. Using a modest legacy from his mother, he made several trips to the Far East and to Asia, travelling first class all the way and writing lengthy letters back to his two sisters. Eventually, in 1890, he returned to England to set himself up as a yeoman farmer with squirearchical overtones. He also continued with his father's development project, borrowing the necessary money to complete it. This sum was charged, using Durrington and Sheering as collateral, to secure not only its own development costs, but all the calamitous Glyn borrowings since Henrietta had first started the process in 1825.

In spite of appearances, Clayton had a very modest net income. In

1892, the Homerston Estate had shown a net loss of £375, which was offset by an equivalent amount of rent from Durrington House. Sheering Estate Farms brought in a net rent of about £500 and his farming activities probably brought in about £200 a year on top of that.

Had Clayton managed to bring the Homerston Estate project to its conclusion, his descendants would have had expectations of over £300,000 on the reversion, at that time some eighty years off. If he had proceeded as he ought, that is to say borrowing very little in anticipation during the early years while the equity built up, so that the reversion would accelerate rapidly in value as it neared its term, Clayton's heirs would have been very wealthy. Unfortunately, Clayton did not keep his borrowings within bounds.

Elinor and her mother were unsophisticated in money matters, and thus judged Clayton's financial position solely on such criteria as the diamond ring from Cartier and the size of the generous marriage settlement he made upon Elinor. They had no idea of the true state of affairs and, even if they had, would probably have ignored it.

From travelling second class, as it were, Elinor was going to marry a man who always insisted on first class. Talk of reversions and of equity would have meant nothing to her. It was enough – more than enough – to a girl who had despaired of finding the perfect man that she had apparently done so. On the one hand Clayton fitted in with her romantic ardour and, on the other, he more than lived up to the high standards first established by her grandmother's snobbish ideals. Romance and cynicism were both satisfied. In marrying Clayton, Elinor knew she would be able to take what she saw as her rightful place in society, becoming a hostess in her own establishment, rather than a permanent visitor in what would, as the years passed and she grew older, have become a decreasing number of other people's guest rooms.

On his part, Clayton knew himself to be in circumstances comparatively so straitened that he had no chance of marrying well – that is to say, for money. So he married to suit himself – for love.

The engagement announced, the date set, Elinor and her mother had no hesitation in going straight to Paris, ostensibly to buy a few fripperies for the trousseau (most of which was, of course, made by Lucy). Mrs. Kennedy could, perhaps, be forgiven for a slight feeling of triumph over the grand French relations. 'My French friends were very pleased with me for capturing a rich husband,' said Elinor, 'and were really impressed with the romantic qualities of Englishmen, who were thus willing to propose to a penniless girl. There must be something fine about a nation which did not require a "dot". "Tout de même, c'est beau," I was told: but they chaffed me for having been deserted by him so soon.'

Elinor and Clayton were married at St. George's, Hanover Square, on April 27, 1892. She was given away by one of the invaluable Fouquet le Maîtres. Clayton gave her a splendid diamond tiara and with unusual poetry he asked her to wear it for the wedding to hold her veil of Brussels lace, as she was 'so like a fairy Queen'. Or did Elinor embroider again?

Lucy surpassed herself dressing her sister, who now looked as if she might well become an excellent advertisement for her clothes. Elinor's dress was generally held to be a triumph. She described it in an unusually detailed sketched catalogue of her clothes which she kept from 1889 to 1895. Each outfit is carefully drawn and equally carefully described. This is what she said of her wedding dress:

> White very thick satin, stretched body, fastening under arm, no seams. Fishnet veil and sleeves to elbow of old Honiton lace. Train from shoulder of thick white satin brocade, lined satin, and edged like skirt with satin ruche. Orange blossom aigrette and spray at waist. Diamond tiara, brooches and cross, and two strings of pearls. Bouquet of gardenia, stephanotis and orange blossom.

Elinor also made a drawing of her going away travelling dress and labelled it triumphantly 'For E. Glyn not Sutherland any more.'

She had, she believed, achieved the end toward which she had striven for nearly ten years. She was always to be grateful to Clayton and she never forgot what she owed him.

They spent part of their honeymoon at Brighton and if Elinor is to be believed (and even her imagination was probably not capable of the task of inventing such an histoire) Clayton hired the public swimming baths for two days for their private use in order, he said, that he might appreciate the beauty of the mermaid he had married.

He made Elinor let her hair down – it came to her knees – and swim up and down the baths naked with her hair streaming out behind her. 'Such princely gestures are almost worth the inevitable reckoning,' she wrote, many years and many troubles later. 'The rather (in those days) improper oriental-fairy-tale atmosphere of the idea fitted superbly into my romantic scheme of things.'

Elinor had developed a tremendous capacity for self-dramatisation and was never above re-writing events to fit in with her romantic or her cynical notions. She invented legends, built out of real experiences, which she would magnify. Then, imperceptibly, invention would become reality in her mind. So it is with slight reservations that we learn from her that on her return to Sheering (which she maintains was Durrington) Clayton's tenants, who had erected a triumphal arch, unharnessed their carriage horses and pulled the coach – to Durrington.

Durrington was, of course, let. Whether the triumphal arch was also a figment of her imagination or no, this period of her life must have been like a dream to Elinor – a fairytale with a happy ending and the final justification for all her capriciousness and her rejection of her other suitors.

ii 'Lucile'

Lucy was always vague about dates and never more so than in her autobiography, in which she blithely compressed five years into one. Thus she gave the impression that 'Mrs. James Wallace', as she originally labelled her clothes and called her business, was an overnight success. But, in fact, it took her over five years to become established and to develop from being a society dressmaker, designing clothes for her friends and making them herself with her mother's help, into being a professional couturière, who employed a large staff and who made a profit.

It is apparent from her letters to her mother in the early years of her enterprise that Lucy was finding it difficult to make ends meet and that Elinor's 'huge Lucile bills' (as Elinor put it later) were vital to the survival of the business. Thus Clayton was supporting not only his wife but, through her dressmaking bills, his mother-in-law, sister-in-law and niece by marriage.

All this rather went to Elinor's head and she began to be imperious in her dealings with her sister. Many letters to their mother demanded that Lucy should execute shopping commissions for her or other little errands. It may be imagined that Lucy resented this high-handed approach from a younger sister who, until she had made an advantageous marriage, had been nobody. Elinor was always at her most unattractive when successful. Adversity suited her and displayed her admirable traits; success encouraged her snobbish notions and the idea that she was invariably correct in anything she said or did.

Notwithstanding their personal differences, Lucy made it her business to be agreeable to Elinor for, finance apart, a younger sister now moving in society was a splendid advertisement for her designs. Elinor's wedding dress brought in many similar commissions, notably that of designing the wedding dress of pretty Maud Cassel, Sir Ernest Cassel's daughter (and future mother of Edwina Mountbatten). This was a very important commission indeed, for Sir Ernest, a clever financier, was an adviser and close friend of the Prince of Wales, and thus the guests at his daughter's wedding were from the

Court and very influential social circles from which Lucy hoped to be able to draw her clientele.

Lucy herself attributed her first success to the clothes she designed for an amateur production of *Diplomacy* which a friend of Clayton Glyn, Lord Rosslyn, got up for charity in 1895. Rosslyn was a talented amateur actor and took the principal part. Elinor played 'Dora' and Mrs. Willie James, a leading member of the Marlborough House set, took the part of the adventuress 'Zicka'. The play was performed very successfully in London and then in Edinburgh and Elinor scored a personal success in the dresses her sister had designed for her now mature and startling beauty.

Elinor recorded the two dresses Lucy designed for this role in her growing catalogue of her wardrobe. One was bright cerise, shot with glacé silk, edged with tiny narrow bands of white satin, each edge done with narrow yellow insertions; it had diamond buttons and a belt of cerise. The other was a tea-gown of white chiné silk, edged with gold and jewelled dragons.

Whether or not *Diplomacy* was the reason, the dressmaking business began to succeed soon after, and Lucy and her mother decided that the Davies Street dining room table was becoming too small for the future needs of the expanding enterprise. It was time, they concluded, to take proper premises and late in 1895, possibly with Clayton's help, they took a shop and workrooms at 24 Old Burlington Street and additional staff were engaged. Among these new employees was a little fourteen-year-old apprentice called Celia who became devoted to Lucy's interests and remained with her for many years.

Now began the golden period in Lucy's life when it seemed as if her needle was enchanted. More and more society ladies found their way to Old Burlington Street, intrigued by the notion of personalised dresses. Mrs. Willie James became one of her most important clients, and where she led others followed. A famous society beauty and noted hostess reputed to be the mistress of Edward VII, but more probably his daughter, she was at that time generally acknowledged to be the leader of fashion in London in an era when fashions were still set by a dozen or so women.

Lily Langtry was another who was always the first to wear any new mode designed by 'Mrs. James Wallace', but Lucy felt that her 'taste was more extreme than that of Mrs. Willie James and women were not so ready to follow, however much they might admire her distinctive type.'

A woman who wished to lead fashion in this era had to work extremely hard on choosing her clothes. The incredible variety of her wardrobe, with outfits designed for every occasion, was almost bewildering in its complexity. On awakening in the morning, the fashionable woman opened her letters and drank her tea in bed dressed in a bewitching deshabillée dressing-gown. On coming downstairs, she would be dressed in a morning gown. If in London, she would then pay calls in a walking dress or suit. If in the country, she would change into a tweed shooting suit to have lunch with the guns. At tea, when she received visitors in London, or took tea with the returned sportsmen in the country, she would wear a tea-gown. The final change was into la grande toilette for a dinner party; an even grander one for a ball, a visit to the opera or the theatre. A Saturday to Monday (as a weekend was then called in society) entailed no less than sixteen different changes, accompanied by hats, gloves, blouses, corsets, shoes, furs, evening cloaks and jewels. Three or four domed trunks were not an unusual accompaniment when such a fashionable woman went to a houseparty.

The fashions of the times were elaborate. The hour-glass shape popularised by Princess Alexandra, with a demi-bustle becoming smaller with each season, was in vogue. In the evening, dresses were very low cut and more often than not made in the finest of lace, tinted to a pastel tone and then oversewn with sequins or garlanded with handmade flowers. Blouses, too, came in for elaborate embroidery and were worn with braided and soutached serge walking suits. And underneath, the most important item of all, the corset. Corsetmakers literally created fashion, for they dictated the essential shape on which the elaborate superstructure depended. For Lucy the fashion accorded perfectly with her preference for handwork and infinite elaboration within given themes.

One innovation that Lucy introduced during her time in Old Burlington Street was the cause of a great deal of fashionable tea-time gossip. It was a room set aside for underwear which she called the Rose Room. But Lucy's underwear was not the dull cambric or heavy cotton underpinnings hitherto thought appropriate by late Victorian ladies (if not their husbands). It was scandalously scanty and rather naughty. She designed and made these little camisoles, knickers, petticoats and nightgowns as carefully as she made her dresses, adding bedspreads and pillowcases to match in the palest of pink crêpe de chine trimmed with lace and garlanded with silk roses. Even her corset covers were embroidered and had lace inserts.

'Half the women flocked to see them though they had not the courage to buy them at first,' said Lucy. 'Those cunning little lace motifs let in just over the heart, those saucy velvet bows on the shoulder might surely be the weapons of the woman who was "not quite nice"? They all wanted to wear them, but they were not certain of their ground. They had to fly in the face of the conventional idea as to how a good woman went to bed at night, and it took a little coaxing for them to do it.'

Some husbands put their foot down, but the majority enthusiastically let their wives order more. With impeccable timing and sure instinct, Lucy had created a symbol of the proliferating clandestine sexuality now beginning to replace Victorian prudery in the boudoirs of society.

At the same time as she was clothing half London society in little nothings, Lucy was also beginning to make a name for herself in a different milieu: the theatre. Sir Charles Wyndham was searching for a costume-designer for *The Liars* which he was planning to produce at The Haymarket. He had heard of Lucy's personality dresses and reasoned that the idea might be interesting when applied to imaginary, as opposed to real, characters. 'He asked me to call and see him and the upshot of our conversation,' Lucy said, 'was that I went away with an order to design dresses for Irene Vanbrugh, Mary Moore and Cynthia Brooke.'

This was a departure from the established tenets of costume design at the time, for stage dresses were, almost without exception, very heavy, thick affairs and were mostly made by traditional costumiers in a theatrical tradition that demanded a certain sort of ponderous magnificence. Executed in heavy velvets, thick satins and stiff brocades, such clothes were not made in the lighter more 'modern' fabrics that had already been introduced into the world of fashion by Lucy in London and Doucet in Paris, fabrics which were considered too clinging for stage use.

When Lucy told Irene Vanbrugh that she intended to make her 'a dress of buttercup yellow chiffon', the leading lady looked doubtful. 'You have a lovely figure,' Lucy told her, 'why try to blur its lines with something that hangs in heavy, lifeless folds?' The finished designs bore a strong resemblance to clothes worn in society drawing rooms, rather than to outmoded theatre traditions. In spite of an initial reluctance on the part of all three actresses to appearing in such revealing gowns, Lucy's designs were extremely successful and started a new era in costume design, with a heightened naturalism rather than 'stagey' effects.

The business continued to expand and by 1897 had become far too big for the house in Old Burlington Street. By now, Lucy was dressing practically every woman with pretensions to fashion in

London and dressing her moreover in original designs, not in pallid copies of Worth or Doucet in Paris as other London dressmakers, such as Jay and Reville, were apt to offer.

The time had come to look for bigger premises. She wanted to remain in Mayfair, for it had none of the associations with 'trade' she so despised, but this wish backfired on her, for many of the houses she looked at were restricted to residential use. Finally she found the perfect solution, a house in which in another time and under different circumstances she might have lived. Now, by a twist of fate and chiffon, she put seamstresses in the maids' bedrooms, turned the drawing room into a salon and drew her designs in what had formerly been the morning room.

The house was at 17 Hanover Square and was owned by Sir George Dashwood. It had been in his family since it was built in the eighteenth century and was 'a glorious house, with wonderfully carved chimney pieces and Angelica Kauffman ceilings whose beauty,' felt Lucy, 'would be an unfailing source of inspiration to me. Although the rent was considerably more than I had intended to pay, I signed the lease then and there.' This move was very typical of Lucy's cavalier attitude towards money. Whenever its lack conflicted with her wishes, she just went ahead anyway.

She decorated 17 Hanover Square as if it was still a private house. In this, as in so many things, Lucy created a new way of doing things. The great couture houses in or near the rue de la Paix did not look like ladies' private ballrooms; they were much more utilitarian and looked far more like huge fitting rooms than salons.

At the time of her move, Lucy dropped the 'Mrs. James Wallace' label in favour of the much grander 'The Maison Lucile' – and here she did copy Paris and overtones of the rue de la Paix. Mrs. Kennedy put up more of her capital to form a limited company and 'Lucile' was launched. The little divorced dressmaker had promoted herself to the status of couturière.

Cards were sent out. Elegantly swagged with flowers copied from an eighteenth-century ex libris design, they told the polite world that 'The Maison Lucile' specialised in 'Picture Frocks and Corsets'.

This might seem to be a strange combination, but it was a shrewd advertisement. Corsets were extremely important to the fashionable wardrobe, and so were picture frocks. These were specifically designed for the wearer to be painted in, and many a Sargent- or an Orpen-lady is clad in one of Lucy's diaphanous gowns decorated with just such miniscule details as would stimulate the brush of a society painter. Carefully conceived in fabrics which would catch the light, these frocks were highly successful.

The size of her business and the number of clients she now dressed meant that Lucy's original idea of personalised frocks was on the whole superseded by models which were not designed with a specific woman in mind but which could, once shown, be adapted or made in a different colour combination. Lucy now stopped working entirely from her own sketches and began to design clothes as the couturiers in Paris tended to do at the time – that is to say, by making them from fabric straight on to a dressmaker's form, or on to a live model. The model would wear crêpe de chine petticoats which would become the actual interlining of the dress. 'I had my own room set apart from the others and here I would shut myself up for hours with yards of material, out of which I would create tea gowns and ball dresses, dainty little frocks for debutantes and sophisticated models that looked the last word in wickedness,' said Lucy who admitted that it was in such moments that she was always supremely happy.

'I was an artist,' she said. 'Nothing more. As the sculptor sees his dreams translated into line, and the painter sees his in terms of colour, so mine were expressed in the drapery of a wisp of chiffon or the fall of a satin fold. It is a lesser form of art, I know, but to me it meant a great deal, my life's work and I was tremendously in earnest over every dress I created.'

Lucy was always an artist first and a businesswoman a bad second. Mrs. Kennedy's original capital was not enough to finance Lucy's plans for expansion. She was soon in difficulties with the large weekly wages bill; she had to find a great deal of money to pay her fabric suppliers. Her clients were either personal friends or at least social acquaintances, and she found out what many have found before and since – that the richer the woman the slower is her bill paid. There were social as well as financial reasons which made it difficult for her to press for payment. Would she surrender the cachet of gentlewoman by pressing her claims as a businesswoman?

Lucy was not her grandmother's child for nothing, and this would have looked a good deal too much like being in 'trade'. Although Lucy really didn't care to move in society, she thought of herself as an artist, not as a tradesperson.

Matters came to a head in the mid 1890s when there was no money one week to meet the wages bill. But one of Lucy's admirers at the time – she referred to him as 'Lord de L.W.' – came to the rescue and guaranteed an overdraft of £1,000, a considerable sum in those days. This near-escape gave Lucy what she described as a 'dreadful jar' and she decided to re-capitalise the business. In order to do so she took in as partners Sir Cosmo Duff Gordon and Mr. Miles of the firm of accountants Jocelyn, Miles & Blow.

Sir Cosmo Duff Gordon was a quiet Scot, the head of a cadet branch of the Gordon family, Marquesses of Aberdeen. Very tall, very good looking, he was notable, in his younger days for a magnificent singing voice and, unusual for the class from whence he came, had trained in Italy. He was also a superb athlete and was to be a member of Lord Desborough's Olympic fencing team. He was, at the time of investing in Lucy's business, in the process of becoming 'a very dear friend'. Unfortunately, he was dominated by his mother, a strict moralist who did not approve of her son's relationship with a divorced woman who designed naughty undergarments for a living.

Little is known of the long-suffering accountant, Miles, who spent the next twenty years vainly trying to control Lucy's worst financial excesses. She never cared to be told what to do, and very rarely paid him any attention.

As her business flourished, so did Lucy's private life. Her new friends lived in the larger world where haute bohemia met society, but Lucy turned away from society more and more as the 'nineties passed. This was due at least partly to her growing realisation of the difficulty of mixing business with social pleasure. Her nature, too, demanded this larger canvas. Unlike Elinor, she was little interested in titles or social position. Lucy was always much happier with theatre people, artists, musicians and writers, for she considered herself to be one of them.

Now began a period in Elinor's life in which she had to make some profound adjustments. As a married woman with an entrée into society, she began to live the life then typical of a leisured member of the country set. Her social round was invariable (as formalised as life at Versailles in the time of the Duc de Saint-Simon) revolving, as it did, between the London and the sporting seasons.

With her international upbringing and romantic imagination, Elinor felt out of sympathy with the Essex country set. 'I thought of my Essex neighbours much as the Beau Monde of Paris looked upon the French people who stayed in the country and never came to the capital – as funny provincials with old-fashioned narrow views and limited interests.'

On their part, most of her new neighbours were intrigued by Clayton Glyn's unexpected marriage to someone they thought of as a colonial nobody. They stared at her Parisian clothes, high heels, long gloves and invariable parasol (Elinor would never expose her face to the sun). But later Elinor came to regret her attitude toward them. 'At the time I glorified in my different appearance and remained blissfully ignorant of the flutter I was causing.' Justifying an attitude she would later realise was 'not in the perfect taste which Grand-mamma would have required of me', she claimed that Clayton always encouraged her to be as smart as possible and paid her heavy Lucile bills without even reading them through. What may have given her pause to re-consider her attitude to her dowdy neighbours was that they, in their turn, considered her sophisticated clothes perhaps a little common for the country.

Not all Elinor's new neighbours were unappreciative of her 'foreign' style. Soon after her arrival in Essex, she became very friendly with Frances, Countess of Warwick, the local grande dame, who lived ten miles away from Sheering at Easton Lodge. 'Daisy' as she was called by her intimates, one of whom was the Prince of Wales, had verve and style and remained a close friend of Elinor until her death. When Elinor first started to go about in society after her marriage, Lady Warwick was always ready to give her good advice; but her influence was not wholly benign in its inadvertent encouragement of Elinor's snobbery and obsession with breeding – what she always called 'race'. These were the years before Lady Warwick developed her socialist principles.

Lady Warwick's half-sister, Lady Angela Forbes, remembered the first glimpse she and her sister had of this exotic figure. In her *Memoirs and Base Details* she gives the distinct impression that Elinor was not yet considered to be of the inner social circle:

> It was at Easton that Elinor Glyn made her first appearance on the social horizon. She and her husband lived at Harlow and had driven over to watch the cricket. I can see her now, coming across to the tent where we were sitting, with her very red hair glistening in the sun. Her frock (I must say it was only made of the very cheapest material) made her look as if she had stepped out of *La Vie Parisienne*; we were all so thrilled over her appearance that we got Daisy to ask her to come and stay. The 'creation' in which she appeared for dinner was another marvel, and after dinner she did the most wonderful imitations, for a select few, of Sarah Bernhardt.

Daisy Warwick's patronage of Elinor led to her being often included in the famous houseparties at Easton. In her memoirs Lady Warwick noted that in one houseparty in the 1890s her guests included Lord Curzon, Elinor and her husband. This was probably Elinor's first meeting with the man who was to be the dominating inspiration in her life.

Thus during those early years of marriage Clayton and Elinor often took the road from Sheering to Easton, driving in a brougham drawn by a pair of horses called 'Pair' and 'Impair' – so christened in memory of their engagement in Monte Carlo. They would be greeted at the door by Mr. Hall, the Groom of the Chambers, who, as Elinor later said, was like Olivier, the head waiter of the Ritz in Paris, who knew everyone in the world and where to place them. Elinor and Clayton, in common with the other arrivals, would then leave their furs and their coats, before being led into the saloon where Daisy and her women friends were to be found 'arrayed in the most exquisite tea-gowns of velvet or satin brocade, trimmed in sable'.

Parties at Easton usually consisted of from twenty to forty people drawn from the aristocracy, Tory politicians (never Liberals), ambassadors, sportsmen, and other distinguished men 'with or without their wives' as Elinor put it. But neither the world of Bohemia (artists, musicians, actors and actresses) nor business people of any kind were ever asked.

After dinner on the first night the men would eventually join the ladies and by the end of the evening at such a houseparty, Elinor realised, it was often obvious which member of the party intended to make it his business to amuse which woman – in a discreet way – during the rest of the visit 'in the hope of who knows what rewards'.

In spite of her many visits to Paris and her vivid imagination, Elinor retained a middle-class prudishness and was, one suspects, somewhat shocked by her first encounters with society's attitude towards liaisons. There was still a streak of naivety in her character which betrayed her as less sophisticated and mondaine than she cared to appear.

In the August of the year she was married, Elinor accompanied Clayton to St. Fillans, a grouse moor near Crieff belonging to Lord Dysart. Unlike Lucy, who loved swimming, Elinor had never been an enthusiast for outdoor pursuits. They could be messy and uncomfortable, and she loathed mud and thick boots.

A severe cough, the result of influenza and unappreciated activity on the moors, won her much solicitude from Clayton (who treated her like a 'Dresden fairy princess') and more time to write daily and at length to her mother, regaling her with her ailments and the fact that a sympathetic doctor had diagnosed a 'faulty heart valve' and excused her going out with the guns.

When not cataloguing her illnesses, she constantly asked her mother to charge Lucy with yet more errands: 'Lucy is to go to Owens for me before she comes up & get me a nice hat & trimming 'cause we shan't have time to stop in London on our way up if the B's have a ball in the house.' These and many other requests to Lucy made during the course of four days were couched in the gracious tone of rich sister. Elinor could, on the other hand, still be sympathetic to Lucy's problems: 'I am too delighted that Esmé is coming, I will certainly pay her journey. Dear little soul. That brute James – what a pity he does not kill himself.'

In June 1893, a year after her marriage, Elinor had her first child, whom she christened Margot after her Fouquet le Maître relation. Clayton was disappointed that Elinor had not produced a son to carry on the Glyn dynasty and so justify his efforts to develop the Homerston Estate.

Not long after Margot's birth, Elinor developed typhoid fever and took a long time to recover. No sooner in good health than she concussed herself while acting in *Diplomacy* – an acted fall turned into a real one, as she hit her head against a bit of furniture when she fell.

Elinor was to suffer intermittent ill health for the next five years. It is possible that some of these illnesses were psychosomatic. Her relationship with Clayton was deteriorating as the fundamental differences in their characters and their interests became more apparent. Clayton liked the sporting outdoor life; arriving at church six minutes late on Sundays in order that the vicar should not get 'uppish'; and all the other minutiae of typical upper class squirearchical country existence of the time. Elinor preferred to read by the fire, wearing 'beautiful indoor clothes'. She began to make scenes, caused partly through boredom, which embarrassed and irritated the stolid Clayton.

Elinor had failed to produce a son, and Clayton may also have been disappointed in her for another reason. It is dangerous to make suppositions about someone's sexuality without firm evidence, but Elinor seemed to conform to a type which derives greater satisfaction from flirtation and provocation than from actual physical passion – a pattern of behaviour no doubt formed by her years as debutante. If this were true, it would explain why, although he was obviously fond of her, Clayton began to go his own way after only two years of marriage.

A hint of this divergence is given in Elinor's autobiography. In 1894, one of Elinor's bridesmaids stayed with them for some time. She enjoyed tramping round the estate with Clayton, leaving Elinor to read by the fire. 'She was pretty and good-natured, of the type who willingly bathes dogs, fetches corn for colts and goes for long walks in the rain, and I was grateful to her for taking over these distasteful duties for me, not being yet wise in the ways of men as I became later,' Elinor wrote.

Clayton's developing indifference to her in a romantic sense was forcibly brought home to her while staying at Easton one weekend that summer. Daisy Warwick's husband Lord Brooke, or 'Brookie' as he was known, began to make what Elinor rather prissily called the 'usual insinuations' and kissed her in the rose garden. One can imagine her reaction. Thrilled on the one hand, shocked on the other. Being Elinor, she lost no opportunity to dramatise the incident:

> I was dreadfully perturbed, wondering if I should tell my husband of his friend's behaviour but fearing that he might make a fuss, and that we should have to leave. However, just as I finished dressing for dinner, my conscience made me go to Clayton's room, next to mine. His servant Billingham was just handing him his coat, I can see it all now – but as I appeared the man discreetly left the room. Clayton turned to the glass to do something more to

his white tie, so I plucked up the courage and told him the story of the awful thing that had occurred. He turned round, his whimsical face lit by a delightful smile. 'No. Did he? Dear old Brookie' was all he said and went back to his tie fixing again.

Elinor's romantic dreams seemed to be at an end. To one accustomed to luxuriate in romance, it was a bitter blow; but her cynical, eighteenth-century mood asserted itself as she began to perceive that her life held many compensations, chief among them being her growing social success.

She was by now a fully-accredited member of society and in 1896, temporarily free of financial worries, she and Clayton began to go out and about a great deal. Clayton took a flat in Sloane Street for the season that year and for the next two years, and life was pleasantly divided between Sheering, London in the season, and trips abroad.

Elinor was presented at Court for the first time, at a Drawing Room in May 1896, a fact that Lucy bitterly resented for the rest of her life, divorce having barred her from this ultimate entrée. Elinor wrote of the experience in her diary:

There were numbers of hideous women there, with – Ye Gods – what skins. Brown or pimply, or red and coarse. One could count on one's fingers the women who could stand being viewed in full regalia in the daylight with impunity. . . . some of the feathers on the heads of the real habituées would have been suitable for the tree one sees under a glass case in a cleaner's window.

Elinor must have looked ravishing in the Court dress designed for her by Lucy. She described it in her catalogue:

White satin peau de soie, the skirt edged with silver gauze ribbon (very bright silver) this edged with narrow lace. The bows on the bodice and the train were of the same ribbon. The Centre of each bow was a rosette of lace with a diamond button. The sleeves were of best old Buckingham lace (three yards in each). The train of white brocade lined with satin and ruched inside with silver ribbon and lace, and trimmed with festoons of wide old Buckingham lace fastened with bows of silver pink.

She carried a bouquet, and wore her diamond tiara, pearls round her neck, with a Pompadour ruche with a turquoise and diamond pendant pinned to it.

Frequent trips abroad were another compensation for the lack of romance in Elinor's married life. Clayton always insisted on staying in the best hotels, and Elinor enjoyed joining a society more cosmopolitan than the small group she now moved in at home. As she always did when she was away, she wrote to her mother almost daily. From Cannes in February 1895, she told her: 'The ball last night was not at all bad. Clayton & I have changed places. He now dances away all night & I look on . . .'

As ever she had various errands for her mother or for Lucy to carry out on her behalf. 'My photo of the model the sculptor in Rome took has come. It is not good so must be altered. If you could get one of Window & Groves' old ones of me before I was married showing the *left* side of my face – I don't know the number and have not one, but they will know.'

She goes on to give her mother a detailed description of a ball: 'Lady Brougham was there last night – toooo awful, dress & figure & look, only dark, exactly of the pictures Lucy used to draw at Richelieu of Mrs. E. McKnight. . . . very tight long basque & tied-in skirts, like that of the Breughels. . . . gross peacock green satin.'

Juliet, Elinor's second and last child, was born on December 15, 1898 and her birth effectively ended Elinor's brief interlude of contentment with Clayton. She was told that she could never have another child. Clayton, bitterly disappointed at the failure of his hopes for an heir, and married to a woman to whom he was now indifferent when he did not find her dramatics intensely irritating, waited just as long as it took Elinor to recover from the very difficult birth before taking himself off to Monte Carlo.

Elinor was left with the new-born baby, Margot aged five, and Mrs. Kennedy, to spend Christmas at Sheering. From this point on, Clayton was a husband virtually in name only. Paradoxically, however, he became much closer to Mrs. Kennedy.

1898 was marked by another event – Elinor's debut as a journalist. For some reason (perhaps because she was Lucy's sister) the editor of *Scottish Life* asked her to contribute regular articles on matters of fashion, to be illustrated by her little pen and ink drawings. Elinor was now to turn her acute observations of sartorial and social appearances (always part of her regular letters to her mother), to great account in these charming if inevitably dated letters of advice to a young girl.

Even in these early examples of her work, she showed that she was potentially a very good journalist, with an incisive turn of phrase and accuracy in recording the minutest detail, talents which were to be largely responsible for the success of her many books.

Les Coulisses de l'Elegance were written in the form of letters to 'Griselda' and signed 'Suzon'. They provided Elinor with the first opportunity to air her views on a number of aspects of fashion and deportment, much of which she had imbibed, as it were, at her grandmother's knee. Thus:

First, I hope to be able to explain to you HOW TO WEAR YOUR CLOTHES, because there is not the slightest use in having the loveliest things in the world if you don't know HOW TO PUT THEM ON. . . . The first principle of good dressing is to clothe oneself suitably for the position in life one holds and in harmony with the occupation of amusement in which you are engaged.

But in spite of this new outlet for her energy, Elinor remained very depressed during the next two years, and, as always, depression was accompanied by sickness. At one of the shooting lunches she now rarely attended she contracted a cold which developed into rheumatic fever. For a time, she was very seriously ill; so ill indeed that Clayton and her mother feared for her life. Mrs. Kennedy was in constant attendance, and Clayton rented her a small cottage on the estate, called Lamberts, to be near her daughter.

Elinor was too weak to be taken abroad to convalesce, and her recovery was slow. But one day she stopped feeling sorry for herself and had what she described as a 'fit of rebellion against the idea of dying young, to which I had hitherto been quite resigned and had, in fact cherished as being rather touching and romantic'.

Perhaps it was her mother who, seeking to divert the invalid, got out Elinor's early letters to her, and her diary, written in the form of letters, of her first visit to France. Or perhaps Elinor herself asked to see these reminders of earlier and, in retrospect, happier days. Re-reading these fragments and retracing her footsteps through her journals from the mid-eighties, Elinor laughed and laughed at the simple young girl she had then been. 'Suddenly, I saw that if they seemed so funny to me, other people might find them amusing also, and that it was worthwhile trying to put them together in a readable form.'

Humouring what was probably felt to be an invalidish whim, some 'nice blue copy books' were procured from the village shop and Elinor began to write *The Visits of Elizabeth*.

Of all her many books, this is one of the happiest, and the funniest. The character of Elizabeth, the debutante reporting back to her mother from a round of country house visits, was modelled partly on Elinor's romantic view of her life when young, and partly on Lady Angela Forbes. Generally regarded by society as being something of an 'enfant terrible', she herself was well aware that she had been the model, for her photograph was used as the prototype of Elizabeth in the book.

'"Enfant terrible" I may have been;' she wrote in her memoirs, 'but I do not think I ever found myself in exactly the same exciting situations as Mrs. Glyn's heroine, though I believe I once made a terrible gaffe, rather on the lines of Elizabeth and the Ghost.' She refers to the episode in which Elizabeth tells her hostess that she has heard a ghost, much to the embarrassment of a philandering male corridor-creeper.

Elinor explained later:

> I pictured to myself how a young girl such as she [Lady Angela] might view the society 'World' if she came into it really unsophisticated, but with a fine perception. With such a type for my heroine, I found the writing of the imaginary letters quite easy. I had no idea of publishing anything, but wrote for the sheer fun of it, much as I had done my little sketch portraits years before.

The book has a superb collection of thinly-disguised portraits of people Elinor had known when she had been virtually a hanger-on in other people's houses. She did not necessarily repay kindness in kind, for one of the funniest and cruellest portraits is 'Lady Theodosia', a corpulent woman with a menagerie of badly-behaved dogs. She gives two dinner parties a year for a mixed bag of county and local vicars. Pairing is done on the Marshall and Snelgrove principle – guests who draw 'Marshall' pair up with a 'Snelgrove'. Lady Theodosia is based, of course, on Elinor's early benefactress, Lady Fitzhardinge.

But Elinor is equally hard on herself, for the adventuress, Miss La Touche, represents herself in the later years of 'going about'. It is Miss La Touche of whom another debutante tells Elizabeth '. . . . [she] will never get married: she is too smart, and all the married women's men talk to her. . . . the best tone is to look rather dowdy.' Elizabeth tells her mother that she doesn't believe it, and would rather be like Miss La Touche.

The Visits of Elizabeth is a humorous gem, springing naturally from Elinor's close observations of manners, morals, decoration and, above all, clothes and general atmosphere. Such observations would always be Elinor's strongest suit – some of her descriptions of interiors and dresses read as if she is looking at them as she writes.

Pleased that writing in her penny notebooks had had such a good effect on both her spirits and her health, and perhaps clutching at any straw to preserve domestic peace, Clayton took the books to London and showed them to a Mr. Jeyes, then sub-editor on the *Standard*, whom he ran into at The Garrick. Jeyes was highly entertained, to the point of reading choice passages aloud in the club. The laughter they provoked made him think again of what he had hitherto regarded as the scribblings of an amateur. He sent Elinor a telegram that made her forget about her sufferings. He asked if he might come down and see her the next Sunday, and added, 'Elizabeth will do.'

As neither Elinor nor Clayton knew anything about publishing, indeed, went to considerable pains to disclaim any knowledge of it at all due to its proximity to 'business', they let the enthusiastic Mr. Jeyes handle *Elizabeth* for them. Shrewdly, he chose to maintain secrecy on the subject of the identity of the author when he sold it to *The World* to appear in serial form.

As the letters were published week by week, society began to get extremely excited about this portrait of a private world, its regulations and transgressions, as it had obviously been written by someone with inside knowledge. But of course it wasn't long before Elinor couldn't resist owning up to a friend who came to see her, full of this mysterious correspondence. 'Even so, she wouldn't believe me for a long time, when I assured her I was really the author,' said Elinor. 'I can hear her now saying so ingenuously "But Nellie darling, it can't possibly be you. A really clever person must have written these letters."'

Under the stimulus of so much success, Elinor felt even better, threw away the sticks she had been hobbling around with and resumed her normal life in society. She took part in the early autumn, for instance, in a charity matinee at Her Majesty's theatre, arranged by Lady Arthur Paget in aid of a South African war charity. Appearing with four other red-haired society ladies – Baroness d'Erlanger, Lady St. Oswald, Mrs. Curzon (Curzon's sister-in-law) and Lady Mary Sackville – Elinor triumphed in a tableau vivant of an imaginary Titian picture, 'The Five Senses'.

So successful had the letters been in *The World* that Jeyes now suggested that Elinor bring them out in volume form, putting forward Gerald Duckworth, a recent acquaintance who was just starting his own publishing house, to launch the book. It is not difficult to imagine Elinor's excitement when Jeyes showed her the following letter, dated August 17, 1900:

My dear Jeyes
I like very much 'The Visits of Elizabeth' & think in volume form they should sell well. Will you put me into communication with the authoress? I should suggest a 15% royalty.
I am induced to Aix-les-Bains for baths & leave London on the

28th. Could it be done before this date, so that I may put things 'en train'.

It was done, and Elinor met the man who would publish her work for virtually the rest of her life. Publication was agreed, but not without a reservation or two on Elinor's part as to whether she should preserve her anonymity. The question was answered differently by the opposing facets of her character. Her romantic, histrionic side craved the notoriety. Her cynical snobbish side feared it was vulgar. The former prevailed, but not before consultation with her social arbiter, Daisy Warwick. 'We decided that my own baptismal and legal names "Elinor Glyn" sounded like a nom-de-plume and would be taken as such outside the circle of my own friends who of course knew the identity of the author in any case by now: so "Elinor Glyn" I have remained, both in public and in private, ever since.' Thus was a nice compromise achieved between social and professional considerations.

The Visits of Elizabeth came out in the New Year of 1901 in a flat-backed apple-green cover with a white label and gold lettering. It was an immediate critical and financial success. The *Manchester Guardian* praised its 'mirthful spirits, always overflowing'. The *Standard* called it 'fresh, amusing and original', while the *Daily News* found it 'thoroughly engaging'.

And so it was. It is not a major work but, in the pleasant literary stream of comedies of manners, *The Visits of Elizabeth* is in the same vein as Jane Austen (whom Elinor never read). And it influenced a major work of fausse naiveté in modern literature – *Gentlemen Prefer Blondes* by Anita Loos.

Elinor had found a new outlet for her abundant energy, her quick wit and ready tongue – an outlet which gave her an identity of her own, beyond that of being Clayton's wife. 'Mrs. Glyn' became 'Elinor Glyn'.

iv *Gowns of Emotion*

Much as Lucy loved the house at 17 Hanover Square, she was not to remain there for long. After two years, during which the line of carriages outside her door grew longer by the season, Sir George Dashwood, her landlord, decided not to renew the lease and Maison Lucile had to find itself another home at a particularly difficult moment. As Lucy remembered: 'It was just before the Courts, and we were in the throes of making presentation dresses.' These dresses for the twice-yearly Court presentations of debutantes and of newly married women were a very important part of any English dressmaker's business at the time and contributed substantially to the profits.

After desperate efforts, temporary premises were found just off Hanover Square, at 14 St. George's Street, but they were dreadfully cramped. Lucy could hope to do only half the business she had done at the Hanover Square house. The hurried move had an unpleasant side effect: it started whispers among Lucy's competitors that her enterprise was failing, hence the move into smaller premises. However, Lucy had a champion in the person of Margot Asquith, the outspoken wife of Herbert Asquith. Margot lost no time in scotching the rumours.

Lucy's first impression of Margot Asquith had been less than favourable: 'She walked into the shop one morning and asked for me. "I hear that you design the most beautiful dresses in London," she began with her characteristic frankness. "Personally, I hate English clothes, so I get nearly everything I wear from Paris, but I would like to have one dress from you, and if I like it I will get some more."' Lucy had found something 'disarming in her candour. . . . her smile was so charming that I succumbed to it at once. I was interested too at the prospect of creating clothes for this vivid, restless creature, and I realized that she could wear dresses which not one woman in a thousand could carry off.'

The first tea-gown Lucy made for Margot Asquith was a great success and she became one of the very few people whom Lucy would allow into her studio when she was designing. Margot was interested in and very knowledgeable about fashion, to the point

where she created an international scandal in 1910 when she invited
the French couturier Paul Poiret to show his collection at 10 Downing
Street. The resulting 'Gowning Street Scandal' made international
headlines, for it was a time when British industry was depressed and
the importation of a Paris couturier provided plenty of fuel for
Asquith's many enemies. Although not a leader of fashion in the same
way as Mrs. Willie James – she was far too individual for that – Margot
Asquith moved in the 'Souls' set, and sent her friends to Lucy, among
whom were Violet Duchess of Rutland, Ettie, Lady Desborough and
Lady Wemyss. These women appreciated the aesthetic sensibility of
Lucy's designs and were an important and influential clientele for a
young English couturiere.

The business carried on in St. George's Street for two years but
eventually 23 Hanover Square was leased. 'It was ideally suited to
us,' said Lucy. 'Because there were more rooms and the big ballroom
was ideal for the main showroom.'

Lucy decorated her new couture house enthusiastically and with
little regard for economy. She shared her passionate interest in interior
decoration with Elinor, though her taste was much better than the
'hot-house' look beloved of her sister. She decorated her new premises
in her favourite eighteenth-century style with pale grey walls and
carpets; she picked out the dadoes and skirting boards in white and
festooned the tall windows with grey silk taffeta curtains, fastened
back and trimmed by hundreds of tiny silk roses – flowers that
always seemed to surround Lucy like a nimbus wherever she lived or
worked.

Her naughty underwear had its own special room, in the middle
of which she put a large day bed, specially imported from Paris and
claimed to be an exact copy of a bed Madame de Pompadour had
owned.

The plainness and airiness of these decorations and the uncluttered
lines of the gilt Louis XV chairs and sofas, which were also up-
holstered in grey silk, must have come as a shock to Lucy's late
Victorian clients. For the prevalent taste of the time was for dark
colours, anaglypta wallpapers, heavy bobble fringes obscuring the
lines of furniture and layer upon layer of carpet. An enormous clutter
of bibelots and photograph frames were but dimly perceived in a
stygian gloom, for daylight filtered through net curtains, with heavy
velvet curtains depending from lowering portières obscuring the
scene even further.

Lucy's pale grey decoration based on eighteenth-century taste
affected many who came to 23 Hanover Square, and it is possible to
see her influence at work in early twentieth century decoration.

Elsie de Wolfe, the decorator and socialite, became a close friend of Lucy long before she, too, had found her métier. As a young girl, Elsie had been presented at Court by Lady Arthur Paget, one of Lucy's customers. Lady Arthur Paget was an American, one of the first 'Dollar Princesses' to marry into the English aristocracy, and she and her mother, the energetic Mrs. Paran Stephens who had been so kind to Elinor in Paris, made up an unofficial marriage bureau for American girls wishing to marry a Title.

Elsie was as strong-minded and convinced of her own taste as was Lucy, and the two women often worked together and helped each other. Elsie's enormous success was based on her revival of eighteenth-century elegance in light, fresh rooms. She was directly influenced in this by the then revolutionary decor at Maison Lucile.

As a style for couture salons, Maison Lucile had many imitators. For example, Norman Hartnell's superb salon in Bruton Street, designed in 1934 by Norris Wakefield who added the modernist element of faceted geometrical wall-mirroring to Lucy's original eighteenth-century model, created a contemporary version of Lucy's look.

But Lucy's decor was not as much of a shock as some of the clothes she now began to design. 'I loosed upon a startled London, a London of flannel underclothes, woollen stockings and voluminous petticoats, a cascade of chiffons, of draperies as lovely as those of Ancient Greece and draped skirts which opened to reveal slender legs. If I never did anything else in my life,' said Lucy, 'I showed the world that a woman's leg can be a thing of beauty, instead of a "limb" (in the parlance of those days), which was only spoken of in the privacy of the fitting-room.'

Many a dowager, who had originally held up her hands in horror at the notion of Lucy going into trade, now had the satisfaction of accusing her of spreading the cult of 'immoral dressing'.

Lucy paid no attention. Nor did her clients who became even more numerous and grand. A triumph against the Mrs. Grundys was to be able to enter the name of the Duchess of York (later Queen Mary) in the Maison Lucile register. 'I see that her first fitting,' Lucy recalled, 'was for a "blue satin dress with tucked yoke and sleeves".' Asked to submit some designs for the Duchess of York's consideration, Lucy had chosen 'simple dresses, beautifully embroidered, but with nothing approaching the extreme in style, for I fancied, from what I had heard of her taste in dresses, that these would be the most likely to appeal to the Duchess.' And appeal they did. The first fitting was a great success, the Duchess choosing two dresses immediately and ordering more.

Lucy had interrogated the fitter, a jolly Irish girl called Mollie, and had been fascinated to be told that the two women had had a lengthy discussion about the best way to get rid of the Prince of Wales's cold. Mollie had been indiscreet enough to tell Lucy that the Duchess wore 'only ordinary cotton underclothing with Swiss embroidery on it "Like my very own Sunday ones. I'm thinking," said the girl, "she keeps her silk for best."' On another occasion, Mollie had dropped her box of pins during a fitting and had been thrilled that the Duke of York (later King George V) had gone down on his knees to help her pick them up.

Queen Mary retained, for the rest of her life, an echo of Lucy's designs. The sweet-pea and hydrangea colours the Queen always favoured, the delicate embroidery, the slim straight skirts with tunics worn over them, the love of old lace – all are hallmarks of Lucile in the early years of the century – a style that became a royal style that lasted for more than fifty years.

Lucy had great success in dressing debutantes. A story had got round that the young Lady Clarendon had 'caught' her extremely eligible husband in a particularly pretty grey satin ingenue dress, especially designed for her first meeting, aged seventeen, with this desirable parti. The dress had been designed by Lucile. From henceforth Lucy was held to be 'lucky' for debutantes.

Scarcely a fashionable mother in London, wishing to fire off her daughter, didn't bring her child to the pale grey former ballroom to be dressed by Lucy for her first season. Before long, 23 Hanover Square had a special department for debutantes' dresses and Maison Lucile was the first couture house in London (Paris too, for that matter) to specialise in these young dresses. As Lucy explained: 'The general rule was that fashions were created for older women, and were only adapted for the jeune fille, often very unsuitably at that.'

But, in these last days of the Victorian age, the most profound innovation Lucy made was to evolve the mannequin. The idea dated from her 17 Hanover Square days.

'Down the steps into that beautiful Adam room with its Angelica Kauffman ceiling, its gilt chairs and couches that had been brought over from Paris, tripped the first of a long line of sylphs, destined to reach down the years, and to survive so long as there are dressmakers whose purposes it is to lure women into buying more dresses than they can afford,' Lucy wrote.

In the days before Lucy's innovation, one paid a visit to one's dressmaker, only to be received into the uncompromising atmosphere of a shop, with perhaps some hard chairs, a few unbecoming mirrors and a door which opened on to a little fitting room. Before Lucy's new approach nobody had thought of developing the social side of choosing clothes; of serving tea and imitating the setting of a private drawing room. Trying on and selecting clothes had been, she said, a thing 'of as much secrecy as fitting a wooden leg might be expected to be'.

In many of the then fashionable dressmakers' establishments – such as Worth and Paquin in Paris, Reville, Busvine and Jay in London – the models were displayed on horrid lay figures. These were dreadful affairs of sawdust with wax faces. Then, greatly daring, some re-sourceful soul, possibly Paquin, conceived the idea of having living models. But as Lucy pointed out: 'There was no parade, oh dear no. Nothing so frivolous. . . . there must be nothing which might shock the susceptibilities of the grandest dames who visited the salons; nothing which might suggest that the poor little mannequin had a personality of her own, that she was capable of any more emotion than the sawdust dummy which she replaced. She must not show the glow of youthful flesh, or the curves of young ankles.' To prevent this, claimed Lucy: 'They encased her in a garment of rigid black satin, reaching from chin to feet, which were shod in unappetizing laced boots. Even the most nervous mamma could safely take her son with her to the dressmaker's when temptation appeared in such unalluring guise, that is to say, if it could be called temptation at all, for as a guarantee of the respectability of the establishment, the director could be relied upon to choose only the plainest of girls to show off his creations.'

The idea grew slowly in Lucy's mind that it might be interesting to put on '. . . . a mannequin parade, which would be as entertaining to watch as a play. I would have glorious, goddess-like girls, who would walk to and fro dressed in my models, displaying them to the best advantage to an admiring audience of women.'

It was not an easy task to find such mannequins. No society girl would even consider it, so Lucy had to recruit her young women from the middle or the lower classes and then train them. Always an expert in the art of seeing hidden possibilities in even the most unpromising woman, Lucy found six girls who would 'do'. After considerable coaching, hairdressing, and deportment lessons (Lucy was no grandchild of Mrs. Saunders for nothing) these girls from

Bermondsey and Balham flowered into the exotic creatures, now named 'Dolores', 'Hebe', 'Gamela', and became an overnight sensation.

While all this Pygmalionish activity was going on, Lucy had been setting the stage very carefully for the first-ever fashion show. 'I had a soft rich carpet laid down in the big showroom and beautiful grey brocade curtains to tone with it were hung across the windows. At one end of the room I had a stage, a miniature affair, all hung with misty olive chiffon curtains, as the background, which created the atmosphere I wanted.'

She then sent out the invitations 'on dainty little cards, keeping the illusion that I was inviting my friends to some afternoon party rather than to a place of business. All my clients were curious to see this new idea. . . . I realised that on this parade of mine I would stand or fall, and as the day drew near, I was terribly anxious. . . .' No doubt Sir Cosmo and Mr. Miles were also anxious, as Lucy had spent a great deal of money on what must have seemed a crazy idea.

But nothing ever deflected her once she had decided to go ahead with one of her inspirations, and at last the day of the show arrived and the ballroom became crowded with curious women. One of Lucy's most influential and faithful clients, Princess Alice (of Hesse) sat at the front. Lucy's old friend Ellen Terry was pressed into service to show late arrivals to their seats and Lily Langtry's entrance caused a satisfactory sensation. Margot Asquith ('young and rather noisy, but always vivid and amusing') was also in the audience.

Not content with introducing her clients to the entirely new notion of mannequins parading up and down, Lucy initiated another custom that has been in use in the world of fashion ever since – the naming of models. Before her show, they were either referred to simply by a number, or as the 'pink silk' and the 'black velvet'. Lucy's imagination was just as over-heated as Elinor's later became, and it offended her sense of the dramatic that some creation of hers, the expression of a mood, should be dismissed as 'Number Nine'. So she gave them all names and personalities of their own. 'The Captain with Whiskers'; 'When Passion's Thrall is O'er' (layers of transparent grey chiffon); 'Give Me Your Heart'; 'Do You Love Me?' She called this collection 'Gowns of Emotion'.

The show was enormously successful and Lucy's reputation was firmly established as *the* dressmaker. Hanover Square was filled with women ordering emotional clothes for themselves and the mannequins became famous overnight due to such headlines as *Lucile's mysterious beauties*. The press had been actively encouraged by Lucy who was shrewd enough to realise the importance of publicity at a time when most dressmakers shrank from it, lest it offend their clients. She was quoted endlessly and was always willing to give a journalist good 'copy', even if sometimes the result was slightly over the top. One such contemporary writer told readers: 'Lucile believes that gowns may express ideas from grave to gay, even emotions and passions. So she has gone to the silent worlds of desires and temperament and sensations and translates their secrets into wondrous colours and entrancing forms.'

However, not everyone was enthralled with pretty, clever Mrs. James Wallace, and her talent for publicising herself and her designs. Beverly Nichols later wrote: 'She was a rather tiresome woman who used to trail around in mauve tulle talking about the "dress of temperament". If she had dressed to match her own temperament she would have worn sateen shorts.'

Lucy was oblivious. She had become well known as a creative artist in her own right. And she had created a business out of thin air, a talent with a needle and a great many clever ideas.

With success, Lucy achieved happiness. She loved the dresses she created 'very much as a mother loves her child, or an artist his pictures'. Forty years later, she looked back with pride and pleasure at some of her 'emotional dresses'. She had designed one particular model 'just after a young man whom I like had left for America. It was in deepest black and became the most popular model for a widow that I ever showed. Every woman that lived in London went into "Consolable Sorrow", and I must say they looked sweetly pathetic.'

v *Distant Warnings*

One reason behind Elinor's illnesses and depression in 1899 and the beginning of 1900 was her dawning realisation that Clayton's finances were not as bottomless as she had thought and were now beginning to show the strain of supporting her love of the luxuries of life.

When Elinor couldn't get what she wanted (a new dress, a trip abroad, new decorations for Sheering) she would have a tantrum. Some of these ragings were so violent she literally bit the rug. In April 1900, while she was recovering from rheumatic fever and writing *The Visits of Elizabeth*, money was so short that she was persuaded by Walters, the family solicitor, to postpone her marriage settlement for the first time. It would not be the last.

Elinor could never manage money. This inability and her refusal to economise in any of the many things she felt made life worthwhile materially contributed to the shipwreck of Clayton's finances and, simultaneously, to the deterioration of their marriage.

She had become accustomed to the life of a rich society woman, with regular visits to expensive hotels abroad, travelling first class clad in extremely expensive clothes made by her sister. The children had a nanny of course and Elinor a personal maid. Costs mounted, to be met by Clayton borrowing further against his expectations. The Homerston reversion, created for the now impossible son and heir, became worth less and less as Clayton borrowed against it, and, as it was plundered, so the amount that could be borrowed against it was reduced, and so on. It was a descending spiral, travelling fairly slowly at first, but gaining momentum as it went.

It was hardly surprising, given her temperament and her disappointment with Clayton as a romantic lover, living in a society which not only condoned but positively encouraged extra-marital affairs, that Elinor fell in love.

She met Seymour Wynne Finch in 1901 and recognised in him a man she might have invented for the hero of one of her books. He had been a Major in the Royal Horse Guards and was also what Elinor would later describe as 'the best type of Englishman'. He was a popular member of the Marlborough House set, unusually charming and handsome and, as his diary shows, a valued guest at smart Saturday to Mondays. He was a sportsman with a ready wit. On hearing, for instance, that a certain lady treated her husband 'like furniture' he asked, without a moment's hesitation: 'Drawing-room or bedroom? It does make such a difference.' Here was the reality that Elinor had mistakenly ascribed to Clayton.

To make matters worse, he fell deeply in love in return. Though his diary is – as one would expect of such a man and the time in which he lived – a model of discretion, there are many mentions of meetings. In 1901, for instance, he visited Elinor on June 23rd, in Bentinck Street, but she was out. He visited her again the next day. On the 25th he saw her at the Carlton, and paid another call on the 27th. On July 14th he lunched with various ladies, including Elinor and Sarah Bernhardt (with whom he had had a passionate affair fifteen years earlier), at a discreet private restaurant, the Amphitryon. On October 14th they were in the same houseparty at the Warwicks. On the 15th all went to Newmarket except 'Mrs. Glyn, Strath [Lord Strathmore] and me'. On October 17th he reminded himself that it was her birthday and on October 19th a group went to Sheering for tea.

Matters were serious. The morals of Elinor's set would have meant that no one would have looked askance at a love affair – as long as it was conducted discreetly. Clayton himself would probably have ignored it, and the cynical side of Elinor's dual nature would have had no scruples at all. But the romantic and prudish side still baulked. Although she and Clayton were by now married virtually in name only, she still clung to the hope that the failure of her marriage was temporary, and that in some unimagined way the money difficulties would be resolved, and that Clayton would turn to her again.

So she sent Seymour Wynne Finch away, and henceforth they met only when social chance threw them together.

Ten years later, Elinor met Sarah Bernhardt again in Paris and they talked of him. 'I was enthralled,' she wrote. 'The only man she is said to have ever really loved – loved me – she and I are of the same group the group of Sirens. . . . We spoke of him and her eyes filled with tears and her voice broke, and yet he had not been her lover for twenty-five years. He is dead and we two are perhaps the only two women he ever really loved when alive – and we are instinctively drawn to one another.' In her diary, Elinor mused on the possibilities in the two ladies 'comparing our loves – hers in fact and mine only in words – because she was a great actress and free and I was the immaculate and well-behaved wife of an English Squire. But we have both had many lovers and seen the souls – base or elevated – of many men. Would I have been happier if I had taken these as facts, as she had done, or only more full of unrest – who knows?'

The parting distressed her greatly and, as always in adversity, a trip abroad offered her an escape from her unhappiness. Deciding to repeat a successful journey to Egypt of the previous winter, she now determined that the whole family must accompany her, and accordingly set off with Clayton, Mrs. Kennedy, the two children, their governess and of course her lady's maid.

Half English society had decided that Cairo was *the* place that winter (which probably determined Elinor's choice). She became very friendly with Lady Newton-Butler and the Duchess of Sutherland who persuaded her to abandon her prejudice against outdoor sports and watch the 11th Hussars playing polo at the smart Gezireh club. Elinor met many interesting people, including Cecil Rhodes and Dr. Jameson (of the 'Jameson Raid') as they were passing through, noting in her diary 'Rhodes and Jameson and those other three men were sitting together at dinner and five more ill-shapen creatures I have never seen. Dr. Jameson's back view is like that of an old rat with pink ears and a bald head.'

But, in spite of the balls and the parties and the admiration, Elinor fell ill again and gallstones were diagnosed. During her slow convalescence, she returned to the recipe that had already proved successful in raising her spirits, and she began a new book. Called *The Chronicles of Ambrosine*, it not only provides interesting clues about how she felt about her life at the time, but also insights about the unpleasing snobbish side of her character. Kind hearts are certainly not worth more than coronets in this book, which has far less charm and high spirits than *The Visits of Elizabeth*.

The story concerns Ambrosine. She is poor, pretty and an aristocrat, brought up by a strict grandmother living in the eighteenth century. Almost on her death bed, the grandmother marries Ambrosine off to Augustus, the common son of the neighbouring nouveau riche family. Augustus drinks, and the marriage is made very unhappy by this and the appalling taste of his parents. Ambrosine falls in love with Sir Anthony Thornhirst, but refuses to have an affair:

> He did not even kiss my finger-tips last night. We parted sadly after a storm of words neither he nor I had ever meant to speak – why the situation is as it is, I cannot tell. In my bringing up, the idea of taking a lover after marriage seemed a more or less natural thing, and not altogether a deadly sin, provided the affair was conducted sans fanfaronnade, without scandal – why did I hesitate? I do not know.

Elinor's own romance had not had a happy ending, but in her books she could re-write her life: without a stain on her conscience she killed off Augustus and married Ambrosine happily to Sir Anthony.

Seymour Wynne Finch found no difficulty in recognising himself and, at a houseparty at Wynyard later that year, Lady Londonderry had him announced to the guests as Sir Anthony Thornhirst. Daisy Warwick also appeared in the book, as Lady Tilchester, and it is a charming portrait of her – she is a much nicer character than the snobbish and humourless Ambrosine.

Elinor was half way through the book when the moment came for the family party to leave for home. Clayton was unusually bad tempered with her as they voyaged to Rome, where Elinor began declaiming about the beauties of art and architecture. Bored with his wife's dramatics, Clayton apparently exclaimed: 'For goodness' sake go and get your ebullitions over while I order lunch.'

If Clayton would not listen, others would. Elinor soon found a sympathetic ear in Lord Grey, later Governor General of Canada. This was one of the first of many friendships with men much older than herself, men who could further her education, and to whom she could look up. Lord Grey took her sightseeing and discussed Gibbon with her. Clayton was indifferent, dismissing the situation with the words '. . . He is only one of Elinor's antiques.'

Another new friend met in Rome was potentially more of a threat. The noted sculptor Waldo Storey, living at the time in the Palazzo Barberini, executed a bust of Elinor and they became very friendly, more on Elinor's side than his, judging by a letter she wrote him the next year, in which she complains that he hadn't answered her letters, and that he hadn't made any effort to see her when he had been in England. She told him she thought he would

> Find me very much changed for the better. I am not nearly so vain in the way that used to irritate you so, do you remember? I believe happiness has altered the bad things – I have had a year of intense happiness. I think I know all emotions now and am no longer the ignorant and bigotted (I can't spell even yet . . .) person you knew. Oh. I would like to see you again and talk, Waldo – do you hear?

While in Rome, Elinor had a recurrence of her gallstones and Clayton took her to see Dr. Axel Munthe, the Swedish doctor then specialising in the problems, real or imaginary, of society women, and later to become world-famous as the author of the semi-philosophical book *The Story of San Michele*. Elinor observed that he had 'a very magnetic – one might say hypnotic personality. . . . I should imagine that he was a man with a lonely soul, seeking for greater things than he could find, either in his surroundings or in himself.' Munthe was impressed with Elinor, and noted in his case-book that she was a 'Syren'.

From Rome, Clayton and Elinor went on to Lucerne and it was here that she saw a magnificent tiger-skin in a shop below her hotel. Scarcely concealing his boredom at Elinor's fits and starts (and probably short of money), Clayton flatly refused to buy it for her. But Elinor would not be deflected. Waiting for her at the hotel was a letter from Gerald Duckworth enclosing a large payment of royalties from *The Visits of Elizabeth*. Immediately cashing the cheque, Elinor bought the tiger-skin. When he returned to their sitting room, Clayton found her lying on the tiger-skin stroking its fur, quivering with emotion, staring at him with smouldering, passionate eyes.

It was a little 'much' for an emotionally atrophied Englishman: Clayton flung out of the room disgusted at this hothouse display. Henceforth they were irreconcilable – Elinor indulging in more dramatics and Clayton retreating to such consolations as the brandy bottle and sporting activities.

On Axel Munthe's advice, Elinor travelled to Carlsbad in the summer of 1902. Alone. Here she found a pleasant society taking the cure from a round of what Victoria Sackville-West once described as 'Those meals those constant meals'. Elinor met Sir Francis and Lady Jeune (later Lord and Lady St. Helier). Jeune was a classical scholar, and during walks through the pine woods he awoke in Elinor all her old enthusiasm for the ancient world. Both he and his wife were to remain steadfast friends of Elinor for the rest of their lives. Elinor had a great capacity for friendship and, now that she was travelling without Clayton, began to make friends who would suit her enquiring mind and cosmopolitan outlook.

Carlsbad proved restorative and, as her health improved, Elinor again took up the work she had started on *Ambrosine*, finishing it on August 20th. To her mother she enthused 'Sir F. Jeune who is a great Literary light says my book is "absolutely delightful" and that there is no living writer my equal. I am in that class by myself. Others have elephant's touches compared to me. He says the critics will fall upon it tooth and nail but I am not to mind in the least, every-one who really knows will appreciate it as it is far ahead of *Elizabeth even.*' Imperceptibly, without realising it, Elinor was progressing from the role of a society woman who happened to have written an amusing little book in her spare time, into an author taken seriously by other authors. An author who was, incidentally, a member of society.

Douglas Sutherland and Elinor Saunders at the time of their marriage

The widowed Mrs Sutherland,
Lucy, Elinor and their Aunt
Henrietta at Guelph

Elinor, Lucy and their mother in Jersey

Elinor's diary of a visit to Paris when she was in her early twenties

Mr Kennedy towards the end of his life

Lucy and Esmé, at about the time
Lucy started her business

James Wallace

Elinor just after her marriage. She is wearing her wedding dress, converted into a balldress

Clayton Glyn at the time of his marriage to Elinor

A Lucile design, about 1895

Maison Lucile, Hanover Square

Sir Cosmo Duff Gordon with his labrador Bombastes

Lucy at the time of her second marriage

Maryculter, Sir Cosmo's family home in Aberdeenshire

Margot and Juliet outside Lamberts

Elinor in her bedroom at her Trianon. She made every silk rose herself

Lord Alastair Innes Ker

Major Seymour Wynne Finch

Elinor at the time of writing *Three Weeks*

Four Lucile theatrical designs, circa 1905–1907

Sir Francis Jeune and another new friend, the popular novelist Sir Gilbert Parker, both liked *Ambrosine*, but advised Elinor that she should try to write more slowly and take greater pains over her style, her English, her grammar and her spelling. This advice was, of course, sound, but it may not have been right for her. Her talent lay in observation and spontaneous creation. Her books did not come from her imagination, they came from her experience. Real people were always her models and her books were outpourings – her best results were always those over which she had spent little time. She made efforts to revise her plots but the actual act of writing was spontaneous. She left spelling, grammar and punctuation to be corrected by her publisher.

Elinor was no longer amateurish about her 'hobby'. But she concealed this cleverly in, for instance, the letter she wrote to *Harpers* magazine in America that same October, on response to a request for biographical details:

Dear Sir,
I hardly know what to reply to your letter. I have several French relations and spent much of my time in France and in Paris, where I went a great deal into society, and at the different embassies saw a mixture of many nations, until my marriage.
My husband is a regular type of the English Squire, and we have a pretty home. We own land round here, and the place has been in the family for about 200 years. . . . I have very few country tastes. I do not like cold or any game or thick boots and mud. . . . I have a very beautiful boudoir and when my social and other duties are over, I spend much time there, reading. I never cared for novels and hardly ever read any. My favourite study is Philosophy and the exquisitely witty works of the eighteenth century – both French and English.
My favourite periods in history are the Early Greek and the eighteenth century. . . . I have never written any books but *The Visits of Elizabeth* and *The Reflections of Ambrosine*. I only wrote *Elizabeth* to amuse myself, without any idea of publishing. . . . I do not care the least about money, and would never write a word, no matter how tempting the offer, unless the 'fit' happened to take me, and it amused me to do so, otherwise I should write rubbish; to me, no forced thing could be good. I must first *feel the thing well done myself* before I would wish to publish it.
I would never promise anything to be finished by a given time,

nor even that I should ever write again – I cannot tell. I might never feel inclined. When I do have the inclination I see the whole thing plain in front of me, and write straight on, never correcting anything but the spelling. I spell very badly – it is quite amusing considering how very much I have read. I have never met any literary people, and do not belong to any 'societies', so I have no a notion of the manner in which real authors write books. They probably take a great deal of pains, but I cannot do that.

The comic side of life always appeals to me. I am never bored, the dullest country dinner party makes me laugh studying people.

I know the world and society very well and all my pictures in my books are drawn from the real thing, nothing is over or under drawn. It is only the story itself that is more or less imagination. It makes me laugh so when some of the more ignorant critics question this point. They say 'Gives quite an erroneous picture of society' or 'Such pictures of society are from imagination' etc., etc. I and my friends are greatly amused when we read this sort of thing.

All this sounds dreadfully egotistical to me as I read it over. But I do not know how else to write the information you want. These are all facts. . . . I am sure you will use them with discretion.

Elinor and Lucy were both expert at manufacturing convenient myths to conceal the rather more inconvenient truth. The trouble with this mythologising was that both sisters ended up believing it.

vi *Lady Duff Gordon*

Sir Cosmo Duff Gordon, a 'good friend' and business partner from 1895, had wanted to marry Lucy almost from their first meeting, but his mother's High Church aversion to divorced women and the threat of her delicate health had stopped him. In 1900 his mother died suddenly and he was free to follow his inclination.

It was almost too late. For Lucy, feeling run down and overworked, had gone with her mother to rest in Monte Carlo. 'After a few weeks I was so much better that I . . . began to go out and enjoy myself at the Casino and at the fêtes which were given at the Palace by the Prince of Monaco, a jolly old man with the bluff manners of a country farmer, and a passion for deep sea fishing,' Lucy wrote. At one of these fêtes, she 'renewed the acquaintance', which had been begun in London, of Lord C. In the ensuing weeks, this anonymous peer fell in love with Lucy and proposed. She accepted, but asked that the engagement not be announced until their return to London.

Was this her way of bringing Sir Cosmo up to 'scratch'? She may have taken a leaf out of Elinor's book (Elinor had also taken herself off to Monte Carlo at the time of her courtship by Clayton).

Sir Cosmo followed Lucy, her mother and Lord C. to Venice, having sent a telegram which said: 'If you are going to marry anyone it is going to be me.' After a furious quarrel with the other suitor, Sir Cosmo persuaded Lucy to change her mind and, on May 24, 1900, Mrs. James Wallace became Lady Duff Gordon, marrying from the house of friends of Cosmo. The wedding took place at the British Consul's. 'It was funny,' said Lucy, 'that I, who had created so many lovely wedding dresses for other brides, should have chosen to be married herself in quite an old frock. I was so happy, and I wanted to forget all about clothes and anything that reminded me of the business for a time.'

The newly-weds spent their honeymoon in Abazzia, bathing all day long, which revived Lucy's memories of her daily swims in Jersey when she was young. 'We were both very much in love,' Lucy said, 'and the place was the most perfect background.' Cosmo, she relates, was surprised that she had only brought two dresses with her, and one of those was a bathing dress. But this was a characteristic exaggeration in her memoirs. No lady would travel in those days with but one change.

Sir Cosmo is a somewhat shadowy figure, largely because there are no surviving letters between him and Lucy. He was a keen sportsman and enjoyed life at Maryculter, the family house in Aberdeenshire, a great deal more than Lucy did, although she spent some time there in the very early years of their marriage. While there, one of his favourite sports was to make the younger members of the houseparty don fencing masks while he shot at them with wax bullets. This was meant to stiffen their resolve. He had lost an eye in a shooting accident but this did not stop him being an all-round athlete.

Unfortunately Lucy's distrust of men was by now very deep-rooted and, when Cosmo tried to encourage her to be more prudent in her financial dealings, she completely misread his motives and started, soon after their marriage, chafing at the bit as several letters to her mother show. In 1901, now living in a rented flat off Berkeley Square, she wrote:

> I think the time has gone by when anything nice or interesting happens to me. I never get a sign of adventure or the salt of life. . . . I only live a Darby and Joan life. I'm happy but it is *deadly* deadly dull. . . . Cosmo talks all the time so I only get a chance of listening.

And she wrote to Mrs. Kennedy from the Ritz in Paris:

> . . . most extraordinarily dull to be with . . . never makes a joke. . . . One can only amuse oneself when one has a nice young man. As I shall never be allowed one I shall never have any real fun again as I'm getting too old and with huge Esmé to drag about, it's awful. . . . I hope Esmé will enjoy life so that I may have some amusement indirectly as all that is over for me now.

Lucy was in the process of finding a house in the country near London. 'I shall have a new interest in furnishing it. . . . I've quite made up my mind it is the best thing for us. Cosmo is like a wild caged animal.' She might have been describing herself.

Lucy was fond of Cosmo – when he did not stand in her way – but only to the extent that she could love and trust any man. Their marriage appears to have been one more of mutual interests than of physical passion. Though in her late thirties, Lucy was not to have any further children, due to an abcess on her womb which would not be diagnosed for another fifteen years.

Cosmo remained devoted to Lucy for the rest of his life. In the few photographs taken of them together he is usually to be observed looking at her quizzically and she more often than not gazes challengingly into the camera with one or other of the young men that she increasingly drew to her. They 'picked up her pins' as her granddaughter put it; they were never sexual partners. Sir Cosmo appeared to tolerate all but one of them, one suspects because they kept Lucy busy and happy, leaving him freer to pursue his sporting activities.

Cosmo and Lucy spent an increasing amount of time apart as Lucile expanded, demanding Lucy's presence in New York or Paris, but it was – at least for the next fifteen years – a very amicable arrangement. In a 1902 letter to her mother, Elinor summed up Lucy's separateness: '. . . Lucy writes in raptures of Versailles and being alone. The best thing and the best place for her. I think she is impossible with other people.'

Marriage to Cosmo may have made Lucy feel trapped, but it endowed her with instantaneous goodwill for her business in the form of a title. She was barred only from being presented at Court. Cosmo, for his part, found himself married to a temperamental but talented and increasingly wealthy woman who was ready to subsidise Maryculter. For Lucy made (and lost) a very considerable fortune.

Lucy confided to her memoirs: 'I suppose every woman remembers some years in her life which stood out more vividly than any others, generally because they were especially happy ones.' The summer season of 1907 was a particularly brilliant one, arguably the most dazzling of all those sunlit years in the period just preceding the First World War. And just when it was at its zenith Lucy scored one of the greatest triumphs of her career. 'A new play was launched, with a new actress who set the whole Town raving over her beauty. . . .'

The play was *The Merry Widow*, the star was Lily Elsie. And her clothes were by Lucile. They caused a sensation, as did their wearer. One particular hat – the 'Merry Widow' hat – made a small fortune for Lucy, for women in Europe and America clamoured for exact copies of it. As a very young boy, Cecil Beaton fell in love with Lily Elsie and acquired a picture postcard of this new star in her black hat. It had a short brim at the front, a large one at the back, adorned with wisps of Bird-of-Paradise feathers.

Although Lucy had already designed clothes for other leading ladies, *The Merry Widow* was her first international success, and one which could be directly ascribed to her reputation for creating beautiful mannequins out of what was known as common clay. George Edwardes, the producer of the operetta, was aware of her skill in what is now called 'making over', and he brought his unknown discovery (christened Elsie Broughton) to Hanover Square because he felt she needed much the same sort of coaching, as well as a wardrobe. Lucy attacked this task with her usual enthusiasm. 'I had to look again to discover that her hair was a wonderful shade of gold, and that her skin was of the real lilies and roses type.' Lucy altered the way Lily Elsie walked, she altered her hairdo, her make-up; and then designed exquisite clothes for her to wear. Cecil Beaton remembered the end result in *The Glass of Fashion*;

> The leading lady's gowns were inevitably made by Lucile and were masterpieces of intricate workmanship. It was the fashion for women to wear high-waisted Directoire dresses, falling straight to the floor, where the wearer's feet would be encumbered by bead-fringes and possibly clinging trains. Lucile worked with soft materials, delicately sprinkling them with bead or sequin embroidery, with cobweb lace insertions, true lovers' knots, and garlands of minute roses. Her colour sense was so subtle that the delicacy of detail could scarcely be seen at a distance, though the effect she created was of an indefinable shimmer. Sometimes, however, she introduced rainbow effects into a sash and would incorporate quite vivid mauves and greens, perhaps even a touch of shrimp-pink or orange. Occasionally, if she wanted to be deliberately outrageous, she introduced a bit of black chiffon or black velvet and, just to give the coup de grâce, outlined it with diamonds. . . . In her heyday, Lucile's artistry was unique, her influence enormous.

Lucy's designs for Lily Elsie were nothing short of triumph. Lily – in her new guise – became a star overnight. She became very friendly with Lucy, possibly because they shared a somewhat derisory view of men and their motives. She once told Lucy that 'she disliked the male character, and considered that men only behaved tolerably to a woman who treated them coldly'. 'I have never been fool enough to give my heart to one of them,' she said, 'and so they think it must be worth having.'

Lily had a fearsome mother who acted as a shield against the stage-door johnnies who hung about outside Daly's theatre every night. Mother and daughter were often to be found barricaded in the star dressing room sharing a picnic of cold ham and salad. However, Lily wasn't above taking the odd gift from admirers, though she returned little on such amorous investments. Lucy remembered that Lily came into the salon once wearing a magnificent sable coat. 'The mannequins crowded round to admire. "Now don't you girls think I have done anything naughty to get this," said Lily, "Jack only gave it me because he thought I might be cold."'

The Merry Widow clothes designed for Lily Elsie were Lucile at its best. In layers of chiffon, they had the higher waist and the tunic over a slit hobble skirt just then being brought into fashion; their handwork was exquisite. Lucy used a palette of pale sweet-pea colours and white, with black accessories to give the pale blonde star an even more fragile air than she owned naturally.

Over fifty years later Audrey Hepburn's balldress in the film of *My Fair Lady* was based on the 'Snow Princess' dress Lucy designed for Lily Elsie's big waltz scene in *The Merry Widow*.

1907 was otherwise memorable for Lucy, for Esmé became engaged to, and later in the year married, Anthony Giffard, Viscount Tiverton, the son of the first Earl of Halsbury, Lord Chancellor of England (and the author of the definitive *Halsbury's Laws of England*).

She met him while they were both acting in an amateur 'sketch' for one of Elinor's charities in Harlow. The Giffard family were horrified at what they saw as a mésalliance and did their best to stop it. Esmé herself seems to have had another suitor in attendance as this undated letter to her mother at the time possibly indicated.

Have you heard the news, and what do you think of it. Do come home soon and arrange matters. I wonder what you think of it all. I expect you are having a very lovely time and don't want to come home but do, as I feel very muddled. I can't think of another word to say. Harry has behaved like a brute. I have told Elsie [de Wolfe] and of course she thinks me a fool, any American would. Oh if only he had been Harry, how lovely everything would have been. I am very depressed, as everyone who knows thinks I am cracked and no one is sympathetic. If only I had Harry. Please write me a nice letter. I have no other news.

From this mysterious missive, one might gather that Lucy's account of Esmé's marriage as a runaway love-match is probably far from the real truth.

Whatever lay behind it, the marriage went ahead at St. Peter's Eaton Square on July 7, 1907. Esmé wore an empire dress of white tulle which Lucy had sewn herself. The marriage further consolidated Lucy's new-found social position, and it also gave her a son-in-law who would become a sturdy support in difficult later years.

In 1909, after a visit to America, Lucy decided to put on a fashion show which was virtually a full-scale theatrical performance.

She called it *The Seven Ages of Woman* and based it loosely on Shakespeare's lines – with a few essential differences. Clients – who included the glamorous Queen Marie of Rumania, the Queen of Spain, Princess Patricia of Connaught, and virtually every smart society woman in London – saw seven scenes. Starting with 'The Schoolgirl' which had but two dresses (one called 'The Beginning of Knowledge', the other 'The Awakening of Youth'), the show then progressed through 'The Debutante', 'The Fiancée' (a large scene, reflecting the importance of the trousseaux in Lucy's business), 'The Bride', 'The Wife', 'The Hostess' (another big scene), and finally 'The Dowager' who was only allowed four rather subdued ensembles with names like 'Eventide' and of course 'Twilight'.

It was 'The Hostess' (in other words, the married woman who entertained, was entertained and who could indulge in the luxury of a lover) who came in for the full hot-house Lucile treatment. Elinor must have sat in that audience and watched with rapt attention. The list of model-names tell their own unwitting tale:

> *Scene A*: The Desire of the Eyes
> Persuasive Delight: The Liquid Whisper of Early Green: Visible Harmony: A Frenzied Hour: A Garden of Sleep: Salut d'Amour: Unorthodox: An Interval: Afterwards: Contentment.
> *Scene B*: Two Pictures: After Vigge (sic) Le Brun: After de Bucourt
> *Scene C*: After Nattier.
> *Scene D*: The Victories of Beauty.
> Echoes: A Symbol of Change and Emotion: The Horizon of Dreaming Consciousness: Fervid Inflorescence: Enchantment: Scented Silence: Passion's Thrall: Nemesis.

Lucy knew her customers and their lives intimately and gave them what they wanted, those amoral luscious ladies of the Edwardian era: stately galleons sailing through life in exquisite handmade Lucile dresses, through a languid sea of houseparties, seasonal dances, amorous dalliance during shooting parties and love affairs conducted in shadowy boudoirs after discreet teas.

Timing is an essential ingredient in the pot pourri which makes up a successful fashion designer. Lucy was right for the Edwardian age, which perfectly suited her particular brand of imaginative and delicate handwork; her fragile laces and huge hats; her clothes which turned ripely mature women into walking reminders of the pleasures of the boudoir.

The best designers flower for a brief, bright season and then begin to lose touch with the veering winds of contemporary taste. Lucy's brief summer happily coincided with the height of the Edwardian era.

NOTORIETY

(1903–1914)

'To some natures security hath no charm.
The sword of Damocles suspended over their heads
adds to their enjoyment of anything.'

Three Weeks

i *Three Weeks*

Elinor's private world was crumbling. By the beginning of 1903, Clayton's financial situation had become so bad that his long-suffering solicitor, Walters, had virtually taken over the management of the tottering edifice of loans and repayments which were, in their turn, financed by further loans. Walters' first statement of account for the year, for instance, shows that after deducting various sums due to his firm, £463 17s 6d could be paid to Clayton – not a great deal of money with which to support a household of three adults and two children, especially when one of those adults was Elinor.

The situation was so bad that Clayton decided to move out of Sheering and let it, and join Mrs. Kennedy in Lamberts, the small cottage he had rented to her on his estate.

Any pretence that Elinor and Clayton were married in anything but name was now abandoned for, as part of the necessary additions to the cottage, Elinor insisted on her own wing, duly built on in plasterboard, connected to the main building by a glass corridor. She described her new quarters in a rather encouraging letter to Waldo Storey:

> . . . I would like to see you very much and show you the new hermitage I am building on to my mother's cottage. Just a sitting room, a bedroom, a bathroom, a room for my clothes and a room for my maid. It is built in a field and is joined on to the house by a veranda; no one is to come in unless I ask them, not even Clayton. And over the door is to be written 'Leave care behind, all ye who enter here.' It is to be a place of peace and quiet and grey walls and soft colours and plenty of green.

She called this extension her Trianon and decorated it in a style similar to Lucy's couture salon. Vaguely influenced by eighteenth-century decor, the effect was extravagantly enhanced by literally thousands of pale pink silk roses made by Elinor, her mother and by Dixie, the girls' governess. The finished effect was Elinor at her most typical.

During her lonely childhood, Elinor had formed the habit of solitude. She liked to live in one or two rooms with a maid to bring her meals and very hot coffee; she was never at ease in large houses or with a great many servants; hotels were her favourite, or very small flats. So the Trianon was, for her, the best of all worlds. She could still be seen to be living with Clayton and the children but in reality had a great deal of time to herself.

Her new independence came at a moment when her looks were in full bloom, having improved with the years. She was now accounted one of the beauties of her day – a day that placed more value on the mature, rather than the emerging, beauty.

Elinor began to discover that there were compensations for a husband who now spent most of his time shut up with his cigars and his brandy. She continued to travel by herself, and to go up to London more often, quartering herself with devoted friends, such as her Carlsbad acquaintances, the St. Heliers.

She still suffered from unspecific aches and pains, probably brought on by the financial troubles she tried to ignore. In 1903, Axel Munthe advised a return to Carlsbad to take the cure once more. It was here she met Lord Milner, who was resting from the heavy burden of his duties in South Africa.

Milner was strongly attracted to Elinor, and she to him, for he was everything that Clayton was not: powerful, famous, solvent and very ready to enter into any fancy she might come up with.

> I have seen him – my old friend. I wonder why in the past I never loved him – he loved me and loves me still. His stern face grew soft when his eyes rested upon me. We talked for hours in the firelight and he forgot his duties and his dinner. We visited the past at Steptaniewarts and the new moon. I gave him a new moon once, of the tiniest diamonds. Cartier I remember designed it, and made it into a pin. He wears it still. We spoke of Nuremberg and our joyous day there, of pine woods, of forests, of walks high up the mountains where, gay as children we used to wander, and he reminded me of our playful afternoon when we got lost and I was childish and pretended there were bears coming out of the dark trees to eat us. And how I held his hand and made him run down into the open early moonlight.

From the vantage point of 1910, when this diary entry was written, Elinor could be gently philosophical about the outcome of this promising new attachment, since she was by then in love with someone else – someone grander, more famous and more powerful than Milner. Seven years after the event she could write:

> His face was at last full of a wistful pain – it touched me – he kept his hands clasped as though he were afraid to let them free lest they

should caress me. And at last he went away and I fear will not come again I cannot love him – I love only one, but even though he will not see me, we shall write. That side of he can safely have – the intellectual. He shall be the friend of my ideals.

At the time, however, Elinor had not entertained such platonic ideas of the future of her relationship with this flatteringly powerful empire builder and highly intelligent man. Her frequent letters to Milner are lost, but his (less frequent) in response to hers still exist, showing him to be often evasive, pleading pressure of state business for failing to have tea or dine with her. But others are full of tender concern, interest in her writings and in her health. This must have been a refreshing change to her, used as she was to Clayton dismissing her work as idle scribblings, roughly on a par with doing needlework.

Milner was under a great deal of pressure, during his visit to Carlsbad, to become Colonial Secretary, a post that had recently been vacated by Chamberlain. Arthur Balfour, then Prime Minister, sent a special messenger to Carlsbad offering him the post, which he refused. Here was a man Elinor could respect. On his part, he obviously enjoyed the company of this vital woman. On his way back to South Africa in December, he was not too busy to write Elinor an eleven-page letter:

I wonder whether you are embarked by now on any new literary enterprises? Not that I intend that remark to goad you on, unless you feel in the humour. Nothing to my mind is more deplorable than the way in all successful writers, or is it their publishers? will never leave well alone. . . . the more genuine any gift of writing is the less possible must it be to force it. So though I should be glad to hear you were writing again, if you felt in the vein – for I am sure the vein would be a rich one, I should not be glad, if I thought you were only doing it because people worried you to.

He ends, rather wistfully:

I hope, if you do write, you will be able to tell me that you are all right again and enjoying life. I shall never forget what a delightful time we had in those Bohemian woods. . . . I feel sure we have still a lot to say to one another. But there must be time for it.

But time to talk or pursue a love affair was the one commodity Milner could not spare. Believing as he did that duty to country came above any personal consideration, he felt all his efforts must be given to affairs of State and Empire, and he was content to conduct a loving relationship with Elinor through letters. Even when they found themselves in London at the same time, he seemed to prefer to keep her at a letter-writing distance.

Their correspondence and occasional meetings continued regularly until 1907; then there is a gap of three years, three of the most important years in Elinor's life. The letters and meetings were resumed briefly in 1910, lapsed again, then resumed on a regular basis until the final letter from Milner, in 1921. The timing of this correspondence with Milner is extremely interesting, for it ceases when Elinor began to get involved with Curzon, the great love of her life. It resumed when Curzon dismissed Elinor for the first time, ceases when there was a reconciliation, and then continues after the traumatic finality of Curzon's second marriage. Clearly Elinor was the prime mover in the relationship with Milner.

It is a tribute to Elinor's personality and her energy of mind that she was admired by two of the most important statesmen of her age. (One affair was platonic, the other was not.) Her sometimes misdirected but nonetheless genuine intellectual inquisitiveness and sense of drama, combined with her extreme good looks, must have been attractive indeed to Curzon and Milner, both outwardly very cold and complicated men.

Elinor first mentions Curzon in a letter to Milner. Milner replied on June 20, 1906. Apologising for not being at a Saturday to Monday at which she had expected to see him, he added an interesting postscript:

> Curzon is very like your picture of him, but as you opine *there is a great deal inside that head* tho' the outward appearance is perhaps unpromising.

Years later, Elinor scrawled across this letter in pencil 'If only he [Milner] had come.' One can perhaps advance the hypothesis that, though she may well have met Curzon earlier at Easton, the Radcliffe party was the first occasion on which she really noticed him – or he her.

Elinor by no means neglected her writing and, in March 1906, she published another book which pleased the growing number of readers who relished her faintly naughty accounts of Edwardian society.

The Vicissitudes of Evangeline was a light comedy of manners, concerning a pretty, penniless adventuress who ended up happily married to the brother and heir of an unmarried Duke. Slight as was the plot, it gave Elinor plenty of opportunity to paint another picture of society, and her considerable public was not disappointed.

Nor was Gerald Duckworth. Each book she now wrote turned in a respectable profit. Duckworth himself had fallen victim to Elinor's charms and spent a great deal of time in the Trianon or in a bower Elinor had constructed in her garden, listening to her read aloud choice bits from her newest offering.

Duckworth and Milner were not the only men now to be ensnared by Elinor. Some time in 1905 she had met and become attracted to a young Guards officer, Lord Alastair Innes Ker. Very much cast in the Wynne Finch mould, though considerably younger, Innes Ker became a frequent visitor to Lamberts. He was a lively and good-looking young Englishman, the second son of the Duke of Roxburghe, and his increasingly close relationship with Elinor was apparently accepted, at least at first, by Clayton, and the trio became accepted as such in society, being invited to many houseparties together. On one occasion, they took part in a tableau together, Innes Ker playing Bothwell to Elinor's Mary Queen of Scots. It is not recorded what part Clayton played.

So much a part of the family had this delightful young man become that he accompanied them all to Paris when they went to put Margot into finishing school in September 1906. Elinor lost no time in showing Versailles to her 'young Englishman of race'.

One can imagine Innes Ker's irritation with her dramatics as she insisted he walk across the great terrace to the steps above the tapis-vert with his eyes shut, so that his first sight of her dream palace should be the full façade. But he complied. 'Now, turn round,' Elinor commanded. 'Gosh, what a lot of lightning conductors,' he said, spoiling her carefully constructed coup de théâtre. Elinor often told this story later as an illustration of her pet theory that young Englishmen were unawake to the finer things of life. But Innes Ker was far from stupid, and was more probably indulging in an Elinor-tease.

A year later even Clayton was beginning to grow uneasy at the fondness Elinor exhibited for her young admirer and prevailed upon her to send him away. In the best traditions of the time, Innes Ker took himself off to India, pausing only long enough to give her an inscribed copy of Laurence Hope's *India's Love Lyrics* as a farewell present. It was to be a final farewell, for Innes Ker married an American heiress, then so often considered an obligation for a titled if somewhat impoverished younger son.

A year later Elinor met his mother in New York, and wrote to Clayton with news:

About Alistair, I think it is too sad. . . . I hear from her friends here, that he is miserably unhappy. . . . she knows he does not

care a pin for her. . . . he has never cared for anyone but me. You
see, my dear old man, after you told him that time he was not to
come after me, he never did, and was quite changed from then.
All last Autumn and winter he was dreadfully unhappy, and only
married this girl because his brother made him, and he thought it
was the only thing to do. . . . I don't suppose we shall ever see
him again, so it does not matter.

Clayton was not entirely unsympathetic and told the children to be
especially kind to their mother after he had forced her young admirer
to depart. A less altruistic motive might have been to avoid scenes
in the restricted atmosphere of Lamberts.

The change this episode had effected now began to show in her
writing. Elinor had been touched by Innes Ker. Previously she had
almost always played the role of adored Princesse Lointaine, even with
Wynne Finch. But Innes Ker had encouraged something in her that had
been without nourishment for many years, and that something was
romance. It was not necessarily sexual passion, for Elinor was, if not
frigid, certainly never a physical woman. But a longing for love, dor-
mant in her for many years, now bubbled to the surface. Her emotional
life, atrophied by her neglected childhood and allowed little scope by
Clayton, now began to take wing at the age of forty-two. This first
became evident in her book *Beyond The Rocks*.

Beyond The Rocks is a bridge between the first period of Elinor's
writing career (in which she developed her powers of observation in
light-hearted comedies of social manners) and her second (in which
she became a novelist trying to deal with the deeper emotions of
passion and romance).

Beyond The Rocks is an interesting combination of cynical comedy
and romance. Described by Elinor as 'A love story', it is similar in
plot to *The Reflections of Ambrosine*. Theodora Fitzgerald marries a
rich old Australian, Josiah, to save her father's broken fortune, but
meets and falls in love with Lord Bracondale, a handsome, well-bred
man of her own class. Scenes are set at Versailles, and at country
houseparties in England, and here Elinor took a very cynical look at
the values of the world in which she lived.

The dénouement is based on a famous story of the time, which
Elinor would certainly have known about. Theodora decides to send
Bracondale away and writes him a long passionate farewell letter
and, at the same time, writes a short note to her husband concerning
her return to London. Her enemy, Morella Winmarleigh, jealous of
Theodora's success with Bracondale, changes the letters over and
Josiah learns of his wife's romance.

The incident on which this was loosely based concerned Lady Londonderry. Adored by her devoted husband, she fell in love with Harry Cust who was at the same time involved with the beautiful and jealous Lady de Grey. Lady de Grey found Theresa Londonderry's letters to Cust and had them sent round to the unsuspecting Lord Londonderry who opened the packet while at luncheon with his wife. Summoning a footman to take them down the table to his wife, he said, 'Henceforth we do not speak.' And they never did. They remained married, entertained, lived in the same house, but he never forgave her. This incident appeared later in Victoria Sackville-West's evocation of the era, *The Edwardians*, but it was Elinor who used it first.

Bracondale is a very good example of the middle-period Glyn hero: young; 'of race'; a typical product of Eton, Cambridge, a stately home and cricket grounds. Elinor found real young men of this type attractive and they, in turn, found her different from the other married ladies of their set, in her dramatic appearance and manner and her insistence on trying to awaken them to romance, poetry and philosophy.

Innes Ker was the model for the most famous hero Elinor ever created, the young Englishman Paul, in the novel that would forever put her without the inner pale of that very society she had so wanted to be part of. The novel was *Three Weeks*.

Three Weeks is one of those rare literary works – a novel which met the emotional needs of a wide readership at exactly the right moment. When the idea first occurred to Elinor, she had no clue that she would create a new literary genre, which would change her life for ever.

At the height of her affair with Innes Ker, the Glyns went to stay with Lord Kintore near Glamis. As was usual at such houseparties, the company sat round a roaring fire after tea and before changing for dinner, and Elinor, who had always been willing to sing for her supper with her Bernhardt imitations or with readings from her books, was asked by her fellow-guests to tell them a story.

She had been watching Innes Ker, a man whom she had discovered to be 'intellectually and emotionally sound asleep', as he lay on the hearth rug, playing with his rough-haired terrier. Elinor wondered what would happen if he were suddenly to be emotionally and intellectually awakened by falling in love with an intense, passionate, knowledgeable woman. A woman such as Sarah Bernhardt in the *Theodora* of long ago. Or a woman such as Elinor now felt herself to be.

Idle speculation, fuelled by her hopeless love for this younger man; residual guilt; the extinction of marital love and the death of former fantasies; Clayton's indifference at home and Milner's admiration from half a world away – must all have contributed to the frame of mind in which Elinor wrote *Three Weeks*.

As she gazed at Innes Ker on that rainy afternoon she might have been musing for a moment on the tiger-skin, across which she had undulated to so little effect long ago. She might have half-remembered the immortal love stories of Lancelot and Guinevere, Tristram and Yseult, read, half-remembered, half-understood when she was young.

Elinor was an emotional time-bomb, primed and now ready to go off. Innes Ker unwittingly became the fuse. She told the whole story of *Three Weeks* at a sitting. The reactions of the audience are not recorded but they must have been sufficiently encouraging for Elinor to take to her rose-strewn retreat in the 'Trianon' in October 1906 and write the novel that would make her notorious.

Unlike anything she had ever written before, the story came straight from her subconscious. *Three Weeks* was Elinor. The romantic side of her, formerly suppressed by the cynical mondaine side and by circumstances, bubbled up. 'It seemed as if some spirit from beyond was guiding me,' she later wrote. 'I wrote breathlessly for hours and hours on end, hardly conscious at times of the words which were pouring out of my brain, until I came to read over the chapters and found that what I had written was exactly what I had hoped and meant to say. The original manuscript shows this, it flows on with hardly a correction or alteration.' *Three Weeks* meant everything to Elinor.

> It was the outpouring of my whole nature, romantic, proud and passionate but forever repressed in real life by the barriers of custom and tradition, and held fast behind the iron mask of self-respect and self-control which had, perhaps fortunately, been locked round my throat by Grandmamma in Canada long years before.

Three Weeks is far more than a catchy title or a period romance. It has genuine fervour.

Paul Verdayne is the typical Elinor-hero who

> Believed in himself – he believed in his mother . . . life was full of certainties for him. . . . He liked hunting better than anything else in the world. He had been in the eleven at Eton and left Oxford with a record that should turn a beautiful Englishman into a perfect athlete. . . . books had not worried him much.

Paul falls in love with Isabella Waring. 'She was the Parson's daughter
. . . . and often in those days between her games of golf and hockey,
or a good run on her feet with the hounds, she came up to Verdayne
Place to write Lady Henrietta's letters for her.' (Shades of that jolly
bridesmaid whom, twelve years before, Clayton had found to be a
congenial outdoor companion while Elinor dreamed over her fire
and reread the *Memoirs* of the Duc de Saint-Simon.) Paul is sent away
to get over this unsuitable romance and goes to Paris which bores
him. 'He did not know its joys and was in no mood to learn them. . . .
visiting Versailles . . . he came to the conclusion it was all "beastly
rot".'

Moving on to a hotel in Switzerland he notices a table at dinner
most carefully laid for one, which he assumes to be for 'one of those
over-fed foreign brutes of no sex'. But the occupant is a woman, and
a mysterious one at that.

> She herself was all in black, and her hat – an expensive,
> distinguished-looking hat – cast a shadow over her eyes. . . . her
> face was white, he saw that plainly enough, startlingly white, like
> a magnolia bloom. . . . she certainly had a mouth worth looking
> at again. It was so red. Not large and pink and laughingly open
> like Isabella's, but straight and chiselled, and red, red, red.

Paul eats his soup. So does the woman. Dismissing her as being 'well
over thirty. . . . I suppose she has nothing else to live for,' Paul
drinks more port than is good for him and then goes out to smoke
a cigar. He hears a sigh, smells tuberoses from the terrace above him
and then sees the woman's face.

> It seemed to emerge from a mist of black gauze. And looking
> down into his were a pair of eyes. . . . a pair of eyes. . . . were
> they black, or blue, or grey or green? He did not know, he could
> not think – only that they were eyes – eyes – eyes.

A game of hide and seek begins, the woman appearing and then
vanishing. This is in line with Elinor's 'now you see me, now you
don't' early attitude towards flirtation. In the book the flirtation is
very much controlled by the older woman, not by the younger man.

Finally, she summons him. 'Come Paul, I have some words to say
to you.' And this is where *Three Weeks* departs from convention, for
the woman has, shall we say, the whip-hand. It is the woman who
teaches Paul about love and life. It is she who dictates the progress
of the affair– who plans its settings and who brings it to an end. This
is a complete reversal of the man/woman hunter/victim relationship
normal in a romantic novel.

Unwittingly, Elinor invented a new balance of sexual power in her romantic fable. It is the leading or active role taken by the woman that horrified her contemporaries, quite apart from the shock of adultery appearing in print. The sexuality on nearly every page might seem quaint to modern eyes, but at the time it lifted *Three Weeks* out of the ranks of the humdrum romantic read into a cause célèbre.

There are other aspects of the book which appear dated, but what still intrigue are the descriptions of the settings of this torrid affair. Here is Elinor's description of The Lady (as the unnamed heroine of the book is referred to) and her surroundings:

> It may have been the usual brocade walls and gilt chairs of the 'best suite' but its aspect was so transformed by her subtle taste and presence. . . . there were masses of flowers – roses, big white ones – tuberoses – lilies of the valley – gardenias – late violets. . . . a great couch filled one side of the room beyond the fireplace. Such a couch. Covered with a tiger-skin and piled with pillows, all shades of rich purple velvet and silk embroidered with silver and gold – unlike any pillows he had ever seen before, even to their shapes. The whole thing was different and strange – and intoxicating.

And later:

> A bright fire burnt in the grate and some palest orchid-mauve silk curtains were drawn in the lady's room. . . . in front of the fire, stretched at full length, was his tiger – and on him – also at full length reclined the lady, garbed in some strange clinging garment of heavy purple crepe, its hem embroidered with gold, one white arm resting on the beast's head, her back supported by a pile of the velvet cushions, and a heap of rarely bound books at her side, while between her red lips was a rose not redder than they – an almost scarlet rose. . . . the whole picture was barbaric.

The whole picture owed much to Lucy, and to the increasingly exotic colours and embroideries she was using at this time. The Lady's clothes obviously came from Lucile too:

> She was garbed all ready for dinner in a marvellous garment of shimmering purple, while round her shoulders a scarf of brilliant pale emerald gauze, all fringed with gold, fell in two long ends, and on her neck and in her ears great emeralds gleamed – a pear-shaped one of unusual brilliancy fell at the parting of her waves of hair on to her smooth white forehead.

This book was written in 1907. Both the decoration and clothes were far ahead of their time. Not for another three years would Leon Bakst's designs for the Russian ballet inspire Poiret's oriental revival and a thousand exotic drawing rooms be furnished with huge heaps of brilliantly coloured cushions piled high on vermilion couches.

In the sexual sense, too, Elinor was ahead of her time. The novel presents a picture (in outline if not in detail) of a passionate and violent love affair lasting only three weeks. The physicality of its descriptions shocked the Mrs. Grundys:

> They were sitting on the tiger by now, and she undulated round and all over him, feeling his coat, and his face, and his hair, as a blind person might, till at last it seemed as if she were twined about him like a serpent.

As the night of the full moon approaches, Elinor excels herself:

> She was seated on the old Venetian chair. . . . the most radiant vision he had yet seen. Her garment was pale green gauze. . . . clasped with pearls. . . . the whole place had been converted into a bower of roses. A great couch of deepest red ones was at one side, fixed in such masses as to be quite resisting and firm. . . . from the roof chains of roses hung. . . . above the screen of lilac bushes in full bloom, the moon in all her glory mingled with the rose-shaded lamps and cast a glamour and unreality over the whole.

This exotic scene climaxes as the loggia floods with moonlight and the rose-strewn couch becomes an unusual marriage-bed. Elinor leaves nothing to the imagination: 'My darling one,' The Lady whispers to Paul. 'This is our souls' wedding.'

To a generation accustomed to romances which ended on the 'Reader I married him' threshold of the bedroom, and a nuptial chamber, moreover, sanctified by a religious ceremony, Elinor's over-heated descriptions of illicit love were horrifying.

After this climactic scene, the novel unravels to a denouement which Elinor believed literally atoned for the earlier scenes of passion. The Lady (now identified as the Queen of an unnamed Balkan country, married to a brutal husband) vanishes. A year passes. Paul suffers, and so does The Lady. Eventually she summons him to her in Constantinople, with the news that she is the mother of his child. But they are fated to be parted. She is murdered by her husband's servants and Paul returns – a broken man – to England.

The final scene takes place in church, in the nameless Balkan kingdom, as Paul observes his son, now aged five, celebrate his birthday. As Elinor saw it, the redemptive power of true love transcended conventional morality. She did not reckon on the average reader, who lost interest once The Lady had met her fate. In a prologue to the American edition, she attempted to exhort the merely prurient in rousing language:

> The minds of some human beings are as moles grubbing in the earth for worms. They have no eyes to see God's sky with the stars in it. To such *Three Weeks* will be but a sensual record of passion. But those who do look up beyond the material will understand the deep, pure love and the Soul in its all, and they will realise that to such a nature as The Lady's passion would never have run riot until it was sated – she would have daily grown nobler in her desire to make her Loved One's son a splendid man.

Noble as these sentiments were, they were completely ignored by the public. With the publication of *Three Weeks* in June 1907, a violent storm broke over Elinor's head. From being a beautiful member of Edwardian society with a penchant for self-dramatisation, a sleepy husband and a conventional life, she herself took on the aura of a Scarlet Woman.

Elinor knew that *Three Weeks* would outrage many people. She had qualms about publishing it. Several of her closest friends were asked to read the book in manuscript or proof form.

Frances Warwick was shocked and advised Elinor not to publish it, warning her that if she did none of her grander friends would ever speak to her again, the rule being that such experiences might be enjoyed but not described in print. Several letters Milner wrote to Elinor indicate that she had decided not to publish. 'I am so glad you have another book shaping in your mind . . . some day perhaps, the suppressed volume will after all see the light of day.' .

But on May 10, Walters had written to say that £8,000 had been offered for Sheering which he found 'unacceptable, as this would leave no surplus for you'. By the 13th, in spite of an increased offer of £9,000, Walters still estimated there would be nothing left.

It may be concluded that Elinor was forced to publish to avert yet another financial crisis. On May 24, Milner wrote, thanking her for the book. 'I shall not write anything till I have read it right through. That will not take long, but I don't mean to rush through it. Literature is not fairly treated so.' Elinor, possibly unnerved by the first storm-signals from her friends, had obviously written Milner an unpleasant letter to accompany the book, for he went on to say:

Pending my further communications, may I respectfully, fondly, humbly, but firmly *protest* against your last letter? If it might not seem disrespectful, I should like to shake you. Why, because the weather turns glacial in the middle of May which is damning but truly English – should you become at once 1) so dolorous and 2) so spiky to your friends? Yes – very spiky and disagreeable. The world after all is not such a bad place, nor in particular, has it treated you so badly.

Three days later, he wrote again: 'I am reading the book and find it very enthralling. This letter is meant as a conciliatory one – an olive branch. I was not unappreciative of your long letter, and never intended to give you that impression, or imply any of the unfriendly thoughts you read into it.'

On June 9, Milner reassured Elinor:

No remarks or comments of any kind have reached my ears with regard to the matter you refer to. . . . Perhaps I am over-critical but remember, if I am critical in the confidence of friendship, to your face, I am certainly not going to join the detractors behind your back. On the contrary. To the *world* I can and will only dwell on the strong points – and there are many. Very likely the book will not meet with the hostility you seem to fear. If it does, I doubt the storm will soon blow over, and your real friends will not be dismayed, or in any way affected by it.

Milner misjudged the strength of the approaching storm, at first a small cloud on the horizon, but soon to become a hurricane.

Gerald Duckworth advertised the book as: 'A Novel for those who are neither old nor young. A study of a strange woman. An episode in a young man's life.' As fast as it was reprinted, it sold out. Everybody read it – in secret. As Anita Leslie perceptively commented in *Edwardians in Love*: 'It did not merely appeal to the romantic aspirations of kitchenmaids, but to the kitchenmaid in the heart of every great lady in Europe.'

Three Weeks was, literally, an overnight sensation. The reviews helped, warning that it was 'emphatically not pour les jeunes filles' (The *Onlooker*); 'The most unedifying study of the spider and the fly. . . . Mrs Glyn has not the dainty touch to make such a record artistic. . . . Mrs Glyn must return to fresher and more healthful themes if she is to retain her hold upon an English audience' (The *Daily Telegraph*). The *Sunday Times* was the only dissenting voice in the general chorus of disapprobation. Perceiving the novel as being 'narrated with too much emotional intensity to deserve the reproach of lasciviousness', it recommended it to readers 'who can tolerate in fiction a defiance of the conventions' and described it as a 'very dainty romance'.

Majority opinion differed. *Three Weeks* was condemned by society and was absolutely forbidden to the young. To Mrs. Denton Carlisle, for example, who, when a very young girl, was invited with her father Sir Charles Gill and Lady Cunard to dine in Marienbad with the King. Not noticing the presence of the still unpresented young girl, Emerald Cunard sought to amuse Edward VII by discussing the relative merits of *The Visits of Elizabeth* and *Three Weeks*. Many years later, Mrs. Carlisle told Anita Leslie that 'the Prince looked thunder, turned his shoulder on Lady Cunard and changed the topic with determination'. Mrs. Carlisle pretended to notice nothing, but she heard later that an equerry had been sent to Lady Cunard with a reprimand which kept her 'banished to her own hotel for several days'.

Emerald's own daughter Nancy read it at the early age of eleven. 'My week with *Three Weeks* in bed in the clandestine hours of dawn was a very great enjoyment. So that was an adventuress – beautiful, perfidious, dashing. She blazed a while across the repressions of my childhood. It also chanced that *Three Weeks* was the first novel I read.'

Nancy discussed the book with the philosopher and mathematician George Moore (at that time her mother's lover). 'I told him that it had thrilled me, but that *Too Weak* [a parody by Montague Eliot] though very unkind, had made me wonder if there were not, well, some exaggeration in it. . . . we must have talked for twenty minutes, while I asked myself how severely punished I would be if the matter were discovered.'

Nancy's governess Miss Scarth did discover the book and reported the discussion she had overheard to Lady Cunard. 'Astonishment and annoyance soon turned into uproar because G. came out firmly on my side, and as I stood there crimson with defiance, saying "Why note? Why not?" there was an increasing vehemence in all his words: "Why should she not read *Three Weeks*? It may not be good literature but what possible harm can come to her from reading it?"'

Emerald Cunard's fury was probably fuelled by the memory of her temporary disgrace at Marienbad.

In spite of every mama's horror at the book – or more probably because of it – it became obligatory reading for the more daring Edwardian young, rather as *Lady Chatterley's Lover* was read by their grandchildren because of the attempts to suppress it. The Headmaster of Eton, Dr. Edward Lyttelton, felt so strongly about the possible corruptive power of *Three Weeks* that he banned it and wrote to

Elinor to inform her of his decision. She challenged him, asking whether he had actually read it, to which he replied that he had not. Being Elinor, she immediately sent him a copy, and he later wrote to her again to say that he had enjoyed it and had been misled by its reputation. He did not, however, lift his ban.

But the worst consequence of the success of *Three Weeks* was to exile Elinor from many of the houseparties she had come to enjoy in the restricted world of Edwardian society. Elinor had gained entry to this world at considerable cost and – though she had delighted in light-hearted mockery – it was desperately important to her.

Curiously, the reason many of her erstwhile friends barred her was not because of the content of the book but because she had written of her own affair with a young man. She had transgressed the code of kissing but never telling.

If she could so reveal herself, society asked, then surely she could reveal others' transgressions too? Had she 'belonged' in the first place she might have got away with it, as Millicent, Duchess of Sutherland, had done in her first novel *One Hour and the Next*, published in 1899. Not as overtly passionate as *Three Weeks*, it did nevertheless deal with a fairly shocking situation and yet the Duchess was not ostracized in the same way as was Elinor.

From now until the end of her life, vague impropriety attached itself to Elinor's name, particularly in England. A famous verse, written anonymously, first amused her, but later dogged her when she wished, as she did ever more frequently, to be taken for a serious author. It went:

> Would you like to sin
> With Elinor Glyn
> On a tiger-skin?
> Or would you prefer
> To err
> With her
> On some other fur?

There were many, of course, who did not desert her. The Duchess of Abercorn and Lady Arthur Paget both wrote charming letters and, as we have seen, Milner stood fast too.

In 1916, nine years after publication and before it went into its first cheap edition, the sale in Great Britain, the Empire and America was just short of two million copies. In addition, the book was translated into virtually every European language, being particularly successful in Scandinavia and Spain. By 1933, Elinor supplied *Everybody's* with the information that, counting the cheap editions and the translations, she estimated that total world sales were over five million copies.

Why did it sell . . . and go on and on selling even in the more liberated 'twenties? Because, in the last analysis, *Three Weeks* is a great love story. A romance with all the stops pulled out, telling of two very disparate people claiming each other beyond the limits of morality, time or space, it still thrilled the post-war generation, even though by that time the high-flown prose in which it had been written was dated.

In the character of the mysterious Lady – who is a Queen, yet counts her rank as nothing in the face of true love; who sacrifices herself that the child of this love may live; who is beautiful, cultivated, worldly; who educates her lover up to her own exacting standards – Elinor created an entirely new type of active, rather than passive, romantic heroine.

It is not surprising that with *Three Weeks* Elinor graduated from her role as a witty commentator on the tiny society within which she had lived, and stepped out on to a much larger stage.

ii   *Lucy and Elinor Visit America*

The summer of 1907 was a miserable one for Elinor. The fuss over *Three Weeks* showed no signs of abating and judicious flight seemed to be the answer. Accordingly she planned a trip round the world, ostensibly to round off Margot's and Juliet's education (a feeble excuse, for they were only twelve and seven respectively). To prepare for the journey, Elinor went to Paris to buy dresses, hats and shoes and to collect Margot from her finishing school, where she had been punished for reading *Three Weeks*. While in Paris, Elinor met Kate Moore, her old friend and the well-known American hostess, who told her how popular her 'shocker' was in America, probably adding that there would be no question of closed doors should she go and visit.

Elinor abandoned her plans to travel to Japan and back with her family. Returning home from Paris with Margot in tow, she sent her mother and Dixie, the governess, in her stead while she set forth alone for America with a new Lucile wardrobe and, among other essentials, sixty pairs of shoes.

Armed with letters of introduction from Sir Coudie Stephen, her old Paris acquaintance, now equerry to Edward VII, and from Kate Moore and Lady Arthur Paget, Elinor set sail on her forty-fourth birthday, and immediately discovered she had a friend on board in Consuelo, Duchess of Manchester. The Duchess had been born Consuelo Yznaga, of an old Southern family, and was one of the Dollar Princesses. Although she was a member of the inner circle that had so disapproved of Elinor's scandalous work, she was more liberal-minded than most of her set and very willing to introduce Elinor to friends in America.

Elinor felt rejuvenated. It was as if she had left all her problems – even her old personality – behind. '. . . it seemed a very big adventure to be thus travelling about by myself in the role of "Elinor Glyn, the famous authoress" instead of in the company of my husband as the rather timid, peculiar-looking wife of the well-known traveller, Clayton Glyn.'

She had found the role she would play for the rest of her life, and one which she naturally enjoyed to the top of her considerable bent.

At last she found herself where she had always, subconsciously, longed to be – centre stage – playing in a drama of her own making.

Warned by the Duchess of Manchester's mother, who was travelling with Consuelo, that she would be mobbed when she arrived, Elinor dressed very carefully for New York. She wore a purple overcoat, purple toque and a purple chiffon veil which she draped around her face, an effect deliberately reminiscent of 'The Lady' and one which had been developed with the help of Lucy, who knew that her sister would be the best possible advertisement for her designs in America, a country which she was beginning to consider as a possibly sympathetic environment for another Lucile establishment.

Mrs. Yznaga had not under-estimated American fascination for the society authoress. On arrival, Elinor was given celebrity treatment and it was not surprising that she scored an immediate hit with the American press. Her path had been paved with fantastic stories about the true identity of 'Paul' and the suggestion that she herself was the heroine of *Three Weeks*. She was bombarded with questions. 'What did she think of America? What were her views on American divorce? How long was she going to stay? How did she react to the change from obscurity to fame?'

The answer to that was obvious. Elinor loved it.

> Until that moment, I had been merely a private person, who happened to write books when she felt inclined: I had only been interviewed once or twice, and thought it a really funny idea that anyone reading the papers would be interested to hear about me. I knew no literary people except Mr. Jeyes and Mr. Mallock and Mrs. Mason, whom I had met at the Jeunes.

Now the centre of attraction in her own right, Elinor found herself in a country which did not present her as an immoral woman, but as someone with her own particular achievement to her credit.

American society was enthusiastic in their welcome of this exotic visitor and even such sticklers as Mrs. Frederick Vanderbilt were keen to invite this 'noble' Englishwoman to their houses, accompanied as she was by a Dollar Duchess.

Elinor found Mrs. Vanderbilt's house on Long Island overdone:

> We were received by our hostess at the doorway of a palatial salon . . . furnished with magnificent ornamental cabinets and chairs of great value but little comfort.

At the tea party which followed Mamie Stuyvesant Fish, another social leader, notorious for her waspish tongue, remarked: 'They say in Europe that all American women are virtuous. Well, do you wonder? Look at those men.' Elinor found her hostess's idea of decoration:

> Splendid beyond all the dreams of avarice . . . even the most humble porcelain accessories were decorated with blue satin bows. There were no books, or any evidence that the bedrooms were ever occupied, and the difference between these super-hotel suites and the intimate cosy charm of those at Easton Lodge was indescribable.

At a lunch given in Elinor's honour by the social arbiter, Emily Post, there were

> . . . heaps of people . . . all agreeable. . . . the men are Working Bees. I can think of nothing else, kind clever creatures who one might go to the end of the world with without feeling one was with men. I call them of the 4th Sex – that is another race of beings altogether.

She was also very funny about a visit to the theatre:

> . . . so well built *everyone* can see but the decoration too awful for words. Exactly like turkey's insides that one has seen on the kitchen table, splodged over the boxes. . . . They call it Art Nouveau, that is the principal thing here – energy, force and an absolute want of the perception of value or symmetry or harmony. The women have mammoth feather hats, broader than their shoulders, tailor-suits with waists at their knees – so long. And short skirts.

The news of Elinor's splendid reception was not long in reaching Lucy who was feeling, as usual, rather restless. Her business was going from strength to strength and, when Elinor wrote in typically extravagant terms of her doings in America, Lucy decided to follow her sister and see for herself whether she should establish a branch of Lucile there.

Elinor sounded a note of caution in a letter to her mother in November. 'Lucy wants to come for December and I think it would be a good thing and splendid for her, if she would ever have enough control of herself to be careful all the time of what she said and did; I never go "off guard" for a moment, it would not be safe.'

Leaving Cosmo and Miles to run the business, Lucy arrived in New York just before Christmas 1907 with the firm intention of finding an American backer should she decide to go ahead with a New York Lucile. In her autobiography, Lucy makes no mention that Elinor was there at the same time, even though she was taken about by her suddenly successful younger sister and indeed stayed with her at the Plaza. This is hardly surprising for Lucy, for so long used to being considered the more successful and 'artistic' of the sisters, had, if only temporarily, been outstripped by Elinor in terms of fame and (or so it appeared at the time) fortune.

In the middle of January 1908, Lucy wrote a letter to Cosmo from the Plaza, headed 'Write here all the time':

> Fancy the controversy getting into the English newspapers . . . not one word of it was true that Nelly is supposed to have said, it was entirely invented by the newspapers. . . . we have had the greatest fun and excitement over it and it has put up the sale of her book to thousands and thousands more. I am rarely mentioned, and then quite nicely. I shall be perfectly happy to be back with you again, and shall tell you lots of things too amusing that strike me. I'm sure we would make a fortune here, if we can find the money. There are such opportunities of wearing good clothes here. Twice this week I have been to luncheon parties of women, one was of twelve, the other eighteen, where they all wore the most wonderful light dresses in white and pale colours. They have to dress like that, the houses are so hot. The Vanderbilt house was in the best taste I have ever seen. . . . I have never had such a time in my life of society and going out. I have not met one American man that you could fancy was a gentleman. They are awful.

Rare light is shed on Lucy's relationship with Cosmo in the same letter – distance did indeed lend enchantment:

> I can't help telling them things about you and I show them your photograph and, darling, have little conversations with you every night when I go to bed, and tell you how I love you. I am so thankful that you are getting better and that I shall hear your beautiful voice again. . . . I do wish you were here, you would be a hero among these women, they would adore you. I hope you will allow me to come again next year as it does me good to feel I am as good and better than other people.

Elinor and Lucy went to Washington, where they were presented to President Theodore Roosevelt, by Senator Warren. Lucy was not impressed.

> The President stepped forward, shook hands with me warmly and said: I'm so pleased to meet you, Lady Duff Gordon. I've just been reading your *Memories*.' He talked quickly, asking me questions and never waiting to hear my replies, and did not listen when I tried to explain that the *Memories* he was talking about were those

of my husband's aunt, Lucie Lady Duff Gordon, who had died in the early 'eighties.

Lucy sailed back to England at the end of January 1908. Elinor stayed in New York for the rest of the winter, and continued to be lionised. She was particularly thrilled to meet Mark Twain, who called on her at the Plaza.

> He told me that he liked *Three Weeks* very much and understood its meaning, and I found that he did, indeed, know it well, for he discussed every point and made a profound analysis of the whole book. He also made many interesting comments of his own concerning human instincts and their control.

Rather pushily, Elinor said she was going to write down an approximation of everything that Twain said, and send it to him to read, presumably with the idea that she could use it as some sort of endorsement by a 'serious' writer.

Mark Twain however had very different ideas and wrote her the following letter.

> It reads pretty poorly. I get the sense of it, but it is a poor literary job; however, it would have to be because nobody can be reported even approximately except by a stenographer. Approximations, synopsised speeches, translated poems, artificial flowers and chromos all have a sort of value, but it is small. If you put on paper what I really said, it would have wrecked your type-machine. I said some foetid and over-vigorous things but that was because it was a confidential conversation.

However, at a testimonial dinner later that winter in New York, Mark Twain made a very generous and encouraging speech about Elinor.

Early in the spring Elinor had to make a quick visit back to London, for Clayton's finances were in crisis once more and Walters had requested she postpone her marriage settlement yet again. She also planned to go to Paris to 'frivole with Lucy' and because Puccini was interested in composing an opera based on *Three Weeks* but this came to nothing – he decided instead to compose 'La Fanciulla del West'. Elinor was agitated at hearing from Mrs. Kennedy (now in Tokyo) that she had been ill. 'I won't admit even that you have colds, *you are perfectly well* darling Gran and *must be.*' Neither Elinor nor Lucy could ever face the fact that their mother was mortal.

Elinor was back in New York in March and immediately set off on a coast-to-coast trip. The further west she went the more she liked it. Her favourite episode, and one which she would use in two of her later novels, took place in a mining camp in Nevada where she found the romantic America she had been seeking. The atmosphere in Nevada struck a responsive chord in one who had been brought up by a pioneering grandmother. Accompanied by Sam Newhouse, described in the newspapers as the 'Utah millionaire', she went to Rawhide, which was all the goldrush clichés made familiar by a thousand cowboy films. Elinor played faro in the Northern, the biggest gambling hall in the town. In Stingare Gulch, the red light district, she witnessed a drunken shoot-out between a prospector and a gambler. The dainty society lady descended on a camp of rough and ready 'nature's gentlemen'. The miners made much of their incongruous visitor and gave a banquet in her honour in the leading hotel, covering the long table with white oilcloth decorated with a centre-piece of yellow daisies which one miner had ridden ninety miles across the desert to obtain.

Elinor and twenty miners sat down to a meal washed down with champagne that had come from the east, ate food that had come a hundred miles by waggon and drank springwater from a source six miles away. She was astonished by the perfect manners of men whom she would formerly have regarded as beyond the pale.

A deputation led by Governor Hutchinson presented Elinor with a tiny gun. 'We give you this here gun, Elinor Glyn,' said one of the miners, 'because we like your darned pluck. You ain't afraid, and we ain't neither.' Pinning the badge of Deputy Constable on her breast, they told her she could now 'arrest any boy in the state'. Her reply was felicitous – she told them she would like to arrest the lot, for they were all so delightful. 'I wish I could be a miner,' she told them, 'because there must be satisfaction in digging the gold from the earth and knowing that you are receiving your wages from nature itself.'

This encounter with the miners, rough children of the West, made Elinor ponder on many of her basic beliefs. She had been brought up by her grandmother to regard manners as the exclusive province of 'born' aristocrats and yet here were men who had acquired such manners not through bloodlines, nor through the accumulated traditions of centuries of authority, nor even through education, but solely through character. Elinor must have compared them favourably with the society that had closed ranks against her in England.

She treasured the little silver gun and the deputy's star for the rest of her life; her granddaughter has them still. She brought two other souvenirs of her visit back with her to England from America. The first was an abiding interest in the New Thought, just then intriguing America. This was the doctrine which claimed that thought force could be harnessed to obtain anything the thinker desired – from a promotion at work to a lover. Elinor was much taken with this pseudo-philosphy and never altogether abandoned its basic principles, though later she came to distrust its more materialistic features. She spread this philosophy to her mother and her sister and, from this time, all her letters sent 'golden light' to their recipients.

She also returned with 'The Secret of El-Zair', the first of many treatments she would use to preserve her youth and beauty. El-Zair was a form of elixir of eternal youth, and over the next few years Elinor carried out the part-mystical, part-medicinal treatment faithfully, keeping a full account of her progress. She persuaded Lucy and Cosmo to try it. The seventy-year-old Lord Redesdale was also recruited, even if the only way he could benefit was in 'youthful exaltation of mind'.

From Nevada, Elinor went on to San Francisco and Santa Barbara, from where she wrote despairingly to her mother of Sir Coudie Stephens' death:

> . . . the only thing I want is to be home again, I am so crushed with grief at the death of the kindest friend we have ever had in life. . . . his unassuming thought for every member of my family even in his last letter. . . . his schemes with the King so that I should be recognised as England's greatest modern writer . . . dear Coudie was to have settled all my new version with the Lord Chamberlain's Office [this was a new version of the dramatisation of *Three Weeks*] . . . and get the King's special support. Alas. I must stand alone.

Elinor returned home via Salt Lake City where she found 'the English butler is the only gentleman', thence to St. Louis where Mr. James Hackett was to produce the first dramatic version of *Three Weeks* which Elinor had written while she was in New York. However, when she reached New York again at the end of her trip, she unwisely signed away the performing rights east of Missouri to Elizabeth Marbury, Elsie de Wolfe's girlfriend. This signing away of her rights for one hundred pounds, caused a great deal of trouble subsequently between Elinor and Lucy, who was torn by her loyalty to her sister and her friendship and business connections with Elsie de Wolfe.

Elinor set sail for home in June 1908. She had not seen her family for nine months and was looking forward to a reunion with them, for she was in an optimistic mood. Her books were bringing in large sums of money, she had travelled by herself, and her visit had been an enormous personal success. She had an idea for a new book which came out a year later under the title *Elizabeth Visits America*, in which she dismissed the eastern seaboard and its social pretensions, and eulogised the Far West. Intended as a return to the comic vein in which she had first scored a success, it produced a much less spontaneous effect and showed signs of considerable reworking. Nor was it flattering to Elinor's hosts, many of whom must have recognised themselves, but it never affected Elinor's popularity in America.

Elinor had not seen her family for nine months and the financial situation at home, very grave before she went away, had become infinitely worse.

In her autobiography and in Anthony Glyn's biography the point is made that she was totally unprepared for the intelligence that Clayton had, in effect, borrowed all that he could on his assets and that henceforth all they would have to live on would be her own earnings.

This was not in fact the case. She had agreed to the postponement of her marriage settlement several times since 1903 and she had also been party to the considerable correspondence between Clayton and Walters. By 1906, for instance, matters had become so desperate that Walters had suggested a loan for £1,000 for Elinor (not Clayton) from Scottish Provident to help pay the Inland Revenue and other pressing creditors. It was turned down and Walters tried again, this time with Law Life, telling Elinor that it would be 'on security of your pin money together with a policy on your lives'. Conclusive proof that Elinor must have been very well aware how matters stood is contained in the condition stipulated by Law Life that she had to agree to be seen by a doctor – a certain Sir Dyce Duckworth.

The history of Clayton's total financial ruin was found, long after Elinor's death, carefully put away in a blue box with a Bramah lock at Miskin, the house belonging to Elinor's son-in-law, Sir Rhys Rhys Williams. All the correspondence with Walters, with the exception of anything relating to the events of the year 1910, was painstakingly organised. She also hid a diary covering a particularly sad period of her life, written in 1910 and subsequently edited by her years later. Obviously, the blue box had been so carefully put away with posterity in mind.

It was clear also that her husband was a sick man. Always inclined to corpulence, Clayton had now become bloated, not with gourmet food, but with his favourite consolation – brandy.

There had been hints that drink was one of Clayton's problems some years previously when he had fallen out with a cousin, Dick Richards, who was also a wine merchant, over a consignment of brandy which Clayton had chosen to regard as a free sample and which Richards was

ungentlemanly enough to charge him for. Clayton never paid and the
family feud thus caused was only to be healed at his funeral.

For the next six years Elinor kept up the myth that Clayton was
independently wealthy and that she worked to amuse herself. The
reality was very different: she had to cast about for money to house,
feed, clothe and educate her children and keep her mother and her
husband in a style which they were unwilling to modify. She was
naturally hurt when one of Clayton's relatives referred to 'Aunt
Nellie's extravagance'. Even though the sales of *Three Weeks* remained
buoyant, she rarely had enough money to re-assume the carefree life
she had led before. She had now to produce books and articles to
make money. Writing, once an antidote against depression, now
became work. Needlework and reading were things of the past.

Now she began to take her work seriously and, typically, threw
herself with great fervour into the role of 'author'. Nothing was
allowed to disturb her when she was writing in the 'Trianon' and
Margot, then thirteen, remembered having to create the right mood
for her mother by playing the 'Valse Triste' over and over and over
again, while Elinor curled up on her bed, writing and writing with
her stylo.

Lamberts cannot have been a happy house. Clayton drinking
brandy in his study; Elinor writing in the 'Trianon'; Mrs. Kennedy
in charge of the girls and encouraging Clayton not to change his way
of life; the girls, one minute ignored by their mother, the next being
caressed extravagantly. 'My mother loved to hug us [Elinor called it
'squeezing'],' Margot said years later, 'and I hated it, so I always used
to stick my bones out but Juliet loved it, being smaller and more
cuddly.'

Despite the success of *Three Weeks* things looked bleak indeed in
1908. *Elizabeth Visits America* was not due out for another year but
there was a need for money now. It was at this low point that a
lucrative possibility arose from an unlikely source. During her visit
to Paris in 1907, Elinor had met the Grand Duchess Kiril of Russia
who had suggested that a good way to put over *Three Weeks'* moral
message would be to turn it into a play.

Elinor had already written a dramatic version, at the prompting of
Elizabeth Marbury, the grotesquely fat and extremely powerful
American theatrical agent whom she had met through Elise de Wolfe,
who had, as already mentioned, purchased the stock performing
rights in the United States for a hundred pounds. Casting around for
profitable schemes, it occurred to Elinor that a private performance

might, as the Grand Duchess suggested, not only vindicate the book and re-establish her in English society but also prompt a theatre manager to mount a commercial presentation.

This was a daring idea, but Elinor went further, casting herself in the part of The Lady (in the original dramatic version, Alla Nazimova had been cast, but this came to nothing). Losing no time, Elinor produced *Three Weeks* as a charity invitation matinee on July 23, 1908. She gave a creditable performance in the main part, leaning on her long-ago memory of Sarah Bernhardt as Theodora. She was supported by a cast of professionals. Paul was played by Charles Bryant, a handsome young juvenile lead. His father was played by C. Aubrey Smith, later to become leader of the English colony in Hollywood and a familiar screen figure over nearly three decades whenever an English colonel-type was needed in films. Sir Charles Hawtrey produced and Lucile provided the dresses.

'I have been rehearsing all day,' Elinor wrote to her mother on July 17. 'Things are going on. Hawtrey is rather casual and *no* one knows their words. . . . It puts me out. "Paul" is beautiful, 6′3″ and quite a gentleman. We shall look lovely at all events. As yet all seems chaos but they assure me it will be right in the end.'

London society, having flocked to what they doubtless hoped was a scandalous performance, found themselves watching a run-of-the-mill melodrama without one snakelike undulation or naughty line. But it went well enough for Hawtrey to make plans for a West End presentation, substituting a professional actress for Elinor's amateurish but heartfelt essay at the role of The Lady. The contract was signed, and Elinor obtained satisfactory terms. But the Lord Chamberlain's office turned it down. No official explanation for the ban was ever forthcoming, but Lord Redesdale later told her that it had been vetoed at the instigation of the Foreign Office and thus on political rather than moral grounds.

This ban upset Elinor extremely for, apart from being a financial disaster (she had personally underwritten the whole production), it also confirmed her position as a notorious woman, as she obviously realised, judging by a letter she wrote to Ralph Blumenfeld, then editor of the *Daily Express* and friend and near neighbour in Essex:

> I want to ask your advice about the sentences printed under my picture in the *Sketch* and *The Tatler*. They say 'prohibited play' and other spiteful things – this does me great injury and may cause the censor to finally refuse the play. . . . it is not true either, as the play was not prohibited or refused as it had never been sent up in its present form.

Elinor had not yet come to terms with the fact that she would always have a somewhat notorious reputation from now on – the days of the 'amusing little Mrs. Glyn' were finally over.

There was one member of the audience that July afternoon who found Elinor fascinating, and that was Lord Curzon. He sent her a charming letter of appreciation of the book, of her acting and of her courage in vindicating her motives in writing the book in the first place.

Elinor was extremely flattered to receive such a complimentary letter from the ex-Viceroy of India and a man who, though at that time living in partial retirement, was not going to be content with life in the political wings for the remainder of his career. Elinor replied as warmly as Curzon had written. What was to become the great romance of her life began. She was forty-four.

George Nathaniel Curzon was, at first examination, a curious man to have been attracted to a woman on the fringe of society who had written a scandalous novel. But further exploration reveals an inevitability to Curzon's and Elinor's affair, an equation that makes perfect sense given the characters of them both.

Curzon was a curiously incomplete man. Shane Leslie in his *Studies in Sublime Failure* analyses what he felt to be fatal flaws:

> He was a mosaic of several great men rather than a single great one. His Foreign Office career disclosed chips of Castlereagh and trimmings of Talleyrand. . . . his character, though not too deep to plumb was a paradox presenting a running unreliability to secretary or to colleague. He could pass rapidly from hysterical rage to bantering burlesque. He lived in an atmosphere of imprudent pride, but at unexpected moments he could show tear-moistened humility. . . . an epicurean one moment and a spartan the next. He could take larger views than any member of the cabinet, yet there was no domestic detail he would not supervise. He chose the books for each guest's room and if a volume was missing, there was an angry inquiry, followed by correspondence. He dusted his own china and shook out his carpets, because it was a waste of time to explain what he wanted to his servants.

Born to a branch of the Curzon family, his father Lord Scarsdale was a parsimonious peer in holy orders. A repressive tutor, following a sadistic governess, were formative influences on the boy's emotional life. At Eton he was taken up by the epicene pedagogue Oscar Browning, a snobbish and unpleasant character who made his rooms a refuge for boys he favoured. Browning's 'irrepressible attentions' to the young Curzon gave rise to much Etonian (and therefore society) gossip at the time.

Curzon went up to Oxford and there spent too much time in debating to achieve more than a Second. Even so, he was consoled by no lesser personage than the famous master of Balliol, Jowett. Curzon took long to get over the disappointment of his degree and threw himself into working for several prizes, taking the Lothian at his second attempt and winning the Arnold over the future novelist Anthony Hope, after a fortnight's unremitting study. Having been elected a fellow of All Souls, he then took himself off round the world. Before he was thirty he had travelled extensively supporting himself by writing for *The Times*. He left Oxford with another legacy, a verse which dogged him all his life, just as Elinor would be dogged by hers:

> My name is George Nathaniel Curzon
> I am a most superior person
> My cheek is pink, my hair is sleek
> I dine at Blenheim twice a week.

During his travels, he went to India and paid a visit to the Viceroy at Calcutta, where he found an omen in the fact that the official residence had been modelled on Kedleston, his family home.

When not on his travels, Curzon enjoyed the company of the 'Souls', a name he unwittingly coined for this small group of friends at a dinner he gave for 'the gang', as they were also known, at the Bachelors' club in 1889. Forty-nine people attended this dinner; they represented the more intellectual members of Edwardian high society – women as well as men. To Curzon, membership of this group was to be of enormous importance. The approval and encouragement of these friends supported him in his triumphs, and in his failures too.

Entering the House of Commons in 1887 as Tory member for Stockport, Curzon was made an Under Secretary in the Foreign Office where he soon demonstrated that he was not over-careful about whom he offended. He showed a glacial exterior to those he felt to be his inferiors and anyone who had done slipshod work. This made him many enemies during his political career. But, in private, with his friends, he was very funny indeed. There is a hint of this in his second wife's memoirs when she quotes Curzon's description of himself as looking like 'a butler out of place'.

In 1895 Curzon married the American beauty and heiress Mary Leiter and in 1898 he was made Viceroy of India by Lord Salisbury. He remained Viceroy for seven years, the last two of which had been made very difficult indeed, through a series of misunderstandings with another leader of the Souls, Arthur Balfour, and with his secretary for India, St. John Brodrick. In 1905, Curzon resigned his glorious position, and in 1906 Mary Leiter died. Curzon was without office, and a widower with three small children. He was lonely and under-employed, but he was biding his time to fulfil his ambition of becoming Prime Minster.

This was the complex, powerful and, to those not his intimates, enigmatic person who wrote to Elinor what would have been called a 'mash' note at the time. Curzon loved beautiful women and before his marriage had a considerable record of affairs and 'spangles' (the Soul term for sweetheart). He was also attracted, so it would seem, to authoresses; he supported the romantic novelist Ouida in her old age, and was very friendly with Pearl Craigie who wrote under the pseudonym of John Oliver Hobbes. He had introduced another authoress, Amelie Rives, to the ranks of the Souls in the 'nineties.

Matters between Curzon and Elinor proceeded quickly after this first note and a rendezvous was arranged in Heidelberg. Here Curzon met Elinor, apparently by chance, as she was on her way back from choosing another finishing school for Margot in Dresden. It does not seem likely that their affair started at this date, rather that Elinor was flattered by the attentions of possibly the most 'superior person' yet to fall into her net, one moreover who shared with her a love amounting to adulation for the aristocratic certainties of the eighteenth century, and who was eager to discuss philosophy with her. Another element was always in the background. Money. Income still fell short of debt and expenditure. Royalties from the American sales of *Three Weeks* had not made up the deficit in the Glyns' finances.

A drama of a different kind threatened Elinor's precarious equilibrium at the end of 1908. Margot caught scarlet fever at her finishing school, and Elinor rushed out to Dresden to look after her, only to discover that she was in an isolation hospital to which Elinor was forbidden to go. Margot's treatment was appalling and she recovered thanks only to the devoted nursing of Dixie, the governess. This episode gave Elinor a lifelong dislike of Germans.

An idea of the Glyns' financial straits at this time may be gathered from letters which Elinor wrote to Clayton. Unfortunately, the other side of this correspondence is lost but, from the tone of her letters, it is possible to gather that Clayton was demanding, on the one hand, and obdurate about altering his extravagant lifestyle, on the other, as this letter of January 22, 1909 shows:

Well, dear old Man, Walters' letter has come with his proposal. I see nothing else to be done and so have agreed to it, but what we shall have to arrange is not to launch out into any single future expenditure beyond what we know we can pay for; any extras we can only have when the money is actually in hand from my work. The terrible anxiety – of knowing every few months a fresh avalanche of money has to be raised to pay for Newton's and gardens and Colemans [probably wine merchants] and things get me so nervous I cannot work properly. I am trying now with all my force of will to write to 'Elizabeth', except for taking Margot out to drive I almost never go out – I refuse all invitations and my head aches and my hair is going quite grey at the sides, from the strain, forcing ideas when they won't naturally come. However, there is no use in grumbling and I have given my word it shall be finished by March. . . . I won't be paid for Elizabeth until about May and we shall have to live on that for the rest of the year, so that is all the bargain I make. Enough to pay Thrupp & Morely entirely, then you can have the rest. £1,500 I believe it is. Life is sickening sometimes, isn't it? I hope Walters has given you the £500 on account. You know I would do anything I could for you, and the thing I am going to work for now is enough for a good season for Margot, who grows more sweet and beautiful and good as the days go on, and she must be beautifully educated. . . . Now I must begin work again, I am so tired and weary I could cry, but to be cheerful is the only thing.

That Clayton paid scant attention to Elinor's ideas for retrenchment is obvious from his correspondence with his brandy merchant in France, Xavier Bernard, culminating – on January 8, 1910 – with an order for seven cases of Cognac Fine Champagne 1856 at fifteen francs the bottle, an order which totalled over two thousand francs.

Late that summer of 1909, with *Elizabeth Visits America* finished, the delivery money paid and most of her debts settled, Elinor went again to Carlsbad where it is likely she had a rendezvous of a more amorous nature with Curzon, for by October 1909, Curzon had visited Lamberts and met Clayton. By November he had offered Clayton financial help; the offer was that he lend Clayton £1,200. Elinor wrote to Clayton on January 13, 1910:

My dear Old Man – I think there must be some mistake because Lord C wrote me 'I have never had a word from your husband since I made the offer and do not know at all what is going on.' This was written on the 6th, so perhaps he expected you to write. *Do* communicate with him or Walters and see what is happening.

The uncertainty worries me so. I do not know what his offer is, and do not want to if it helps you. I know he means in every way to be kind.

One is left with the impression that Elinor started her relationship with Curzon with the idea of financial help at the back of her mind. But something unexpected happened to her. She fell deeply in love with him.

In her autobiography, Elinor glosses over all this:

On one terrible occasion, in 1911, I discovered that Clayton had supplemented the income which I gave him by borrowing £1,000 from a friend. I felt particularly humiliated, for it was a friend who had often paid attention to me, and who had never ceased to show his devotion. The idea of accepting money from such a quarter was intolerable to me, and I went to see Mr. Blumenfeld, then Editor of the *Daily Express*, and begged him to help me to earn £1,000 at once.

However, the contents of the 'blue box' disprove this pleasant fable, and so do the contents of a book which Elinor wrote many years later.

Did She? is a curious work. Bernardine Forteville is holding the family fortunes together by working under an assumed name, as a sales assistant, when the rich Adrian Vandene spots her and immediately asks her to pose for a portrait, for which he will pay her five pounds an hour. He falls in love with her, but she is far more preoccupied in paying off a final mortgage demand for ten thousand pounds.

Bernardine strikes a bargain with Vandene that she will live in a flat he provides, and be totally dependent on him for everything, including her clothes. 'I suppose there is no question as to what I should have to pay for ten thousand pounds. . . . he has warned me he does not think he will keep to just friendship always. . . .' During this time she falls in love with him, and they eventually make love, after which he goes away, as he is married.

Bernardine does marry Vandene eventually, the obstacles – a wife and a lunatic son – having been removed by the simple expedient of a car crash. Life, however, is rarely as neat – or as kind – and it was not to be in Elinor's case. Having set out to ensnare Curzon, she became ensnared herself.

iv *Lady Muff Boredom*

As the Edwardian age drew to its close Lucy estimated that she was making a profit of nearly £40,000 a year (equivalent to £1,400,000 today) out of the business that she had started on a dining room table. Her short visit to America had not only made her aware of the possibilities that existed in New York but also restless with Hanover Square, and the repetitive business of producing clothes for the season: for Ascot, for Drawing Room, for Saturday to Mondays. Lucy was a woman who thrived on adversity and was bored when everything was going smoothly.

At the end of 1909 she went back to New York, ostensibly for a holiday with Elsie de Wolfe, but in reality determined to set up an American branch of Lucile – whatever it might cost and more than likely against the advice of the more cautious Cosmo and Miles. Elsie introduced her to some important potential sources of backing at a Christmas dinner at the Waldorf Astoria.

Elsie de Wolfe had developed into a social power. Born of middle class parents (her father was an improvident doctor), she had been endowed with indifferent looks but a tremendous will which, as one of her friends once said of her, 'persuaded you that she was beautiful'. Having been presented at Court in the late 1880s Elsie had not 'taken' and had eventually come back to New York unmarried, with very poor prospects but an extremely stylish wardrobe, much of it made for her at Lucile. Elsie was never really interested in men. Now she launched herself on a stage career via amateur theatricals, mostly slight drawing-room comedies in which she was reviewed for her dress sense rather than for any thespian talent she might have possessed. It was not long before the producer, Charles Frohman, discovered her and sent her on tours on which she achieved fame as the 'best-dressed actress on the Frohman circuit'. But this was not enough to ensure Elsie the power and attention she craved.

One weekend she acted in an amateur performance at Tuxedo Park, a rigidly exclusive country club, and it was here that she met Elizabeth (always known as 'Bessie') Marbury. Bessie was immensely wealthy, a socialite and, rare for the time, a successful woman theatrical agent. It was not long before Bessie installed Elsie in a house in Washington Square which Elsie decorated in a light, bright style inspired by what she knew of late eighteenth-century decoration. The two friends then set themselves up as sapphic salonnieres. Anyone who was anyone in the political, theatrical, social and literary worlds of New York could be found at their tea-time 'conversaziones'.

Bessie and Elsie had two close sapphic friends who both belonged to inner New York society and who were instrumental in ensuring the success of whatever venture they undertook: Anne was the daughter of the financier J. P. Morgan and Gertrude had been the wife of a Vanderbilt. The four ladies were known as 'The Four Horsewomen of the Apocalypse'. It was through these powerful allies that Elsie was given the commission to decorate the Colony Club – the first women's club in New York. Her scheme single-handedly revolutionised smart interiors everywhere and established her in a completely new career – that of interior decorator. The Colony Club was light and pretty and Elsie mixed eighteenth-century furniture with country house chintzes and white treillage.

Elsie persuaded Lucy that the ladies of New York were ripe, as it were, for the sartorial plucking, just as they were ripe for the decorative schemes she was devising for them. Lucy was eager to respond, as she recorded in her autobiography:

> . . . Elsie and I began to talk about clothes and pick out the dresses which we liked the best. We decided that most of them were copies of Paris models, but that their wearers had chosen them indiscriminately and without taste. 'If you knew how much they have cost you would probably be astonished' (said Elsie) 'we pay far more for clothes here than in Europe but we have no really good designers, and we have to buy models brought over from France. American women will love your dresses, and they will think it absolutely the last word in chic to be dressed by an English society woman' Elsie insisted.

Inspired by missionary fervour and Elsie's flattery, Lucy took a house on fashionable West Thirty-Sixth Street. It was not quite as roomy as the always extravagant Lucy would have liked but was pronounced 'excellent for a start'. Pausing only to commission Elsie to decorate it in a manner similar to Hanover Square and to install her faithful assistant Celia as manageress, Lucy sailed back to England to prepare the collection.

Elsie and Lucy had much in common, in addition to their passion for the eighteenth century. They were both adept at manipulating the press and had a thorough realisation, rare at the time, of how useful 'mentions' were. It took little persuasion on Elsie's part for Lucy to embark on a massive promotion campaign to bring the name of Lucile to the attention of the American public. There may, too, have been an element of tit-for-tat, for Lucy had been envious of Elinor's American publicity.

A publicist was hired. Elsie insisted that Lucy's title and aristocratic connections should be emphasised. Numerous articles started appearing with headlines such as '*Lady Duff Gordon, first English swell to trade in New York*'. It was as successful as it was crude – so successful that even the publicity-crazy New Yorkers got tired of reading about Lucy and she was satirised as '*Lady Muff Boredom*' in one newspaper.

Lucy ignored Elinor's press coverage: the jealousy between the sisters was at one of its periodic peaks. But Lucy's title fascinated the American press just as much as Elinor's scandalous book.

> There were stories of myself and of my husband's family, even the Duff Gordon family ghost had half a column to itself and the coat of arms was reproduced in a dozen illustrations. There were pictures of the illustrious ladies I had dressed in London, of my royal clients and the dresses they had bought.

Lucy was of course delighted but would have preferred the publicity to be directed on her artistic achievements – her dresses – rather than on her social qualifications. Elsie and her group were surprised at Lucy's demur: people would go to her 'just for the sake of being dressed by a woman with an English title. Afterwards,' they pointed out, 'you will stand on your own merits and people will come to you because they like your clothes.'

Writing in hindsight, after her career in America had come to an end, Lucy was candid about the power of publicity in America:

> The one thing that counts . . . is self-advertisement of the most blatant sort. . . . the louder you blow your own trumpet, the more likely is it to be heard above the noise of your neighbour's. . . . everything you are and say and do will be taken at your own valuation.

The publicity affected Lucy. She came to believe in it and to regard her American venture in the light of bringing civilisation and art to the savages.

At the end of February 1910, Lucy set sail for New York on the *Lusitania*. In just under two months she had designed over a hundred and fifty new dresses which she had shown at a farewell fashion parade for a thousand guests, among whom were the Queen of Rumania and staunch supporters such as her old friend Margot Asquith, now ensconced in Number 10 Downing Street as the wife of the Prime Minister, Herbert Asquith.

Lucy took four of her best mannequins with her – Gamela, Corisande, Florence and Phyllis. The American press went overboard for these statuesque beauties. Gamela was described as 'tall and shapely and stately, her unfathomable eyes shining with light'. Corisande was 'exquisitely English, fair and slim, pink and white, graceful and sweet and gentle, who ought to sit dreamy-eyed on a marble seat in an old world garden thinking unutterable and tender thoughts'. Florence's eyes were 'wandering diamonds and her smile is born of wit. She is life – she is spring – with a dazzle of sauciness.' Phyllis tempted the soft-centred gentlemen of the American press to place her in a picture frame at once: 'She should hold a young lamb and lift up her eyes to heaven forever.' As if this prose, so deep purple it was almost worthy of *Three Weeks*, wasn't enough, the girls were collectively described as 'crusaders of the Dream Dress given a mission of mercy, the great mission of spreading among New York's Four Hundred the cult of the dream dress, the wondrous product of the genius of Lady Duff Gordon'.

Leaders of society, such as Mrs. Stuyvesant Fish and Mrs. Vanderbilt, took this extravagant bait. Far from being put off by Lucy's insulting missionary attitude, they were agog to view these extraordinary mannequins and eager to see what all the fuss was about. Lucy's publicity man had done a very good job indeed – of course he did have promising and willing material to work with.

Lucy could not have timed her foray to America better. In these last years before the First World War women were spending literally fortunes on their wardrobes, following the extravagant lead of their Parisian and London counterparts. The social stranglehold of the old patroon families, with names like Stuyvesant and val Rensselaer, had been giving way to a new society of incredible wealth obtained in railroad and property development, in mining and steel. The wives of these millionaires were ready to spend money in seemingly limitless streams to achieve social prominence, and who better to dress them than an English aristocrat? Capitalising neatly on this, Lucy delicately advertised some of her models as 'Money Dresses'. 'Though I have always set my face against ostentation . . . I called them "Money Dresses" because it takes so much to buy them,' she explained in her advertisements, lest Americans failed to understand what she was trying to tell them.

Her arrival in New York was a triumph – she was met with placards on street corners informing the crowds that the '*Titled Dressmaker and Her Golden Girls Arrive Today to Show Americans How to Dress*'. It is a wonder that she was not sent back on the next boat.

Elsie had followed Lucy's wishes in decorating the house, 'a lovely big brownstone with massive doors, imposing staircases and high ceilings. . . . at one end of the showroom the miniature stage, a replica of the one in Hanover Square.' From the moment Gamela parted the misty blue chiffon curtains and stepped out on the little stage, a vision of beauty in a ballgown of undulating aquamarine blue, Lucile was a triumph. At the end of the first day, orders had been taken for over a thousand gowns, none of which cost less than three hundred dollars.

Lucy herself was triumphant for she had discovered an interesting new way of earning money by charging five hundred dollars for a 'personal' consultation – there was no lack of takers among the wives of the new rich. Typical of such customers was a certain Mrs. Van Valkenbergh, who had been christened 'The Ten Million Dollar Widow' by the popular press. Her entry in Lucy's ledger recorded her purchases on one occasion alone as:

> Evening Wrap, Four thousand dollars
> Evening Gown, Four hundred dollars
> Afternoon Gown, Three hundred dollars
> Afternoon Wrap, Four hundred dollars
> Parasol, One hundred dollars

This was the era in which the fashionable 'pouter pigeon' silhouette was giving way to a slim, high-waisted look, influenced by Directoire clothes, but very much more elaborate than the simple wetted muslins worn by Madame Récamier. Overskirts became three-quarter length tunics, split in the front to show an underskirt. Made of supple chiffons and laces, these exquisite dresses were then minutely embroidered with paillettes, even semi-precious stones. Evening wraps were sumptuous; one example was made of coral silk velvet and silver bullion lace, then over-embroidered with silver thread, the whole lined in finest pale pink crêpe de chine. The quality and variety of handwork was extraordinary in its diversity and accomplishment; clothes like these had not been seen since the end of the eighteenth century and to Lucy's new customers four thousand dollars did not seem too much to spend on such display.

Having seen her new house established, Lucy went back to London to design her next collection (at that time she did not have a design studio in New York) leaving her new branch in the hands of an English manager and an American business manager.

The following May, having completed her orders for the London season (quiet that year, after the death of Edward VII), Lucy returned to New York. Noticing, as she went through customs that her luggage was examined with more than usual thoroughness, she thought no more of it and went to the Ritz. The next morning Elsie de Wolfe came to breakfast and the two women were astonished to see a headline in the paper which read: '*Lady Duff Gordon Chairman of Lucile, noted dressmaking firm, concerned in alleged customs fraud.*' This was publicity indeed, but of a kind which horrified Lucy and Elsie.

The two managers were accused of falsifying the firm's invoices with intent to avoid the payment of duty on the dresses and other fripperies imported from London. Storming down to West Thirty-Sixth Street, Lucy found that ninety-four dresses had been impounded by the customs, as well as several crates of hats, underclothes and other London imports. She was then told that a civil suit was being brought against her in the Federal Courts for the recovery of nearly fifty thousand dollars.

At first Lucy dismissed this as beneath her notice but, luckily, Elsie insisted that she employ a very good lawyer (Bainbridge Colby) to defend her. Lucy found herself arraigned in front of a Grand Jury, in spite of an offer to settle out of court which had been of no avail. 'If you have the courage to go before the jury you will probably win your case,' Colby told her. Lucy never forgot the morning when her case was heard. 'It was raining . . . the streets looked so unfamiliar and unfriendly and I had such a longing suddenly to be back in London. I pictured the house in Hanover Square, with the long lines of cars in front of it and the showrooms filled with women choosing gowns for Ascot. It seemed so far away.'

Dressed in black, with none of the extravagance associated with Lucile, she impressed the Grand Jurors and was fined only ten thousand dollars. This debacle hastened her return to London, already prompted by her desire to open a branch of Lucile in Paris.

v *Kidnapped*

Elinor went to stay with Count Cahen d'Anvers on her return from her rendezvous with Curzon at Carlsbad in the summer of 1909. While in France, she received a telegram from the Grand Duchess Kiril of Russia, asking if they could meet in Munich.

Her curiosity vying with her snobbery, Elinor hastened to accept and discovered that the Grand Duchess and her mother-in-law, the Grand Duchess Vladimir, wanted to invite her to spend the winter at St. Petersburg with a view to writing a novel based on life at the Russian court. Both admirers of *Three Weeks*, they told Elinor that they felt she would be able to do justice to their small society. As the Grand Duchess Vladimir put it: 'Everyone always writes books about our peasants. Come and write one about how the real people live.'

The need to produce another novel was now urgent. Having no wish to labour yet again in the country houseparty vineyard, Elinor accepted eagerly. She paused only to order an entire new wardrobe from Lucile and hats from Reboux, the leading Parisian milliner of the time, and then set out, arriving on December 18, 1909.

If Imperial propaganda was what the two Grand Duchesses had in mind, they had chosen the right person. In her first letter home, written a day or so after her installation in the Grand Hôtel de l'Europe, Elinor already felt able to describe the peasants: '. . . they all have such mild kind faces and look quite content. I am sure the stories of the agitations must be greatly exaggerated.'

The Grand Duke Michael had just died in Cannes and the court was observing two months' full mourning. The Lucile dresses remained in Elinor's wardrobe, and all she could wear were the two black frocks she had brought with her, one for day and one for evening. Even her black Reboux hats would not do. Lady Nicholson, wife of the British Ambassador, had had the foresight to order Elinor an appropriate (but not nearly so becoming) black crêpe morning bonnet with a long flowing veil.

Elinor loved Russia and all the attention she got from the Grand Duchesses, who spent a great deal of time with her. When they were not at banquets or smaller dinner parties, she read aloud to them from her books. She must have been a great novelty. For the first two months she gathered material for her book, eventually published as *His Hour*. The fruits of her careful observation are very apparent in this novel, a romance between an Anglo-Russian widow, Tamara, and the Heathcliffian Prince Gritzko. The story is slight, but the descriptions of aristocratic Russian life, just before it would be swept away for ever, have Elinor's usual grasp of minute detail and of atmosphere. She swallowed the romance of Imperial Russia hook, line and sinker, and in *His Hour* took the opportunity to make some unfavourable comparisons with an England that she felt had rejected her:

> What struck (Tamara) first was that dark or fair, fat-faced or thin, high foreheads or low, all the ladies were coiffed exactly the same – the hair brushed up from the forehead and tightly ondulés. They were beautifully dressed in mourning, and no one seemed to have much of a complexion, from an English point of view. . . . Afterwards when she knew them better she realised that here was one place left in Europe where there were no parvenus and no snobs or if there were any, they were beautifully concealed. Such absolute sincerity and charm can only stay in a society where no one is trying 'to arrive' all being there naturally by birth. There could be no room for the métier adopted by several impecunious English ladies of title – that of foisting any one, however unsuitable, upon society and their friends for a well gilded consideration.

The Russians, for their part were impressed by Elinor, in particular by her knowledge of some not generally-known details about the Winter Palace, which she explained away by the astonishing claim that she was the re-incarnation of Catherine the Great.

Elinor had only lately become fascinated by re-incarnation and was apt to make such extravagant statements when she was centre-stage. Probably she had done some research before she went to Russia.

Throughout January and February 1910 she worked hard at the novel and went to banquets and card-parties at night, admitting in a letter home that she was becoming very tired. The descriptive parts of the novel were going well, but the hero was proving a problem – she could not find a model among the Russian aristocrats she had so far met, most of whom were rather stolid with nothing of the wild charm she was seeking.

Eventually the Grand Duchesse Helene came to the rescue by suggesting that she might use as a model Prince Gritzko Wittgenstein, who had been recently killed in a duel. This was a very good idea indeed, for Elinor had met him years before at the Khedive's ball in Cairo, and remembered that he had held her so close when dancing with her that his bandolier had pressed into her chest. A suitable hero indeed, and one who immediately inspired Elinor to start the narrative in Egypt before moving it to Russia. But in order to do this, she needed the volumes of her diary which dealt with her experiences in Egypt in the 1890s, and these were at Lamberts. A visit home was thus explained, though the real reason for her return was a fresh financial crisis which was looming, thanks to Clayton's inability to retrench – a crisis confirmed by Walters who had written worrying letters.

The Grand Duchess Vladimir suggested she return to England via Moscow which she had not yet seen and which she wished to be able to describe from life in her novel. Elinor was flattered by the Grand Duchess's thoughtfulness when a court official (one whom she had never seen before) called at her hotel and explained the arrangements for her journey, which would take her via Moscow, Warsaw and Berlin. These arrangements were meticulous. A sleeper had been arranged on the night train from Moscow to Warsaw; a carriage would meet her at the station as it would be too late for cabs; a room would be reserved for her in the Hotel de l'Europe. She would take the train to Berlin the next morning.

The true Russianness of Moscow, differentiating it so sharply from St. Petersburg, thrilled Elinor, who was treated as an honoured guest and conducted through palaces and museums. Reaching Warsaw the following evening, she walked through the station, carrying only her dressing case, to find the promised carriage awaiting her, with two men on the box. As the court official had indicated, there were no cabs. The man beside the coachman climbed down and asked if she were Madame Glyn. Elinor then climbed into the carriage and leant back. She was tired, so it took her some time to grasp the fact that they were travelling very fast through poor streets which could not possibly lead to the hotel in the centre of town.

Realising that something must be terribly amiss, she opened the window and screamed, the wind carrying her voice away, the carriage by then going too fast for her to throw herself out of it. It could have been the scenario from one of her novels – but Elinor was never to use it, for it was too real, and too frightening. The carriage, rattling on to who knew what sinister destination, and by now beyond the outskirts of Warsaw, was overtaken by two riders who forced it to a halt. One of the riders, whom Elinor assumed to be Polish police (an assumption never confirmed, nor denied) took the place of one of the men on the box and the carriage returned to the city.

When the Hôtel de l'Europe was reached, Elinor found that they did not expect her arrival, having never received a reservation. And the Berlin Express went out the same night, and not the following morning, as she had been told. Elinor hurried back to the station where she found a saviour in the reassuring shape of Sir Savile Crossley (later Lord Somerleyton), an acquaintance from Hillersdon visits. Begging his protection for the rest of the journey, she travelled back in his company.

The care taken in the planning of the kidnap gave Elinor food for thought. If someone considered her dangerous, what better plan than to dispose of her en route? For by the time she was missed, the trail between London and St. Petersburg would have gone cold.

But why dangerous? One answer that occurred to her, and to others, was that someone at the Russian court might have thought that she knew more than was good for her about the Czarina, and that *Three Weeks* might have touched on something near the truth.

Elinor had a fertile imagination. But it is certain that Elinor's dramatisation of *Three Weeks* was banned at the instigation of the Foreign Office for the possible reason of not upsetting Russia – an important ally. Lending weight to this theory is the further curious fact that when *Three Weeks* was made into a film in 1923 (a much less prudish era) it was allowed to be shown in England, but the title was banned, the censor insisting that there be no mention of it even in the credits. The mystery has never been solved.

Back in London, Elinor obtained an advance against *His Hour* (which she had not yet actually begun) and visited Walters to instruct him to pay the advance to the most pressing creditor (probably Clayton's brandy merchant). Then she had lunch with Curzon and persuaded him to back an I.O.U. of Clayton's, after which she could write reassuringly to her mother: '. . . . here is £300. . . . let me know when that is used up. All is well. Lord C. lunched and stayed till 4. Very kind. Very tired and worn out and in great pain with his back and leg, but *so* kind and dear, he has settled everything and I can go in peace.'

Curzon's motives are unclear. He was not a vastly rich man by the standards of the time and he was extremely prudent with money. But he was obviously attracted to this wilful, passionate, beautiful woman, enough to want to fund her for at least a small amount. It might have appeared to him as a worthwhile investment in keeping Elinor under obligation, hidden in the background rather than insisting on moving to her natural position at the centre of his life. Under such circumstances, £350 and the sums he later lent could well have been a useful guarantee of discretion. Henceforth, however, Elinor and the man with whom she was deeply in love were bound not just by the ties of physical passion and mental affinity but by the more obligatory ties of money.

But, to Elinor, it was a welcome tie, and his generosity only increased her longing for this strange, remote, proud man.

Before she returned to St. Petersburg, Curzon and her old friend Lord Redesdale warned her not to discuss her strange experiences, the latter promising that the Foreign Office would look after her en voyage.

She took Margot with her and they found a court that had come out of mourning and thrown itself into a hectic round of parties, banquets, balls and other divertissements. Writing to the family in March 1910, she was clearly enjoying herself:

We had a most delightful evening. The Duchess of Edinburgh was at Tsarksoe Selo at the great banquet for the King of Bulgaria and returned at eleven, and like a child recounted to us all the party. It is so amusing to hear the royalties talking amongst themselves of 'Nicky' etc; meaning the Emperor. I often wondered how they were when one has read of them in the papers and now I know – as simple as children. The dinner was good, she said, so she had brought me the menu. She had rushed back because she wanted to hear me read. . . . She showed us her perfectly divine jewels. She was dressed too vilely and coiffée too, but the jewels beyond description. 'Poor Marie' the G.D. [Grand Duchess Vladimir] said, before she came in 'Has no more idea of dressing, she wears a flimsy gown tonight with those jewels of the genii, so splendid! And she will stick to her old corsets, the despair of her daughter! Consequently you will see! The jewels fall into the crevasse between her stomach and her breasts – quite dreadful – but she won't have straight fronted corsets, she adores that stomach! The troubles we have!!!' I nearly died laughing and when she came, I saw it was true, and the G.D. whispered 'You see, thousands of rubles and rubies have fallen into the gulf and the brooch can't even be seen!!!!'

However, not everyone approved of Elinor. The ubiquitous German court lady, Baroness de Stoeckel, met her at a dinner at the Orloff-Dawidoff palace and remembered: 'Mrs Elinor Glyn, the authoress, was supping next to my husband and in an awed voice said: "When do the orgies begin?"' She had, wrote the Baroness, 'come to Russia to write a novel on that country and wanted excitement'. Elinor found it – and she approved, as she revealed in a letter to her mother, which shows Elinor at her most vilely snobbish. 'Sometimes the coachmen become insensible (from the cold) on the boxes waiting. No consideration is expected for them, you can keep them out all night . . .! It is, in short *my country* –!! A real autocracy.'

Returning to London in April to deal with fresh problems of finance, Elinor went back for a third time in May taking Margot with her again and was enchanted to find the country that she had left covered in snow was now green with the famous Russian spring. It was now, deeply in love with Curzon, that she started to write a special diary which she kept up until the beginning of 1911. It is unlike anything else she ever wrote, not concerned with externals, but with her own thoughts and longings.

> Everything seems intended by nature to be happy – and that is where the hurt comes to man – after years of disillusion – the spring time hurts – with its mockery – why cannot we too throw off winter and forget and be gay – surely in these woods there must be a tinkling stream of Lethe to quaff – surely if we look up at the sun he could smell the frozen ache in our hearts?

His Hour was published in October 1910 and many a young heart beat faster when reading of the masterful and tempestuous Gritzko. Reviews were generally favourable but Elinor did not like a prescient notice from Sidney Dark, the *Daily Express* reviewer:

> The curse of British fiction, as of British drama is sloppy sentimentality. Mrs Glyn is a realist. She realises that life cannot be supported on the dead husks of convention and that the real things are not always the 'nice' things. . . . her pictures of Russian society are very acute and very interesting.
>
> We know something of the sunless horror of the life of the Russian village and the Russian factory from Gorky and others. We know something of the curious hopeless yearnings of the educated middle class. Mrs Glyn tells, from the inside, the time-killing devices of the rich and highly-placed. She writes without prejudice (that and her all-round understanding and her virtues as a novelist) but her picture is appalling for all that. As one reads, one thinks all the time of Versailles before the Revolution, with its elegant Voltaireian immoral aristocrats dancing while their doom was being prepared. I have always been sceptical about the possibility of a Russian revolution. But Mrs Glyn has almost persuaded one that it is inevitable.

Elinor returned to England with Margot in June 1910 to pick up the tangled threads of her life. After the excitement, luxury and grandeur of life at the Russian court, the claustrophobia of Lamberts must have been palpable. Clayton was no better and his deterioration added to Elinor's distress, as an entry in the 1910 diary shows:

> What is the shadow which hangs over this house? I wake with a start out of uneasy dreams and creep to the window. There is always a light in that other window, no matter how late, even to the dawn. What is happening there? Are ghosts talking to one who suffers?

Clayton, now a bloated figure, old before his time, was slowly but surely getting through the Cognac Fine Champagne. Elinor tried to be cheerful. 'To jest, to laugh, to keep the ball rolling that is the duty and my heart is aching and torn and sometimes starving.'

Her deep love for Curzon was now the only reality – a reality which reduced her domestic life to the condition of a dream, if not a nightmare. For the first time in her life she had found someone who embodied all that she admired without qualification. But he was out of her reach. She was beginning to realise that Curzon would never marry her, even if she did the unthinkable – and divorced Clayton.

> Day after day the same life, incomplete, hungry, with no aim or end, only to get through it. A strange nameless excitement is in my veins. There is a magnet here in England and I am a needle and between the two are all sorts of paltry obstacles and some great ones, and I feel I could scream to the night 'Tear me a path, sweep them aside, let me be free to follow my bent.'

She owed Curzon money.

> For ever a battle with circumstance. What tears I remember in this bed – what planning to avert or alleviate this or that – what exercise of will to dominate sorrow and pain, and how seldom peace or joy and something is hurting my pride, and I will not admit it, even to myself and something pathetic is wringing my heart and

it must go on daily, and there is no possibility of solace. . . . . Alas! Alas!

In mid-June, Curzon asked Elinor to Hackwood, the Palladian house near Basingstoke he had taken. She was not asked to a houseparty (she never would be), but to stay for a clandestine night, or as she put it:

> A king dwells in the stately house and he is a wizard because he touched a poor sad and weary travelling Queen – who had never been allowed a throne in her own land – and lo! – she became a Queen indeed, reigning with crown and sceptre and her kingdom was his heart. . . . and the dream lasted a night and a day and left a memory of soothing sweetness.

In August, Elinor took Margot to Cowes, leaving Clayton in the care of Mrs. Kennedy. In such a gathering there were the usual little scandals to be discussed, one of which prompted Elinor to confide some bitter conclusions to her diary:

> Lady O, one of the sweetest of women is deploring the defection of her second lover, who has just married a girl of seventeen. . . . I do not think any other nation leave women with the perfectly callous brutality an Englishman can show. It is a perfect fallacy that a woman can be more attractive to a man when she is his mistress than when she is his wife – no one can exert her full powers when she is *unsure*. When she knows full well the man will be off like a snipe the moment the fancy takes him, or any small circumstance ruffles him. Unless a woman is thoroughly bad, with a cool head and no heart, she will never hold a man as his mistress . . .

After Cowes, Elinor went to stay with Billy Grant at Hillersdon, scene of many a conquest in the early days before her marriage, after which she and Margot joined Curzon at Crag Hall, Derbyshire. Here, she first met Curzon's three children: Irene (later Baroness Ravensdale in her own right); Cynthia (Cimmy) later Lady Mosley, who was to become the closest to Elinor; and Alexandra (Baba) who was six years old at the time. Elinor made every effort to fit in, planning picnics in the woods and playing the 'history game'. In the evenings, Curzon read Aristotle aloud to her. But photographs taken by Margot reveal a different story: Elinor looks tragic, Curzon ill-at-ease. The atmosphere was tense and Curzon distant. The presence of his children and of Margot may have had something to do with this. (Margot, now seventeen, was not 'out' but accompanied

Elinor everywhere as, in a sense, a chaperone – a role she came to resent bitterly.)

By October 17, her birthday, Elinor confided in her diary that matters were improved: 'I have seen a vision – away with all sorrow or weariness or despair! Away with all sad depressing things, the glory of it has gilded all the horizon. All is well – never again can dark thoughts come to me.' Had Curzon admitted his love for her? We shall never know, for Elinor burnt all his letters to her and he (most unusually, for he rarely threw anything away) burnt hers to him and went so far to expunge her from his life that he scratched her name out of the Hackwood visitor's book.

Curzon's vacillations continued and Elinor was driven either into the depths of despair or the heights of elation.

Last week for a short while you made me quiver with a sullen sudden anger and resentment – when I had poured my box of ointment at your feet, and told you of something very near my soul – and you answered with airy irrelevance and treated the ointment pouring as naught and with silence. But the feeling passed, for of what use to fret over such things . . . and as long as we can taste of joy when you allow fate to permit us, what else matters? You had unlimited power over me once. Ah! well, the new order of things is far happier than the old . . .

Resignation set in by November, and continued to the end of the year.

For two whole years I banished every creature from my life . . . to lavish worship at the feet of my idol – but the idol has suddenly torn the veil from my eyes and showed me my folly and that love, not worship is the medium of happiness. And thou Lord, what of thou? I wonder what the new order of things will seem to you. Will you miss at all the worship of my soul? Or will the joy of love and the material pleasures demanded of all sentiment, be enhanced for you? Who can tell. I at all events am much happier and at rest.

In the 1910 diary, Elinor often addresses Curzon directly. Was he eventually meant to read it? Possibly. Elinor certainly used it as a means of expressing herself to him as she would never have dared in reality.

At the same time as Curzon was obviously blowing colder, matters at Lamberts had reached so desperate a pass that Walters advised Clayton to leave the country to avoid his creditors. Elinor sent him, her mother and Margot ahead to find a suitable hotel in the south of

France, and they finally decided on the Hotel Beau Rivage at St. Raphael. Elinor joined them briefly, then went back to London to see Curzon and hear him address a public rally. Ironically, Milner was also on the platform. Elinor was thrilled:

> Oh! My heart! To see you there, master of those ten thousand people, calm, aloof, unmoved. To hear your noble voice, and listen to your masterly argument. To sit there, one of a rough crowd, gazing up at your splendid face and to know that in other moments that proud head can lie upon my breast even as a little child. Ah! me. There are moments in life worth living for,

But so uncertain was Elinor of her future with Curzon that she re-opened her correspondence with Milner – a correspondence which had ceased at the time Curzon came into her life. Again, it was she who made the running – it is highly likely that she thought of him as re-insurance policy. Whether Curzon knew of this or not, there was no love lost between him and Milner, rather an antipathy which found expression some years later in a sharp exchange between these two immensely powerful men over the correct manner of wearing the Order of the Garter.

In late November or early December Curzon came to a decision and told Elinor that their affair must end. So painful was this that when Elinor was editing the 1910 diary much later in her life – her motive clearly to prepare it for posterity – she tore two pages out completely. In Paris, on her way back to the south of France, Elinor sat in a familiar room:

> Like a person who has risen from the dead and who can look back upon his former life and weigh and analyse the aspects of it – is it only a week since I was warm, and living, and loving and believing? And the part that hurt most of all was that in the decision you came to, oh! my heart, there was no thought for me – no tender regret that you must cause me pain . . . you must have nothing to disturb your great thoughts, you said.

Curzon gave Elinor a pair of emerald and diamond ear-rings as a parting present, a further gall as sapphires had been 'our stone of love and faith'.

Later that week however, Elinor began to recover her equanimity:

> The atmosphere of Paris suits me here, and in Russia. There are no quaintly jealous women, they understand and appreciate what are good enough to call 'my esprit'. I have my place, conceded with homage. . . . I wonder if you saw me here, the desired guest of all that is highest in France, the favoured of all these Russian

Imperial Highnesses would it make any difference to my value for you? I had grown so accustomed to having to know you in secret and to be completely ignored as an acquaintance in the world, that I wonder what it would feel like to meet you in some great society. Someday perhaps I shall know.

Curzon had told Elinor that his servants were talking. His real reason for ending the affair may lie behind the words 'quaintly jealous women', surely a reference to Curzon's female friends among the Souls. Lady Desborough, in particular, would have objected to the prospect of the brightest star in her constellation becoming entangled with a notorious novelist who had never been admitted to their circle. Elinor had never been introduced to his friends, never been to his house at Carlton House Terrace, never been included in a dinner party or a houseparty.

Curzon, though in the political wilderness at this time and living in semi-retirement, was confidently expecting to make a come-back and was being very careful indeed to give none of his political enemies grounds to criticise his public, or indeed his private, life. Jane Lady Abdy (co-author with Charlotte Gere of *The Souls*) confirms that Curzon probably considered Elinor to be déclassée. 'I think he would have married her if she had not written *Three Weeks* and published it,' she believes, 'because he felt that a Prime Minister could not afford to have a wife who was notorious.'

Elinor on the other hand, counted the world well lost for love.

In Paris Elinor, wearing Curzon's parting present, the contentious ear-rings, was painted by Marietta Cotton. She found another admirer to take her about and make much of her. She referred to him as 'the American Napoleon', and it is possible that this new devotee was the department store magnate, Gordon Selfridge (famous for his simultaneous generosity towards both Dolly sisters), but there is no concrete evidence to support this – simply family rumour. She treated him with indifference, but was flattered by his attentions.

Flattery of a different sort awaited her when she re-joined the family in St. Raphael in mid-December, for she met Professor F. H. Bradley, the most distinguished metaphysician of his age. T. S. Eliot, for instance, was to write his Harvard Dissertation on aspects of Bradley's metaphysical thoughts, subsequently using certain of those ideas in *The Waste Land*. It is a measure of Elinor's personal magnetism and her powerful, if untutored, mind that Bradley sought her out, was intrigued by her, treated her as an intellectual worthy of his attention and became a faithful if unlikely friend. His admiration must have provided a soothing balm for Elinor's battered self-esteem. As they wandered together through the pine-woods round St. Raphael, discussing philosophy and reincarnation, she must have remembered happier times with Jeune and Milner in the forests round Carlsbad.

The elderly philosopher and the titian-haired authoress suffering from the pangs of unrequited love sat in the sunshine reading each other's works: Elinor struggling with *Appearance and Reality* and Bradley reading *His Hour*. Bradley set himself the Herculean labour of improving Elinor's spelling; in this he never achieved Hercules' success.

On December 15, she confided in her diary that she had received a letter from Curzon, noting that he complained that a party was tiring, that the house was full of memories of joys with her, and that such memories could never die. 'How can two people,' she asks Curzon rhetorically in the diary, 'the very sight of each other causing them to flame with passionate desire, suddenly be friends, even tender friends, at a distance!'

At the end of the year she was philosophical, a state of mind no doubt helped by her conversations with Bradley. But back in London in January 1911 she spoke to Curzon on the telephone and his 'voice was cold as it always is when you speak so . . . and I say what I do not mean to – I find my breath comes quickly, I cannot remember what I was longing to ask about . . . my heart beats, and I say quickly "goodbye".'

In February, Elinor had to make a brief visit to America to complete arrangements in connection with the dramatisation of *Three Weeks*, which was being handled by Bessie Marbury, as a vehicle for another of her sapphist circle, Alla Nazimova. The 'American Napoleon', hearing of Elinor's travel plans, arranged to take the same boat. Whether Curzon knew of this and became jealous or not is debatable, but he arranged a meeting. Elinor confided in the diary:

> I am afraid of suffering, but I must be joyous for of what good to be tortured? The moment might come when you would again think only of what was *best* for you and then what would become of me? If I see you, and you are cold and stern, the revulsion may come, but what will it be if, as ever, your much-loved face moves me to the passionate tenderness of old. Surely I am strong, surely my will has not been all in vain.

She saw him again and realised her feelings had not changed. 'I know that however it goes for this world, I can never love you less. You are my darling. My Beloved Lord.'

The last entry in the 1910/1 diary is dated February 1, Mid-Atlantic:

Sometimes I have felt it can only be because you have grown to love some other woman that you are so cruel to me. But you yourself when I asked you, told me it was not so, and you would never lie to me to try to deceive me. You said also it was nothing I had done, and that you loved me the same as ever, only it was circumstance and your life – and then, when we met, you took me back again. So there it is!

Did the 'superior person' love her? The answer is surely 'yes'; but with all the contradictions and the arrogance that were so much a part of his personality. He loved her, but he would not marry her. This first separation, entirely at his instigation, and the resumption of their affair, taught Elinor a bitter lesson: that she would never be part of his grand design. She would see him only when he had time for her; she would never meet his friends; she would always be kept in a secret compartment. American Napoleons would never compensate for Curzon, but she would have to concentrate on getting on with her own life and being content to see Curzon only on his own terms.

In a profound sense this suited Elinor although she never admitted it. She liked to be alone, she had formed the habit of retreat, and her nature was far more suited to intermittent moments of grand passion that to the calmer waters of an overt and settled relationship.

Elinor enjoyed her brief visit to America though plans for the production of *Three Weeks* came to nothing due to problems both with Elizabeth Marbury and with Nazimova.

The trip proved to be a lull before the onset of what she described to her mother as an 'avilanche'. For on February 22, Walters called on her in London to say that Clayton had once again borrowed money from a moneylender,

. . . again the same tricks, got £200 or £300 with a promise to pay £600 for it . . . it is up to £1000 now and he has applied to Lucy . . . it is too disgraceful, the whole thing. I am *heartbroken*.

Two days later she wrote a very long letter explaining everything to her mother:

. . . It appears at the end of the Curzon affair C. gave his written

word of honour he would never do any of these things again. . . .
then as soon as he was out of his troubles he *immediately* collected
£200 to gamble with when you took him to Monte . . . he lost,
then renewed his bill at 100 per cent . . . the Jews will make him
bankrupt if he cannot settle . . . it is *wanton* of him . . . I believe
he has some clot on the brain to do such things. He then wrote
behind my back to Lucy – one letter after another with long
explanations asking her for £500, and she naturally thought it was
queer and consulted Cosmo & Cosmo went to Walters who said
it was infinitely better to let him be bankrupt this time as *nothing*
could hold him.

I arrived yesterday and Lucy broke it to me at lunch. I was
stunned. I went down to Lennox Gardens from Hanover & there
heard the whole details from Cosmo & we sent for Walters. . . .I
felt so dreadful I asked Walters to at least try & collect the bills to
see how much it is but Walters said if he admits to £800 or £1000
we may be sure it is double.

Meanwhile Lucy admonished her mother, probably for the first time
in her life, over her attitude towards Clayton, which had always at
best been indulgent and at worst, conspiratorial:

> . . . How exactly is Clayton's health? . . . I am so sick with him
> . . . I do not consider he is a responsible person . . . everyone is
> too afraid to tell you anything for fear of worrying you, but really
> you must pull yourself together and face things. . . . He's been
> borrowing money again from the Jews in the most childish manner.
> Not much, but enough to have them after him and he is now in
> terror that they will come down on him and seize Lamberts and
> the furniture but as long as he is abroad he is safe. It is a pity he
> does not give *me* a bill of sale on Lamberts to make it safe.

Two days later she is telling her mother not to let Clayton have any
extra money 'or else he will only go to Monte and gamble or spend
it on dinners for Mrs. Hall . . . as regards money you know that he
is no longer a sane person.'

Elinor went to see Curzon to ask his advice:

> He said it was absolutely useless to try and help further; that a man
> who could break his sacred word of honour must have some
> uncontrolled thing in his brain & was irresponsible and this time
> it was my duty to let him be made bankrupt.

Rejecting such plans as pawning her emeralds (Curzon's present),
Elinor told her mother that Clayton had written 'this morning that
he wants to go off on a trip to Algiers as he is tired of St. Raphael!!!!'

The plan was for Clayton to go to Paris as he would be easier to get at – but he took matters into his own hands and decamped to Constantinople, leaving no forwarding address. Meanwhile Elinor mulled over various possibilities, which included selling Lamberts and taking a tiny flat in Paris, if Clayton went bankrupt. 'With the disgrace of the bankruptcy there would be no good Margot coming out in England.' Making a heroic effort she told her mother: 'In spite of all this I am not feeling depressed. I am sure of my star, and something will turn up but the *wanton* foolishness, to call it by no worse term, of C has crushed all my pity for him . . . I would not let Lucy pay the £1000 kind as she is, it would be bondage for the rest of my life,' adding that 'she has a way of doing kindnesses that don't always make one feel happy about them.'

Meanwhile, Clayton was seeking to mend fences with Mrs. Kennedy (who still had some residual sympathy for him) and wrote from Constantinople: 'I have poured pure blood from my right nostril till that arm ached and then started on the other one with equal success . . . my room looked like a hospital surgery.' He told his mother-in-law he found Constantinople to be 'a pretty badly kept 2nd class-all-round place' and that he was looking forward to going home 'as soon as I hear from you that you have opened for the season . . . I will come back to my two rooms and give as little trouble as I can.'

No such soft-soaping was in store for Elinor. 'He wrote me a letter,' she told her mother, 'proving himself an injured creature and plainly proving "a wife with a motor car and smart clothes" it must be her fault and that everyone would say so . . . you would think it was an injured angel with an extravagant wife who took all and left him without enough to buy his enlarged boots for his illness with. I have grown into a stone and I am frozen with the cruelty and injustice of all things.'

Elinor determined to try and pay off Lucy and Curzon. So she applied for help to Blumenfeld, the editor of the *Daily Express*, who promised to pay her a thousand pounds for the first British serial rights of a new 'Elinor Glyn' novel – provided that it were delivered within three weeks. He specified that it should be at least ninety thousand words. Elinor blithely told him it would present no problem; after all, she had a half-finished novel in a drawer at Lamberts. She did; but it was her 'serious' novel *Halcyone*, and she was not going to give Blumenfeld the first book she had ever written as a serious writer. She accepted Blumenfeld's offer and started from scratch.

It meant writing thirty pages a day.

It is a superhuman strain but I had to accept it . . . when I have finished this lurid tale for the *Express* I then have to have a week's rest and begin on *Halcyone* again . . . besides this I have to send the article to the *Cosmopolitan* about Girls at £70 an article of 3500 words . . .

Elinor retired to the Trianon. Guarded against interruptions by her maid Maria, fortified with coffee and brandy in between meals in bed, she dashed off *The Reason Why*.

Ever after, Elinor considered it the worst book she had written. 'My only choice on this occasion,' she revealed in her memoirs, 'seemed to lie between the degradation of myself or of my pen. *The Reason Why* is my witness that I chose the pen.'

She under-estimated it, because of the crisis that had engendered it. It has all the ingredients of a popular Glyn romance. The tragic and beautiful heroine is forced to marry the hero by the wicked millionaire uncle – in order to support her little half-brother and his extravagant stepfather. It has a passionate and happy ending. The contempt the heroine feels at first for the innocent hero is doubtless a faint echo of Elinor's feelings for Clayton. It was an entertaining story and was thoroughly enjoyed by readers of the *Daily Express*. In its subsequent publication in book form, the *Globe* called it a 'penny novelette' but the *Daily Telegraph* said that the story was 'marked by those qualities of vivid and forcible narrative which her readers are accustomed to expect'.

To Elinor, whose heart had been set on the higher tone of *Halcyone*, the 'penny novelette' was a shaming exercise. She felt she had betrayed for money that she wanted to regard as her art.

By the end of April, by dint of this superhuman effort, possibly augmented by a loan from Curzon, Clayton's immediate creditors appeared to have been paid off and he (now back at St. Raphael), Mrs. Kennedy and Juliet were able to return home to England. April and May found Elinor and Margot taking a trip through Italy; Elinor planned to finish *Halcyone* in Sirmione 'where we can live on 7 or 8 francs a day . . . "My friend" [Curzon] won't have a chance of coming now until after the Coronation,' she told her mother, 'he has been in such terrible pain that he fainted, and with all this doing his duty to England as well he is a noble man, and the tragedy of the separation from me makes us both miserable, but such is fate – we both feel it less when I am far away out of England than when near and impossible.' She hated a 'hole and corner life' in Italy, but if her mother could 'stand' Clayton until the work had been done on *Halcyone* she would be 'too grateful'.

On May 20, Clayton and Elinor both signed a deed whereby she purchased Clayton's whole remaining interest in the Homerston Estate. The long-suffering lawyer had somehow compounded with the creditors and raised over £13,000 which included £700 from Lucy. But he told Elinor: 'You will see that there is only sufficient to repay £1,200 of Lord Curzon's debt.' He concluded his sorry accounting by telling Elinor that she was now the owner of the property 'subject to the mortgage of £12,000 and your husband will have nothing left but his furniture and personal chattels to pledge. I do not think it matters leaving the lease of Lamberts in his name, as it is of no value.'

A month later, after her return from Italy, Elinor made the final break with Lamberts and with Clayton, who was now living there partly on her earnings and partly supported by Mrs. Kennedy's private income, Elinor took a small suite at the Ritz by the year, at a special discount, keeping it for the next two years. She never forgave Clayton for accusing her of financial advantage in the purchase of the remaining interest in the estate. It was in reality the end of their marriage. The way was now free to see a great deal more of Curzon.

In August, Elinor and Margot were asked to Hackwood again. It was a happier visit, for Margot had become friendly with Curzon's daughters and he behaved towards her as something between an uncle and a stepfather. She apparently felt her mother's relationship with Curzon to be quite normal, even giving him the affectionate nickname 'Milor'.

Elinor was enthusiastic about spiritualism and Curzon obligingly produced a medium to entertain her. The medium was a Russian peasant woman with a seventeen-year-old daughter who reputedly had remarkable psychic gifts. But Margot remembered that she 'smelt very strong after dinner!' The medium raised the table round which they were sitting and made ping-pong balls move at her bidding in mid-air.

Halcyone, which she was just finishing, was intended to prove Elinor's worth as a writer and as an intellectual. It was a love story, the dénouement of which would reveal her finer feelings, her cultivated attitude towards life – and, of course, her fitness to be Curzon's mate. She designed it, subconsciously or consciously, to show off her education and her love for classical Greece. Unfortunately for Elinor's ambitions, the book did not fulfil her intentions. It was a thinly disguised picture of Curzon, portrayed as John Derringham, a rising politician, ambitious, egotistical and with a tendency to deliver pompous lectures on the necessity for aristocratic government. The heroine Halcyone was Elinor when young, uneducated, but with a mind and taste ready to be cultivated. A retired professor (Bradley), nicknamed Cheiron after the wise centaur of antiquity, is persuaded by Halcyone to give her the rudiments of a classical education. She meets John Derringham, who regards her as a child, and she falls in love with him. Many years later, she meets him again, now wooing a rich American, Mrs. Cricklander, who will finance his political career. But Derringham falls in love with and proposes to Halcyone.

He insists that their marriage would have to be kept secret since, if it was known that he had a wife, he would have to keep her in the splendour which his position demanded and which he cannot afford. Elopement is planned but Derringham stumbles into a ha-ha and knocks himself out. Halcyone, distraught at his non-appearance at the rendezvous, is taken off to London by her legal guardian.

Nursed back to health by Mrs. Cricklander (an extremely unflattering portrait of an American heiress in English society), Derringham becomes engaged to her, though realising that she only wants him for his position. Cheiron takes Halcyone off to Italy to nurse her broken heart, while Mrs. Cricklander jilts Derringham, as his party is about to fall and she does not wish to be married to a man on the Opposition Benches. Derringham pursues Halcyone and begs her forgiveness.

Bearing in mind later events between Elinor and Curzon, *Halcyone* is a remarkable piece of prescience. Curzon must have recognised this unflattering portrait, but as Elinor told her mother:

> my joy is that 'my friend' is enthusiastic over Halcyone the first time he has given me the impression that he is really impressed with my brains!! He used a lot of grand words about it in a tone of deep respect and then said 'not that I do not always think you write well but this is masterly in its restraint and superlative knowledge of human nature.' This is a supreme joy to me as you can think. He is very well and childishly pleased to have me in England again.

Readers were discouraged by its high 'tone' and the book was financially one of her least successful.

The relationship between Curzon and Elinor did not end, though with the passage of time she developed resignation to a fine art. She started to encourage other admirers and take a more realistic view of the affair. It is difficult to ascertain how financially dependent she was on Curzon in these last years before the First World War. She had money earned from the reprints of *Three Weeks* and her other books, she wrote articles on a regular basis for newspapers; but she had never lost her love of luxury and spent an increasing amount of money on interior decoration, which had developed from an interest to something approaching mania.

In the spring of 1912, Elinor decided to take a house in Green Street in order to bring out Margot, now eighteen, as best she might with the funds at her disposal. She had another reason for taking the house and that was in order to entertain Curzon in a manner as similar as possible to that in which he had entertained her, for she had still not entirely abandoned the idea that he might marry her. The longer their relationship lasted the more promising it appeared to her:

> He is so enchanted that I am wearing his splendid brocade train and his sapphires. He is always thinking of some kindness for me and his appreciation of my work and his constant love and sweetness make life a joy, now that I am in England and London and can see him without tearing up for the day or scheming and worrying

She redecorated the house (which she had on a short lease) so lavishly that poor Margot had to make do with a 'cut price' season although she was presented at Court and was able to entertain a certain amount. Clayton, rotting at Lamberts, was never seen in London. Margot, who was now old enough to draw her own conclusions, and had begun to resent the fact that Elinor competed with her for the attention of young men, would usually go back to Lamberts for the weekend. She adored her father and helped Mrs. Kennedy to look after him.

In the summer of 1912 Curzon gave Elinor a magnificent sapphire and diamond ring. But they still met only in private. It is hard to see how the situation could have changed. Divorce from Clayton was unthinkable and to live openly together even worse. Elinor had to be content for Curzon to come and dine at Green Street, though he did so less often than she had hoped and he certainly never treated the little house she had so painstakingly decorated as a second 'unofficial' home. After four years, he still blew hot and cold, sometimes being passionate, more often complaining of pain or of boredom.

vii *The Titanic*

May 1912 was the beginning of the London season. There had never been so many dances; the Courts were more crowded than ever with debutantes being presented. A new musical comedy, *The Sunshine Girl*, was hugely successful at the Gaiety and Pavlova's matinees at the Palace were drawing enormous audiences to see her *Dying Swan*. But overshadowing all this gaiety was a drama being played out in the prosaic surroundings of an Inquiry held by the Wrecks Commissioners, into the sinking of the ship that had been christened 'unsinkable'.

The *Titanic* sank on April 14. The Inquiry investigated, among other matters, accusations of cowardice of a particularly reprehensible kind. Two thus stigmatised were Sir Cosmo and Lady Duff Gordon.

A month earlier, Lucy had been in Paris setting up her new branch of Lucile in the rue des Penthièvres, when unspecified, but urgent, business called her to New York. At short notice, the only available berth was on the new White Star liner the *Titanic*. Afterwards Lucy always said that she had been worried at sailing in a new ship. Whether this was hindsight or genuine foresight is debatable, but she was so reluctant that she refused to book the passage there and then, and returned home to tell her husband of her fears. Unusually, he volunteered to go with her (they rarely travelled together except to Scotland) and she consented willingly, 'little knowing that by so doing I was to expose him to a storm of censure and ridicule that well nigh broke his heart and ruined his life'.

Taking her secretary, one in a long line of faithful handmaidens, Lucy thus set sail with Cosmo on the most luxurious ship ever built, of which it had been said that even God could not sink her. At first, Lucy was delighted with the magnificence of their surroundings.

Everything aboard this lovely ship reassured me, from the Captain with his kindly, bearded face and genial manner . . . to my merry Irish stewardess with her soft brogue and tales of the timid ladies she had attended during hundreds of Atlantic crossings.

And yet she still felt unreasonably apprehensive, taking her fear to the point where she refused to undress completely at night and her 'warm coat and wrap lay always ready at hand, and my little jewel case, with a few of my most treasured possessions, was placed on a convenient table within my reach'.

Unfortunately, these 'treasured possessions' did not include a magnificent pearl necklace which Lucy had on approval from a jewellers in Venice. Neither paid for nor insured, it was kept in the Purser's safe.

The day before the disaster was cold but bright. So cold that Franks (as the secretary, Miss Francatelli, was affectionately known) and Lucy switched on the electric stove in the cabin. When they went down to the restaurant they both kept on their thick day clothes instead of dressing for dinner.

Twenty years later Lucy described her memories of that meal:

> We had a big vase of beautiful daffodils on the table which were as fresh as if they had just been picked. Everyone was very gay, and at the neighbouring tables people were making bets on the probable time of this record-breaking run. Bruce Ismay, Chairman of the White Star Line, was dining with the ship's doctor next to our table, and I remember that several men appealed to him as to how much longer we should be at sea . . . at another table sat Colonel Jacob Astor and his young bride.

Lucy had been in bed in her first class cabin on A deck for about an hour when she was awakened by 'a funny rumbling noise' and then she heard 'people running along the deck outside my cabin, but they were laughing and gay. "We must have hit an iceberg" I heard them say. "There is ice on the deck."'

She went across the corridor to Sir Cosmo's cabin but 'he had heard nothing and was very annoyed at my waking him up'. Reassuring her by saying that, even if they had hit an iceberg, it could not do much damage because of the water-tight compartments, Sir Cosmo told Lucy to go back to bed. She went and looked over the side of the ship, but could see nothing amiss. She then returned to her cabin, but the roar of the high-pressure steam being vented continued to alarm her. This then stopped, as did the engines, and Lucy rushed back to Cosmo, who eventually got up and went to find out what was going on. He ran into Colonel Astor on the bridge and the two men agreed that they should ask their wives to dress.

Lucy put on the warmest clothes she could find, including a mauve silk kimono and a squirrel coat. As she was dressing, Franks came in, very agitated: there was water in her cabin and they were taking

the covers off the lifeboats. A steward knocked on the door to tell
them that Captain Smith had ordered all passengers to put on lifebelts.

According to Lucy's memory, everything had appeared orderly up
to this point, if alarming. But as Cosmo, Lucy and Franks came up
on the port deck, they found a

> scene of indescribable horror. Boat after boat was being lowered
> in a pandemonium of rushing figures fighting for places . . .
> trampling women and children under foot. Over the confusion,
> the voices of the ship's officers roared 'Women and children first.
> Stand back' and I heard the sharp bark of a revolver.

Lucy was offered a place in a lifeboat but she refused to leave without
Cosmo and the three of them went round to the starboard side.
There, Lucy saw with amazement that nearly all the American wives
were leaving their husbands 'without a word of protest or regret,
scarce of farewell'. (A misinterpretation typical of Lucy who had
always mistaken reticence for indifference.) 'When two officers came
up and tried to force me into one of the boats, I refused.' Cosmo
pleaded with her 'while three or four boats were launched, and the
crowds round the side thinned'. But it was no use. Lucy had never
listened to any but her own dictates, and only said: 'Promise me that
whatever you do you will not let them separate us,' and clung to him
until, at last, 'seeing it was no use resisting me he gave in, and we
stood waiting there with Miss Francatelli, who refused to leave us.'

As Lucy recalled later at the Hearing, and later still in her memoirs,
the people in their vicinity suddenly disappeared except for some
sailors who were launching a little boat which turned out to be the
Captain's emergency boat. One seaman, George Symons, was put
in charge of five firemen and stokers by an officer, William Murdoch.
Among these firemen was the one called Hendrickson who would
testify against the Duff Gordons at the Hearing.

It was said that Sir Cosmo had not acted like a gentleman in observing
the tradition of 'women and children first'. Lucy explained at the Hearing that Sir Cosmo had asked Murdoch whether they might get into
the boat, and had received permission which was also granted to two
American men who came up just as it was about to be launched. This
was corroborated at the Hearing by George Symons, the seaman assigned to command of the boat, in the following manner:

> Mr. Murdoch asked who was assigned to the boat, and I said I
> was. The chief officer asked if there were any more seamen present
> and Horswill replied that he was assigned to the boat. Mr. Murdoch
> then gave the order for five firemen to jump in, as no passengers

were around the deck at the time. The remaining members of the
Crew who were there were getting the cover off the surf (or
collapsible) boat. Just as Mr. Murdoch gave the order, I saw two
ladies running from the forward end of the top saloon deck toward
the boat. They asked Mr. Murdoch if they could get into the boat
and he said 'Jump in'. After that I heard three gentlemen come
running out and ask if they could get into the boat. Mr. Murdoch
said 'Jump in'. The chief officer looked round for more passengers
and so did I. But there were none to be seen.

One of the many myths that later titillated society held that Sir
Cosmo had been allowed into the collapsible boat because he had
been dressed in clothes belonging to his wife. But Symons' evidence
disproves this ridiculous story. Cosmo was nearly a foot taller than
Lucy, bearded with a short haircut. He could never have fitted
convincingly into even the most flowing Lucile tea-gown. Murdoch
called out his last instructions to the crew. 'Pull off away from the
boat, as quickly as possible, at least two hundred yards.'
    As they were rowed into the night on the Atlantic swell, Lucy
started to suffer from deadly sea-sickness. To try and keep her mind
off it, she fixed her eyes on the ship.

I could see her dark hull towering, like a giant hotel with lights
streaming from every cabin porthole. As I looked, one row of
these shining windows was suddenly extinguished. I guessed the
reason. . . . when I forced myself to look again, yet another row
disappeared. After what seemed long hours of misery a sharp
exclamation from my husband aroused me from the stupor into
which I was sinking. 'My God, she is going now!' he cried.

'We saw the whole thing and watched that tremendous thing quickly
sink,' Miss Francatelli wrote to a friend after her rescue. 'There was
then terrible, terrible explosions and all darkness, then followed the
awful cries & screams of the 1600 dear souls, fighting for their lives
in the water. *Oh never shall I forget that awful night.*'
    Lucy remembered:

On that night of horror when we rowed away from the place
where we had seen the vast bulk of the Titanic *sink slowly beneath
the sea as though some relentless hand had drawn her under, we scarcely
spoke to one another.* Our ears were too full of those terrible cries of
despair from the poor souls she had carried down with her for us
to want to break the silence which succeeded them. There was
only the plash of the oars as the men rowed harder than ever,
seeking perhaps to get away from their thoughts, and now and

then a muttered silence as they strained their eyes into the gloom
ahead, looking for some sign of the other boats.

There were twelve people in their boat: Symons, the five firemen,
and six passengers. The boat could have held another twenty to thirty
people, but it did not turn back to rescue those in the water. Almost
a whole day of the Inquiry was spent on this: if they had heard the
screams of the drowning, why had they continued to row steadily
away from the *Titanic*?

Two conflicting stories emerged. Henrickson maintained that it
had been Lucy who said that if the boat went back it would be
swamped; but the seaman in charge, Symons, maintained through
extremely severe cross-examination that he had ordered the boat to
be rowed away 'at his discretion'.

When Scanlan, Counsel for the Wrecks Commissioners, examined
Sir Cosmo, he took an accusatory tone, and it seemed to many of
those present as if more than an iota of class antagonism was creeping
into the Inquiry. Resentful murmurs were heard from the spectators
in the gallery.

Scanlan asked whether there was any discussion among the passengers and crew in the small boat as to whether or not they should go
back to pick up the drowning. Sir Cosmo replied: 'I said that after
the *Titanic* sank there was a dead silence.'

Of course, the ship's officers had believed that, when the *Titanic*
finally floundered, she would suck down with her any boats in her
immediate vicinity. As it happened, she slid away, the boilers having
exploded and blown a vast hole aft, and she created very little, if any,
suction.

As the boat rowed away Lucy lay stretched out along the side,
scarcely conscious from violent sea-sickness. When the men rested
on their oars, as they did from time to time, they 'chatted of little,
unimportant things, as people do when they have been through a
great mental strain'.

As time went on, Lucy said, she managed to feel sufficiently better
to tease Franks about the odd assortment of clothes she had put on.
The sailors did not, apparently, think it funny. 'Never mind,
Madam,' Lucy remembered one of them saying, 'you were lucky to
come away with your lives . . . don't you bother about anything
you had to leave behind you.' He was echoed by another member of
the crew who said: 'You people need not bother about losing your
things, for you can afford to buy new ones when you get ashore.
What about us poor fellows? We have lost all our kit and our pay
stops from the moment the ship went down.'

It was then that Cosmo unwittingly made a grotesque blunder. 'Yes, that's hard luck if you like,' he said to the complaining crew member. 'But don't worry, you will get another ship. At any rate, I will give you a fiver each towards getting a new kit.' Later, Lucy said of this promise:

> It was said with his characteristic impulsiveness, and I don't think anybody thought much of it at the time, but I remember every word of the conversation, for it had a tremendous bearing on our future. I little thought then that because of those few words we should be disgraced and branded as cowards in every corner of the civilised world.

At the Inquiry, Harbinson, Counsel for the third-class passengers, rose to cross-examine Sir Cosmo on this point. The tension in the court increased further, as the tone of this Irishman (many of whose compatriots had been third-class passengers) unmistakably once again brought a note of class warfare into his examination. So obvious was this that Lord Mersey reminded the Counsel: 'Your duty is to assist me to arrive at the truth not to try to make out a case for this class against that class.'

Harbinson asked Sir Cosmo: 'Was not this rather an exceptional time, twenty minutes after the *Titanic* sank, to make suggestions in the boat about giving £5 notes?'

'No, I think not,' replied Sir Cosmo. 'I think it was a most natural time. Everything was quiet; the men had stopped rowing; the men were quite quiet lying on their oars doing nothing for some time, and then the ship having gone, I think it was a natural enough remark for a man to make, "I suppose you have lost everything?"'

At dawn, after the long night, matters looked grave indeed. The sea was getting up and boat Number One was too frail to stand much buffeting. But then the steamer *Carpathia* appeared on the horizon. 'The men were rowing now for all they were worth, and one of them began to sing. We were all nearly hysterical with the reaction from our miseries of the night,' Lucy wrote, adding, 'as we saw other boats rowing alongside of us, we imagined that most of our fellow passengers on the *Titanic* had been saved like us; not one of us even guessed the appalling truth.'

On their second day on the *Carpathia* Cosmo said to Lucy, 'I must not forget that I promised those poor fellows a fiver each towards getting a new kit if ever we were saved, I shall write them cheques and give them to them tomorrow.' Lucy agreed with this plan, adding that she was going to ask them all to 'write their names on my lifebelt before we get ashore, for I should like to keep it in memory of our wonderful escape.'

So an informal presentation to Symons, Henrickson, Taylor, Collins, Pusey, Sheath and Horswill took place on the promenade deck, and all wrote their names on Lucy's lifebelt.

News of the survival of Cosmo and Lucy was slow in coming, causing their family great grief in London. Writing to her sister on receipt of the news that they were safe, Elinor revealed her growing adherence to the dotty principles of New Thought and the near-nonsense she could indulge in when under great stress. The letter was dated April 19, five days after the disaster and it was addressed to Lucy in New York. Elinor headed it 'Our Narrative'.

> . . . I felt uneasy and did not like the idea of a maiden voyage for the ship. . . . On Monday morning I was choosing brocades when Maria called me on the telephone, and began like this 'All the passengers are saved, but there has been an accident to the *Titanic*'. My only thought was 'Those greys don't match!' I suggested going to Blumenfeld [editor of the *Daily Express*] while Tivy [Lucy's son-in-law] went to read the tape at the club. Blumenfeld was ill but the sub, Mr. Wilson saw me, and read all the telegrams, just those ones saying all was well . . . no mention of anyone being drowned. I felt much happier until I saw one telegram that he was trying to keep his hand over, which said the *Titanic* wireless message was urgent, help wanted the end of the message was blurred and 'ended abruptly'. I then felt the first horror, but underneath for some reason had no depression or fear, I knew whoever else went down you would be safe.

But the next morning, when the papers came, Elinor was 'staggered at the news in them saying the ship was sinking . . . the *Express* kept telephoning more and more grave news about women saved but men not . . . there seemed to be an angel in the room who told us your great occult strength had pulled Cosmo through too.'

When the mid-day editions came, the Duff Gordons were listed as having been drowned, but Elinor knew better:

> I have never felt more calm and certain in my life, not a tremor shook me. We were certainly sustained by those beyond because every fact seemed to prove you were drowned . . . then the *Express* rang to say your names had just arrived as saved – this was about one o'clock . . . the Lucile girls who had been crying and weeping

and fainting all the morning were also wild with joy only feared for Miss Franks . . . the angels were in the room all the time.

Comforted by the news, Elinor took Margot to a ball in Essex, then motored on to Lamberts to reassure Mrs. Kennedy and Clayton: ·

Gran was perfectly calm. Just think of the change New Thought has wrought in her – she too had the angels' assurance you were perfectly safe.

Elinor went to the memorial service in St. Paul's, calling in at the *Express* office on her way home. One telegram that had come in said '. . . a Miss Something told the reporters (who "could not locate Lord and Lady Duff Gordon") that Lady Duff Gordon "had told her that in her boat they had sung songs all night partly to keep their hearts up and partly to drown the cries of those on the *Titanic* when they realised the ship was really sinking . . ."'
Elinor completely missed the point.

Bainbridge Colby, the lawyer who had defended Lucy over her Custom Fraud case, and who had by this time become both her and Elinor's legal representative in America, waited in New York for Cosmo and Lucy.

We had a period of great anxiety here until their names appeared on the list of survivors . . . I met the *Carpathia* on its arrival. It was a most solemn and tense moment when its gangplank was thrown ashore . . . Sir Cosmo and her Ladyship sauntered off in apparently excellent condition of health and courage. Their baggage consisted of two life belts which they are preserving as mementos of their terrible experience.

Cosmo and Lucy were also met by Elsie de Wolfe, Bessie Marbury and Mr. Merritt, the editor of the *Sunday American*. They drove to the Ritz and at dinner that night 'were all very gay, and drank champagne'. It was now that Lucy made a grave error. Fortified by a heady mixture of champagne and relief, she described what she now regarded as a dramatic adventure in typically colourful and exaggerated terms to her friends – and to Merritt.
'Had you any idea of publication at that time?' Lucy was asked at the Inquiry by Sir Rufus Isaacs, the Attorney General. Lucy replied:

After Mr. Merritt had left he telephoned to me, and said "Mr. Hearst has just rung me up. We must have your story of the *Titanic* in tomorrow's morning newspaper. May I tell your story as I heard it?" I said "Yes." He told me afterwards that he telephoned to their head office all he knew about it, and then a clever reporter put all that into words, and it appeared in the *New York American*.

The 'clever reporter' had coloured Lucy's story even more, adding touches of pathos and misquoting her with sentences such as, 'I said to my husband, we may as well get into the boat, although the trip will be only a little pleasure excursion until the morning,' and 'Numbers of men standing by joked with me because we were going out on the ocean.' At the Inquiry Lucy was cross-examined on these and other statements contained in the story which ran, without her seeing it, under her bye-line.

The newspaper story sensationalised their escape at a time when few facts were known about the disaster. Wild rumours were spreading. 'Everyone looked for a victim to blame for the tragedy, and class hatred "ran high",' said Lucy later.

Soon, the blow fell. A certain Robert Hopkins, a seaman on the *Titanic* (but not on boat Number One) gave an interview to the press in which he threw light on the mystery of the 'millionaires' boat'. He stated it was occupied by Sir Cosmo Duff Gordon, Lady Duff Gordon and eleven others, only two of whom were women. A man, whom Hopkins said was an American millionaire, had promised the boat's crew to 'make it all right with them' if they 'would get right away from the ship', which they did. Hopkins concluded that each member of the crew received a cheque for £5 on Coutts Bank when they were taken aboard the *Carpathia*.

In spite of counter-statements from people in the Duff Gordons' boat, the rumours gathered momentum and, when they started being printed in the London press, it was imperative that the Duff Gordons should appear at the Board of Trade Inquiry to clear their names. They sailed for London on May 7.

The headlines they saw from the boat train were horrific: *Duff Gordon Scandal, Cowardly Baronet and his Wife who Rowed Away From the Drowning, Sir Cosmo Duff Gordon Safe and Sound While Women Go down in the* Titanic.

As Lucy put it, many years later:

The charge we had to face was a moral one . . . the real issue at stake was to both of us at least infinitely more serious. As one of the papers put it: 'The audience were not to be cheated out of the smallest particle of what has become *the* scandal in England.'

They stood accused of getting off in a lifeboat which was half-empty; of leaving to drown others whom they might have saved; and of subsequently bribing five firemen and one able seamen with £5 apiece to row away from the stricken ship. Moreover, it was put forward by one of those seamen, Hendrickson, that their real motive in the bribery was to silence those who could have accused them of persuading the other occupants of the boat to abandon other survivors to the freezing waters of the North Atlantic – and to death.

The Scottish Hall in Victoria, where the Commission sat, was crammed with distinguished visitors, their minds already made up. Prince Albert of Schleswig Holstein was con; Lady St. Helier, Elinor's great friend, was obviously pro, as were Mrs. Asquith, Prince Leopold of Battenberg (a friend of the Duff Gordons), the Russian ambassador Count Benckendorff, the Earl of Clarendon and several Members of Parliament who were attending during a brief recess. The *Daily Telegraph* reported the court was far more crowded than on any previous day. They had all come to see the Duff Gordons give their evidence.

It was a lovely spring day as Cosmo and Lucy drove to court. 'It was difficult to believe that we were not going to some pleasant social function, for there were such rows of cars outside.' Possibly remembering the effect she had had on the American Grand Jury in her customs case, Lucy looked fragile in a huge black hat, and gave her evidence clearly.

In spite of the extremely hostile cross-examination both had to endure, they stuck to their guns, and earned the sympathy of many who were there. This attitude was voiced by Ashmead Bartlett in an article which was published in *The Academy* under the title 'Inquiry or Star Chamber?' He wrote:

> Every fair minded person must deplore what passed at the proceedings of the *Titanic* Court of Inquiry last week . . . it was surely never intended that it should resolve itself into a species of Court of Star Chamber . . . or that efforts might be made to stir up class against class in order to prove that undue preference was shown to the aristocrat and the wealthy . . . Torquemada never placed his victims more unfairly on the rack of the Inquisition than have Sir Cosmo and Lady Duff Gordon been placed on the rack of cross-examination.

They were vindicated completely by the Court of Inquiry, but not by their peers.

For years afterwards, Lucy was used to hearing people who did not know her whisper, 'That is Lady Duff Gordon, the woman who rowed away from the drowning.' Cosmo never got over it. It ruined the rest of his life. The rumour has followed him beyond the grave.

His name has become (and remained) the personification of cowardice under pressure. In 1947, for instance, Evelyn Waugh asked Nancy Mitford in a letter whether she had '. . . heard of Ed's Duff Gordon escape from drowning?' Mark Amory, who edited Waugh's letters, appended the following footnote: 'Lord Stanley was an enthusiastic sailor. Sir Cosmo and Lady Duff Gordon escaped from the Titanic rather early in an underloaded boat.'

Even more recently, Bernard Levin, writing in *The Times* in 1984 in an article entitled *In Extremis and In Character,* said:

> Catastrophe then, does not alter people, but it makes the highlights and darknesses of their nature more pronounced. You cannot, I think, read Walter Lord's *A Night to Remember* . . . without sensing this truth.
>
> On that tragic occasion, the cool and the brave behaved more coolly and more bravely than ever before, the weak and the cowardly more like weaklings and poltroons. Lightoller . . . plainly had no idea of the resources of bravery and selflessness in him, but he displayed both in exceptionally great measure, which – to put it with positively excessive moderation – Sir Cosmo Duff Gordon did not. But I do not suppose Sir Cosmo either, knew his own full character until it was tested under such extreme conditions.

Perhaps Cosmo should not have listened to Lucy's pleas; perhaps he should have stayed bravely behind. But given both their characters and their relationship to one another – Lucy being the dominant character – his conduct is not surprising.

viii *Escape*

It was fortunate for Cosmo and Lucy that a ready excuse to spend time away from London presented itself in the plan to open a branch of Lucile in Paris, right in the midst – in fashion terms – of enemy territory. This plan had been maturing slowly for over a year, and in the summer of 1912 the final moves were made.

The house taken in the rue de Penthièvre had been done up in the flamboyant (and expensive) style Lucy had come to call her own. Both Lucy and Elinor had become increasingly addicted to interior decoration as a means of artistic expression and also as a gauge of their success. The new Maison Lucile came in for typically lush treatment: 'I decided to have more colourful decorations in the house . . . and I had the broad staircase leading up to the showroom carpeted in purple.' Lucy did, however, keep to the grey scheme in the main salon.

Mauve invitation cards were sent out to 'le tout Paris', and Lucy filled this new spider's web with lilacs, roses and carnations; she imported Gamela, Hebe, and Dolores from London to astonish the Parisians; and everything was ready for her grand opening.

The entrenched couturiers of the rue de la Paix watched sceptically as this interloper prepared to show her first collection. They were generally of the opinion that the English could make riding-habits and 'tailleurs' but could never aspire to the artistic and artisan heights of a true Parisian couturier.

1912 was the year when Poiret, a relative newcomer to the ranks of couture, showed his 'Minaret' collection of oriental revival dresses in violent colours, whose general effect he described as a 'blow to the head'. The Ballets Russes had inspired Paris to break out in a rash of Schehezerade outfits, hobble and harem skirts, tunics slit over harem pants and heads invariably swatched in lamé turbans. In launching his new silhouette Poiret, in common with most other couturiers, had abandoned the corset, substituting constriction from the hips upward with constriction at knees and ankle, in the shape of tightly hobbled skirts.

Lucy had ideas very similar to Poiret's, and the keynote of her first Paris collection was a series of dresses which were a development of the tea-gowns she had been concocting for London society's off-duty moments for the past twenty years. Throats were no longer encased in whalebone and net; dresses with V-necks were banded high under the bust. Lucile's new clients at first demurred at showing their necks – for many years invisible in the daytime and covered by dog-collars in the evening (a fashion set by Queen Alexandra when Princess of Wales). Lucy quoted Sir Joshua Reynolds as her authority for beauty, extolling the loveliness of a woman's neck in glowing terms.

Vogue was enthusiastic:

> Lucile's opening . . . was quite charmingly on the order of a *thé dansant*, with music, tea, and tangoing. The dancers were Lucile's pretty, English mannikins who wore Lucile's smartest tango frocks – and most wonderful of all things wonderful – tango hair! Some of them wore green hair, some red hair and some blue hair!

Singling out for special attention a green tango dress, *Vogue* called it 'the gem of the collection. The skirt was of green and silver gauze with a tunic slightly stiffened on the edge and bordered with glittering rhinestones. Black-and-white striped velvet was used for the long-sleeved bolero, and the frock was trimmed with bands of ermine.'

Lucy described the tango hair as a 'queer exotic caprice of mine, but it caught on . . . every smart woman wanted to wear one of these *tête de couleurs* as they were called.'

By the end of 1912, the Paris branch of Lucile had proved extremely successful. Lucy never dressed the 'quiet' Parisienne woman of fashion – she never dressed anyone quiet. She left that to Worth, Paquin and Doucet. But she was extremely successful with actresses, with the stars of the demi-monde and with her rich American clients, who came to Paris twice a year for clothes with the Paris touch.

The staff was doubled, and the business was now so enormous that Lucy did not have time to design every model for the three houses. She thus built up in each house a design team that worked under her supervision, sketching their ideas for her approval or translating Lucy's ideas into models for their particular clients.

'My grandmother was regularly surrounded by queer gentlemen who were designers in their turn, picked up pins and did her bidding,' remembers Lady Flavia Anderson, Lucy's granddaughter. These 'young men' scurried around Lucy, executed her ideas, listened to her plans, walked the tribe of chows and pekingese without which she never travelled. They acted as confidants, business- and social-secretaries, and generally kept Lucy company. One of these young acolytes (and there were many over the years) was a young Irishman, Edward Molyneux, whom Lucy brought with her from London to work in the Paris house. 'He had been brought to me while he was still in his teens, a pale, delicate boy with a passion for drawing and a still greater love of beautiful colours . . . before long I realised,' said Lucy, 'that here was someone who had more than mere talent, he had a genius for designing clothes.' Known affectionately as 'Toni', Molyneux was not only the most talented designer Lucy ever worked with, but one of the most loyal. He stayed with her until 1920.

Cécile Sorel, the actress, appreciated Lucy's lush designs as did pretty little Gaby Deslys, famous for her staggering collection of jewellery. The great courtesans, or 'grandes horizontales', of the day were also her clients: la belle Otéro, Monna Delza and Mata Hari were frequent visitors to the purple and grey salons and, as these women were much copied in matters of dress, they always received Lucy's personal attention.

As soon as the house in the rue de Penthièvre was running smoothly, Lucy decided to find herself somewhere to live in Paris. She now regarded her Paris house as her new headquarters, London being relegated in her mind to the status of a subsidiary branch. This had much to do with the *Titanic* episode. But in separating herself more and more from the business side of her activities, Lucy became increasingly divorced from financial reality.

Life in Paris suited Lucy. She found an apartment for herself – a studio on top of a house on the Rond Point – and there she established the custom of giving little informal parties for her friends on Saturday evenings, inspired no doubt by Elsie de Wolfe's *conversaziones* in New York. Guests were drawn from the more bohemian fringes of society, the theatre and the smarter reaches of the demi-monde, but not from the old-established 'gratin' (those families who still lived in private houses on and around the Faubourg St. Germain).

The actress Réjane was a regular visitor and would often recite at the soirées. The ragingly extravagant Comte Boni de Castellane, still married to railroad heiress Anna Gould, was another. Leon Bakst became a close friend. 'He used to come to my studio and play with the gorgeous silks and brocades there, draping himself up in them, running the delicate materials through his fingers in an abstracted way.'

Lucy was in her element: 'I gathered round me all the people whose society I liked best of all; people who did things, artists, writers, sculptors, musicians.' An important entrée to this world of ideas was again provided by Elsie de Wolfe who, with Bessie Marbury and Anne Morgan, had set up a menage à trois at the 'Petit Trianon', on the edge of the park at Versailles, where they ran a salon. Lucy met

Sardou (she had costumed adaptations of his plays in London) and
Bernhardt, who took to her and came to the studio for dresses. 'You
must not try to make me forget I am an ugly old woman,' Bernhardt
said to Lucy once. 'As a matter of fact I was an ugly young one too,
but it has not made men love me any the less.'

One of the reasons Paris suited Lucy in the closing years of the
Belle Epoque was that there were many strong, independent women
(for example, Sarah Bernhardt and Isadora Duncan) in and out of
society and the demi-monde – such women Lucy had always admired
and felt comfortable with.

But Duncan could be difficult: Howard Greer, one of Lucy's
'young men', was told to design an evening gown for this free spirit.
'You poor deluded child,' Isadora said. 'How awful being brought
up in this false atmosphere. Being led to believe that these ridiculous
modern clothes are flattering or beautiful. Where is the freedom the
Greeks knew? Where is the rhythm of flowing drapery and the subtle
hint of a divine form beneath?' Showing the bewildered young man
stone and plaster goddesses, pointing out the soft and clinging folds
of their draperies, she pronounced: 'Today, everyone seems bent on
deforming the human figure. If you can make robes for me as simple,
as classical, and as feminine as these, you will make me very happy.'

While Lucy was rebuilding her life and her confidence in Paris,
Elinor's life too was changing, as an era came slowly but surely to
an end.

Margot and Elinor went once again to Cowes that summer, and
in the Squadron garden Theresa, Marchioness of Londonderry told
Elinor a story of a society scandal which she immediately turned into
a novel, called *The Sequence*. In this, Elinor returned to English
country house society as the setting for a story of a terrified girl of
sixteen, Guinevere Bohun, married off to a selfish, domineering
general, far older than she. Fourteen years later, she falls in love with
her handsome neighbour, Sir Hugh Dremont, and the book tells of
the struggle she has with her conscience over the next seven years;
of her rejection of her sister's cynical advice to be like everyone else
in their milieu and have an affair with him. She finally succumbs,
only to give him up in a fit of remorse, whereupon Dremont marries,
to ensure his succession, Lady Kathleen Catesby, a beautiful sensual
girl with a hard heart. A few days later General Bohun dies, leaving
Guinevere free. Hugh's marriage to Kathleen turns out to be a sham,
and he is embittered by her free admission that, far from being
blue-blooded, she was in fact an octoroon – an invention which was

to have an ironic sequel when in 1922 Margot married a man thought by many to have a little coloured blood and was apprised of the fact by a woman in the crowd watching her enter the church for her wedding.

The story reaches its climax at Cowes, where Guinevere finds that her son Algernon is Kathleen's lover. *The Sequence* is a trivial tale in all but one instance: the portrait of Guinevere, waking from her numbed existence into love and life, and then tortured almost beyond endurance by the hopelessness of her love, rings true and has depth. Once again, Elinor had drawn on her own life, and Guinevere remains one of the most convincing characters she ever created.

Elinor wrote *The Sequence* at one of her bolt-holes, the Hôtel des Réservoirs, at Versailles, where she had gone as she often did, as a substitute for the enclosed world of her 'Trianon' at Lamberts, and the bustle of life in Queen Street. She finished it at the end of 1912, and then returned to England to prepare for the annual winter migration to the Riviera. She expected Clayton to join the party in Cannes, but this time he never came.

Having rapidly disintegrated into an overweight wreck as a result of his drinking, Clayton suddenly disappeared. No one knew where he was until a letter arrived, not addressed to Elinor, her mother or his children, but to Dixie, the governess. It gave instructions about his clothes and revealed that he was again in Constantinople, his previous hideaway.

Elinor's marriage was now formally at an end after ten years of expectation that Clayton would mend his ways – years during which Elinor had had to earn enough to pay his debts, to support his children and to give him an allowance. It had not, in all respects, been a disastrous marriage. In the beginning, Clayton had delighted in giving Elinor everything she craved. Luxury, position in society, stability at home – none of these would have been hers if Clayton had not married her. She would have been the frustrated virgin of her early tale – getting a little crabbier every year, probably ending as a maiden aunt, pensioned off, first in her mother's, then in her sister's house. As a spinster, she would not have been able to publish her books. As a spinster, she would have been ridiculous in her self-created role as expert on romance. Clayton never gave her the passion she craved like a drug, but he gave her his name and status and she never forgot her debt to him.

No news materialised of Clayton's plans or whereabouts and so Mrs. Kennedy, Elinor and Margot returned to England early in the spring of 1913 to give up Lamberts, which suited Elinor as she had never really liked Essex. In the early summer, news came that Clayton was ill at a hotel at Interlaken and Margot, en route for Carlsbad with her mother, made a detour to nurse him. When he recovered, he returned to England where, on the allowance Elinor made him, he took a small house in Twickenham. Here he lived, bought more brandy off M. Bernard, and was visited on occasion by Elinor, though more often by Margot.

As the tenancy on 36 Green Street had come to an end and the house was to be pulled down, Elinor decided that she too would now live mainly in France. On September 1, 1913, she wrote to Blumenfeld:

> Oh! How much water has flowed under bridges since we talked!! I have been through a sea of trouble about Clayton, but I have just shut my teeth and hoped to come through. One cannot altogether blame him, his illness has affected his brain and I believe made him unresponsible. Now all is over, the Jews are going to make him bankrupt for their 175 per cent!! The actual loan at 10 per cent having been paid into court, and I have paid all his private debts. Do you not call it hard? He went off and left us all, and now is to live by himself, and I am going to make a home for myself and the children in Paris, where I shall have a peaceful life and try to forget all these sorrows. I have taken a very quiet house at Boulogne-sur-Seine, just at the edge of the Bois, and there I am going to work hard.

Elinor and Margot lived in a garage and ate at a local bistro while the house, No. 5 Avenue Victor Hugo, Parc des Princes, was decorated. So lavish was Elinor's scheme, with specially woven brocades, that the builders' bill alone came to more than a thousand pounds. Thrift was something that neither Elinor nor her sister would be able to develop – especially when it came to interior decoration.

A further reason for this move to Paris was that it would give Elinor the opportunity of seeing Curzon away from the prying eyes he dreaded so much. He would also see Elinor surrounded by mondaine, society people who appreciated her talents and taste. But, disappointingly, he was not to come until the spring of the following year, whereupon Elinor immediately took him to Versailles, leading him with closed eyes across the tapis vert, as she had led Innes Ker years before.

'Now,' she said, turning him round. Curzon gazed at the great facade for a long time, without speaking. Finally he delivered himself of his considered opinion. 'Architecturally correct, but monotonous.' Elinor was disappointed. The king had rejected his palace. The most wonderful man in her world did not appreciate the most wonderful building.

Decorating had produced the usual horrific crop of bills and once again Elinor had to write a new novel, in the intervals of bringing Margot out in the Faubourg society so despised by Lucy. She entertained her old friends, and at one such party, reclining on a sofa in a purple alcove, read aloud from her works, both in the original and in French, to an aristocratic assembly of enough Royalty and titled guests to satisfy even Elinor. There were the Duchesse de Luynes, the Duchesse de Rohan, the Marquise de Mun, the Vicomtesse de Noailles and the Comtesse de Ségur – Cécile Sorel. While Curzon was in Paris he commissioned Philip de Laszlo, the well-known society portrait-painter, to paint Elinor in her sapphire ear-rings (the emeralds had been changed by now).

Curzon had previously commissioned portraits of women he had admired – as a gift to posterity. He told de Laszlo that he thought he could 'make a good thing out of the red hair, white skin and green eyes'. Elinor had her own ideas. She wanted to be painted sitting on a long-haired Manchurian tiger whose orange coat would have matched her hair. She explained to de Laszlo: 'If you knew the strange effect tiger skins have on me! the touch of the tiger awakens some far-off savagery – some former life when I was unhampered, and could kill – or love – when I desired, without having to consider civilisation. Now I am in a cage and live off bread and milk, and wear sapphires.'

'All through that last brilliant pre-war summer Paris amused herself, spent recklessly, gave wonderful fêtes, laughed, danced and made love as though she had not a care in the world,' Lucy said of the summer of 1914. Lucy loved living and working in Paris, and, early that year, committed herself even further to living out of England by taking the lease of an exquisite little house in Versailles near Elsie's and Bessie's 'Petit Trianon'. Called the 'Pavillon Mars' it had been given to the actress Mademoiselle Mars by Napoleon. It had a small formal garden reputed to have been planted by le Nôtre as part of his grand plan for Versailles. Here Lucy and Cosmo spent many happy hours with their St. Bernard, Porthos, and Mr. Futze, the peke, giving parties. Lunch parties. Dinner parties. And the new-fangled cocktail party.

But not everyone in Paris danced unaware. Early that spring Henri Bernstein, the playwright, had been discussing with Lucy the mania for the tango and the absurd way it had gripped Paris. 'I do not like it Madame,' he told her. 'People always feel this mad impulse to dance all day and all night, just on the eve of war.'

When war was declared, the reactions of the two sisters were, as always, entirely different. Elinor became ultra-patriotic in her Pallas Athene mood. She went back to England immediately and spent the next year trying to get permission to go back to Paris as a war correspondent. In the meantime, she worked in a canteen washing dishes.

Lucy, on the other hand, regarded the war as an irritating interruption to her work and decamped to America. She afterward maintained that her directors had made her do this, as they felt the increased profits resulting from her personal attention to the American house would compensate for the fact that the Paris and London branches had virtually to close down. She sailed early in 1915, alone. Cosmo followed her later that year, to persuade her to come back and rejoin her family, and to curb her spending which was reaching unprecedented levels – even for Lucy. Lucy turned a deaf ear, as a letter Elinor wrote to her mother at the time shows:

> I had a long letter from Lucy today . . . apparently in the same wonderful spirits as ever, sure that she is expressing *herself* and longing for Cosmo to return safely on an American ship!!!! She never means to let him interfere with her again – she has 'found herself' etc. etc. So I suppose she will settle it as she desires. In any case, they have had it out, and he knows everything from her point of view, so we must hope for the best. She loves America – it is exactly her affair. She means to live there . . . she is entirely satisfied with herself and every aspect of life.

Elinor must have expressed herself fairly forcibly to Lucy on the subject of what she must have felt was Lucy's defection, for Lucy did not write to Elinor again until late 1916, and Elinor told Mrs. Kennedy it was '. . . a sweet letter, the *first* one since she has *been in America* which contains no sting, no innuendo, and no selfish inference – too wonderful.'

The sisters' relationship always improved when conducted from a distance.

MATURITY

(1915–1920)

'He was a man you see, Paul; so when he had won her
love, he did not value it – he threw it away.'

Three Weeks

i *Follies*

New York was also in the grip of a dance craze in 1914. Irene (a Lucile client) and Vernon Castle were ruling dance-mad socialites from their nightclub 'Castles in the Air', backed by Bessie Marbury and decorated by Elsie de Wolfe. Lucy's New York coterie were still extremely powerful and helped to eradicate the adverse impression left by the *Titanic* stories. The dancer Florence Walton, partnered by her husband Maurice, was exclusively dressed by Lucile and proved to be a splendid advertisement for the business.

It did not take Lucy long to realise, on her arrival in New York, that there was even more money around than there had been two years earlier in 1912. But Lucy had a mission very far removed from dressing high society, as she explained in a letter to Esmé:

> I'm getting dead sick of working for the 'few' rich people that go into the four Luciles with their personal fads. They don't like this and that. I am going to work for the millions. You and Margot and Juliet and Gran are in the world to be good wives and mothers. But I have been no good as a wife and mother and I loathe any idea of 'society' or 'titles'. I'm going to be a help to the great 'Middle Class' of America; the workers and the great struggling poor. I'm not thinking of England or France. I don't count on our helping them, they are too old and finished for me to be interested in them . . . I'm sure any drop of English blood of my ancestors has missed getting into me. Ask Gran about me when I was a child. I loved the American child 'Zaïdi Ball' who came to visit dirty little Guelph and adored the idea of her paying ten dollars – a fortune then – for her bronze boots. I have always loved anything 'American' all my life. It always called to me, its push and go. I love its tearing down every five years its skyscrapers to build bigger and higher ones – whereas poor dirty little Guelph is exactly the same as it was forty years ago, even the same streets and shabby houses.

Lucy made herself perfectly plain to her mother in 1916. 'Is Lord Curzon going to be governor of Canada??' she asked. 'I can't believe he'd do such a thing – such a ghastly middle class throng to govern.'

Her new missionary life in America commenced with a stroke of misfortune: during a reconnaissance visit to Chicago where she intended to open a new branch of Lucile if Sir Cosmo and Mr. Miles would agree to it, Lucy developed acute stomach pains. An abscess on her womb was diagnosed, requiring immediate surgery. During her convalescence Cosmo was 'at his very best . . . he fusses after me all day,' Lucy wrote to Esmé. 'The dear fellow, he adores me while I am perfectly hopeless like this . . . I only pray it may go on.'

It did go on – for a while. Forbidden by the doctors to travel back to England for three months, Lucy and Cosmo took a small summer house at Mamaroneck, and moved in, complete with dogs, servants and Lucy's new 'young man'.

> Our Russian boy friend who we call 'Bobbie' [because he looked like an Airedale of the same name] has been the most devoted angel to me all through it – a joy to us all. Cosmo loves him already and they go about all the time. Cosmo chaffs him, and he loves Cosmo . . .'

This idyllic state of affairs did not last. Bobbie became more and more entrenched and Cosmo did not like it. Matters reached such a pass that, in spring 1915, Cosmo returned home alone, or as Lucy put it in response to a question from her mother:

> Cosmo went off and left *me* – alone, ill, in a strange country and with a great danger [Bobbie] so he thought, threatening me – to fight out out *alone* because of a petty personal pride and spite . . . poor Cosmo – how awful to feel as he does – I am sure he is very unhappy.

Cosmo may have had very good reason to be unhappy at Lucy's growing attachment to Bobbie, an attractive young Russian émigré whose real name was Genia d'Agarioff. Bobbie's past was none too good but Lucy would hear nothing against him, as is clear in a letter to her mother of February 1916:

> . . . I want you once and for all to get out of your mind the idea that Bobbie's past 'bad reputation' as you call it could ever 'injure my fame'. Just cut that idea right out of any of your thoughts. I know just exactly the serpent that told you this tale and the vile unkindness of it, only told you to worry you . . . even if it were true, which it is not I know from *himself* every incident in his life . . . the day will come when Cosmo will have to acknowledge he has behaved vilely both to him and to me . . . he [Cosmo], has quite done for himself here in the eyes of all the men who knew about his flight . . . they think him such a coward to go as he

seemed really to believe that my dear boy was a scoundrel of the deepest die. So his going made it worse in their eyes . . . you evidently believed him (instead of me) about 'bad reputation' living on women, and so on and so on.

On his return to London, Cosmo did not go back to Lennox Gardens, but moved into the Hans Crescent Hotel. He and Lucy never lived together again.

It was, in a sense, inevitable and had been coming for a long time. Lucy was much happier leading an independent life surrounded by the young men who picked up pins, for they took her at her own valuation and, if she became bored, she could send them away, which was not possible with a husband. Cosmo liked Scotland and the life of a sporting country gentleman. Circumstances had pushed him into the world of fashion – a world of epicene young men and powerful women – and he had never really fitted into his wife's favoured milieu of High Bohemia. Her disavowal of England and virtual adoption of Bobbie were the last in a series of straws. For the next ten years they would quarrel constantly over the business, but eventually they would become friendly, if distant.

Lucy started to re-organise her life. She took an apartment on Central Park South which she rented furnished while she found something more permanent. She spent a great deal of her time at Mamaroneck, or in one or another of a whole series of summer houses near the water, surrounded by her 'doggies' – and by Bobbie and his friends, including the 'Maestro', an Italian pianist called Patricola, paid by Lucy to give her music lessons. The devoted Franks sometimes lived with Lucy as her companion and sometimes not, especially after she incurred Lucy's ire by suddenly marrying a commis-waiter of German Swiss descent. Despite her professed lack of snobbery, Lucy considered this a mésalliance.

In December 1915, Lucy wrote rather defiantly to her mother: 'I like being alone, just with a few amiable boy friends to do with joy my slightest wish.' There was never any question of an affair with Bobbie. Lucy liked devoted companionship – she was no longer interested in passion, if indeed she ever had been. The faithful Edward Molyneux ('Toni') came over to America to help her whenever he had leave from the Front and she spent a great deal of time persuading him not to go back, for her attitude to the war was that it was a nuisance and a waste of time.

Another young acolyte, Howard Greer, first made his appearance in 1915. One day Lucy received a telegram from this unknown, ambitious to become an assistant to the famous Lady Duff Gordon. His only experience in fashion was as a window-dresser in his local store in Lincoln, Nebraska, from which he had been dismissed for purloining an artificial pearl necklace. Intrigued, she had replied to his telegram: 'Meet me in Chicago Thursday, will give definite answer.' Greer responded: 'Death alone will keep me from you Thursday.'

Greer, arriving in Lucy's hotel suite, saw a small figure with red hair dressed in white linen and surrounded by pekinese and fluttering assistants. Scenting another willing slave, she hired him at once and he stayed with her for several years. For however much she protested, Lucy was lonely in America and her band of young male assistants became more and more essential to her, both at work and at her parties. She treated her constant companions half as the sons she had never had and half as awe-strick acolytes. They had to be ready to turn their hands to cooking for her, arranging flowers, playing the piano, dog-sitting and even dressing up en travesti to amuse her guests. She referred to them in letters to Esmé as 'my boys'. Their uncritical devotion with no counter-balance now in the form of Cosmo or Esmé (both of whom had always stood up to her as far as was possible), did nothing to lessen her belief that she was always right.

Suitable premises were finally found for the fourth Lucile in Chicago at 1400 Lake Shore Drive 'right in the middle of private houses of millionaires', and next door to Mrs. Potter Palmer (the acknowledged queen of Chicago society and an old acquaintance of Elinor's). Lucy left the panelled walls and inlaid floors as they had been in the time of the house's previous owner, but delighted as always in decorating this new outlet for her designs. She put thick purple rugs bordered in emerald on the floors and draped the windows with curtains of grey satin.

The meat-packing heiresses of the Middle West loved it. Telling Esme that the inaugural fashion show was 'the best we have ever had', Lucy enthused about the theatrical staging; 'the room behind the actual stage was so big that we got wonderful effects of a pathway down which the most beautiful dresses walked through three veils of different shades of blue chiffon . . . we had a scene on the stage called after the song "Love's Garden of Roses" . . . Bonza and Bobbie sang the duet from "Thais" . . . and just yesterday we took in three thousand pounds of orders.'

Early in 1915, encouraged by her continuing success, Lucy took much bigger premises in New York, moving Lucile from its original location on 36th Street to a former private house on the corner of 57th Street and Fifth Avenue. In this, she was following the move her society clients had begun to make up town, a trend spear-headed by Bessie Marbury's and Elsie de Wolfe's move to Sutton Place. This new house served as both showroom and couture ateliers for Lucy's private clients. Lucy herself avoided visiting it, for she had lost interest in her couture clientèle and had begun to have very grandiose ideas, fired by her missionary ideal, about making wholesale fashions for the masses.

In late 1915, she took in American partners to finance this new venture, out of which she confidently expected to make millions of dollars. She exhibited a hundred and fifty of her designs at a wholesale show in New York. It was not a success, but this did not deter Lucy whose attitude toward failure was to ignore it.

She now did most of her work at her model studio, which occupied a loft just below the Flatiron building on Lower Fifth Avenue. Here, life was very different from the scented hush of the couture house. The space was taken up, not by eighteenth-century chairs, but by worktables, dressmaker's dummies and seamstresses. Partitions at the back of the studio gave the four assistant designers a bit of privacy as they sketched ideas. Next door was a room in which the mannequins relaxed in their grey crêpe kimonos while waiting to be called for fittings. Across the front of the loft, looking out across Fifth Avenue, was a suite of grey-panelled rooms littered with rainbows of colour where, in the words of Howard Greer, 'the outstanding phenomenon of her day conceived, changed, worried and perfected the gowns that defined new trends.'

No one entered this holy of holies unbidden. In the corridor outside, employees walked on tiptoe and greeted each other in whispers that genius might be left undisturbed. Lucy was so impressed with a sense of her own importance that no other tenant in the building was allowed to enter one of its public lifts when she was in it. Fortunately for the other tenants, she came down to the studio only three or four times a week, arriving around ten o'clock in the morning from the house in Mamaroneck.

She must have been an impressive sight as she led her maid, Franks and a procession of the inevitable pekinese and chows into the building. Lucy had developed a species of uniform for herself which in the summer consisted of a white linen suit with a short flared skirt worn with white suede Russian boots. Mrs. Kennedy, amused, christened them 'Lucy's brigand boots'. To this basic ensemble she added flowing chiffon veils which covered her by now bright carrot-coloured hair and, to complete the effect, what she referred to as a

'Tosca walking stick', an accessory bearing a marked resemblance to a very long eighteenth-century walking-stick, which she sometimes decorated with ribbons or flowers as the fancy took her. In the winter, the white linen became black serge, the white boots brilliant green or red and the chiffon veils intertwined with furs. Lucy had never been greatly interested in her own clothes – quite often buying cheap black dresses off sale rails in department stores. But by now she was very well aware (more than likely from earlier observations as to the effect Elinor's looks had had on her reception in America) that this was a country which judged more from outward effect than inward truth.

It was during this time that she adopted at least one custom of the country – she chewed gum, and created a nuisance by spitting it out of the windows of her studio on to the heads of passers-by in the street below. They were not pleased, but Lucy was, as always, completely indifferent to complaints.

All through 1915 and 1916 Lucy was at pains to assure Cosmo and Esmé that she never went out, that she spent most of her time working. She was becoming more and more reclusive. Perhaps her experiences after the *Titanic* had soured her. She was always present, however, at the opening of her collections. She had brought four of her famous mannequins from London – Dolores, Hebe, Phyllis and Arjamand (the first really svelte mannequin ever to model fashionable clothes). To these she added American beauties such as 'Dinarzade', a statuesque brunette from Knoxville, Tennessee.

A Lucile opening was an important social event in New York and, although Lucy made no secret of her preference for Haute Bohemia, this did not deter her smart customers. On opening day, these clients were met by a social secretary, dressed in the inevitable grey taffeta, who checked the admittance cards. Once they were all seated, Lucy swept in a royal last and sat in a chair placed forward from the front row facing the chiffon-draped stage. This was the cue for the string orchestra to play a waltz and for another Lucile show to begin.

In the autumn of 1915, the society audience saw the beginnings of a change in the Lucile silhouette. For the past three years she had designed clothes with a strong oriental influence. But now she abandoned her draped, straight line with a high bust and hobbled skirts, and went back in history to 1828 to create elaborately frilled, bowed and furred dresses with a natural waist, invariably accentuated by a sash and a shorter bell-shaped skirt. Her choice of materials changed, too. Abandoning the lamé and brocades she had been using, Lucy returned to much lighter, transparent fabrics. She used lace as priceless as it was delicate and then re-embroidered it; chiffon; georgette;

muslin. She based her designs on paintings of the era, and her trimmings became more and more lavish. These dresses were made in many diaphanous layers, one colour on top of another creating a shimmering diffused effect. She had been using black velvet edged with rhinestones to trim dresses; now she started to use bands of fur or jewelled embroidery.

'Lady Blessington' for instance, worn by Hebe, had a 'small black taffeta skirt and over it is a very full long skirt of steel net with flounces of silver lace and a tight black satin boned bodice with a silver lace "Bertha" and a bunch of white flowers. She looks,' Lucy told Esmé, 'a dream of beauty in it!'

Lucy's lingerie and tea-gowns were as popular as ever. A New York version of Hanover Square's Rose Room was duly installed. 'Its walls were hung with pink taffeta, over-draped with the frailest lace and the pink taffeta curtains at the windows and around the day bed were caught up with garlands of satin, taffeta and jewelled flowers,' Lucy wrote in her memoirs.

Lucy's list of clients read like a combination of the Social Register, a silent film set and Broadway. The Dolly sisters dressed identically in lace crinolines, Irene Castle in drifts of chiffon and pailettes, Isadora Duncan in Greek draperies, Norma Talmadge in ruffled net. Vanderbilts and Astors jostled Lily Langtry and Fanny Brice in the elegant fitting rooms.

Mary Pickford, just starting her long career in films, was employed by Lucy for the then enormous sum of one thousand dollars to advertise a Lucile dress – encouraged by her venal mother. But as she grew more successful Mary too became a paying client and, when she went on a bond-selling tour of America late in 1917, wore a specially-tailored khaki uniform designed for her by Lucy.

Not content with her continuing success as a couturière, Lucy launched herself into a secondary career as a fashion journalist – however, she wrote only of her own collections. Most of these articles appeared in *Harper's Bazaar*, owned by William Randolph Hearst. Here is what she had to say about fashion, late in 1915:

The boudoir fantasies of a dainty woman are ever a delightful theme: I write of them with pleasure. This winter, the dressing gown is a dream of coziness and beauty. I'm using for its outer surface a soft, silky material called 'Zenana' which I like with a blanket-like wool of matching colour. Broad bands of satin bind the neck, sleeves, front panels and hem. Pink in its lovely range of flesh to deepest rose, I use for these robes intimes, as well as the paler hues.

For the belle who would seek her couch without delay, but
would wait awhile before she sleeps, I have designed a dear little
bed jacket of warm velvet. In deep rose bordered with ermine, it
is inexpressibly adorable . . . You ask me for a prophecy; I rejoice
in the newest trend of fashion – the return of frills and bows and
furbelows . . .

Clearly, when it came to lush prose, Lucy felt herself more than a
match for Elinor.

In spring 1916, Lucy departed from the normal practice of showing
her collection in her salon and mounted a series of *tableaux vivants* in
a theatre. The tableaux were called *Fleurette's Dream at Péronne* and
concerned the trials and tribulations of 'Fleurette' in the war-torn
town of Péronne in France.

Belatedly, Lucy was beginning to develop a conscience about her
attitude toward the war. Elinor was working very hard as Vice
President of a society called the Secours Franco-Americain dedicated
to bringing relief to devastated battle areas. Péronne lay in one of
these areas, and Lucy decided that she would raise money for it,
through selling tickets to her tableau-fashion show.

The tableaux starred the statuesque Dolores and were presented at
the Little Theatre. Billie Burke, then married to Florenz Ziegfeld,
was a customer and brought her husband to one of the matinees. So
impressed was Ziegfeld that he asked Lucy whether he could employ
Dolores (dressed, naturally, by Lucile) and several other mannequins
in his current *Follies*. 'But they do not know how to sing or dance,
let alone talk,' Lucy is reputed to have said. Ziegfeld assured her that
all they would have to do would be to walk around and carry her
beautiful costumes, just as they had in *Péronne*.

Thus was born a great American tradition: the Showgirl. Dolores
became the most beautiful star the *Follies* ever featured, taking the
town by storm dressed as 'Empress of Fashion, The Discourager of
Hesitancy', in a scene entitled 'Ladies of Fashion – An Episode in
Chiffon'. So successful was this innovation that Lucy designed the
Follies costumes until 1920. She created siren gowns, Egyptian costumes (for a Cleopatra scene), Chu Chin Chow Chinese costumes;
she dressed showgirls as bouquets of flowers, as nautch girls. She
dressed the leading ladies: Irene Castle, Billie Burke, Marion Davies
(Hearst's mistress), Peggy Hopkins Joyce (the blonde showgirl who
was one of the prototypes for Lorelei Lee in *Gentlemen Prefer Blondes*).
The *Follies* gave Lucy a new outlet for her fantasy designs.

But not content – never content – with being the most famous
fashion and costume designer in America, Lucy was persuaded to go

The only known photograph of Lord
Curzon and Elinor together (third and
fourth from left)

The *Titanic* telegram

WP. 25   6-35 8

newyork   24

22 APR 1912

CABLE OFFICE 5, ROYAL OPERA   PALL MALL S.W.

To Glyn Lucilation Ldn
all through horrible experience
new thought kept me perfectly calm
and hopeful all of us now quite
well fond love
~ Lucy.

The *Three Weeks* invitation

Mrs Clayton Glyn

requests the pleasure of

Company at a Private Performance of her Play,

"*Three Weeks*"

to be given at the Adelphi Theatre on the afternoon
of Thursday, 23rd July, at 3 o'clock.

A fashion show, circa 1910, at Lucile

A Lucile design, circa 1912

A Lucile design for Lilie Elsie in
The Merry Widow

The bathroom at the Pavillon
Mars, designed by Elsie de Wolfe

A fashion show sur l'herbe at the
rue de Penthievre, 1913

Lucy in Bobbie's uniform at boot camp, 1917

Bobbie, Lucy and an unidentified friend on Long Island

Lucy as 'Russia' at the Allies Ball, 1916

'My Dearest', an afternoon frock designe by Lucy for the Sears Roebuck catalogu 1917

...yton, bloated and self-indulgent, in the south of France in 1913

Elinor, in *Three Weeks* mood and Lucile dress at Montacute in 1916

Elinor, Margot and Juliet on their tour of the battlefields, 1918

John Gilbert, Elinor and Aileen Pringle — a publicity photograph for *Three Weeks*, 1923

Elinor (in background) on the set of *Beyond the Rocks* with Gloria Swanson and Rudolf Valentino

Elinor in amateur dramatic mood in Hollywood

Elinor with her 'walkers' in Hollywood — 'all over 6 feet 2 inches'

John Wynn

Elinor and her mother in London, in 1924

Elinor on the set of *Knowing Men*; on her left, the playwright and scriptwriter
Edward Knoblock

Lucy at the time of the
publication of her memoirs

Cecil Beaton's portrait of Elir
taken in 1932. She was sixty-e

on stage herself, by the manager of the Keith Theatrical Circuit. He proposed that she should take *Fleurette's Dream* on tour round the vaudeville theatres in his circuit, at a salary of five hundred pounds a week for six months. The tour dates fell between collections and Lucy jumped at the chance, but with less than happy results. The *Variety* reviewer found that 'Madame has lost her poise somewhere en route . . . her "Washington Cocktail" story was indelicate to say the least . . . Holiday Harlemites did not take kindly to Madame's extreme models and laughed at them instead of absorbing their artistic values.'

There was a dark note at this time: the war in Europe. Lucy was constantly being reminded of it by Cosmo and Esmé, who urged her to come back to England. She had absolutely no intention of exchanging the delights of her charming little house on Long Island Sound, her sumptuous new flat on Park Avenue (newly decorated in the Chinese manner), adulation and devoted companionship from 'the boys' and as much money as even she could spend, for England at war and the rigours of Zeppelin raids.

Lucy tried to persuade Esmé to take her part:

> The whole of America is now beginning to talk about me and I am coining money. What possible good could I do in London? The talent that is coming out of my brain just now is not saleable in London, where all is mourning and economy . . . Miles and Cosmo are of course hypnotized by the war, and cannot imagine conditions here at all . . . if they are so shortsighted and selfish as to wish me to make the crossing in a nerve-wracking anxiety for ten or twelve days, never knowing when a blow-up might come, I owe it to myself and to you all to refuse to cross.

Esmé refused to see her mother's point of view and joined her entreaties to those of Cosmo and Miles. Lucy replied:

> My eye . . . what a serious letter of sad reproof you wrote me. Why, I can see I must never write you any letters but serious dullness. Evidently you have so much misunderstood anything I've said.

Elinor had also written an admonishing letter and, as usual, Lucy communicated her displeasure through the medium of her mother:

> I've had a letter from 'Elinor Glyn' of such a condescending patronizing superior being sort of tone written from her aristocratic surroundings of ruby silk and divine panelling!!! Listening to

peaceful English church bells ringing!!! etc etc. with Marquesses and Lords hanging around – to her poor commonplace ordinary being of a sister . . . full of clap-trap sentiment and pity for me and of all they are doing for the war and apologizing continually for talking such grand truths to me – to me – !!! But that she has 'Such intense vibrations of solemn requiem in the air and the Dead March of Saul thundering thro' everything??!!! that she cannot think of ordinary things (such as writing to thank me for a pair of cheap boots that I sent). Really a perfectly ridiculous letter . . . it would have been so much nobler if she had written a splendid War Romance and sold and given the proceeds to one of the many charities for the 'noble soldiers' she talks to me so much about. The £1000 I have given this year has done the noble soldiers more good than 'Elinor Glyn.'

The London branch of Lucile was failing; Lennox Gardens, the house Cosmo and Lucy had lived in for nearly ten years, was sold with most of its contents in 1916; the flat in Paris went shortly afterwards; and the Pavillon Mars lay deserted and empty, its decoration ruined by a tenant who had done her cooking ('and everything else' as Elinor put it) in the bedroom. There was nothing, as far as Lucy could see, to draw her back to Europe. America was such fun. So she disregarded Esmé's plea and stayed put.

There was another reason: income tax. The family solicitor, Tweedie, had warned Lucy that she was liable for a large sum. She ignored it, telling her mother she could not be bothered 'monkeying about with Tweedie and the English government'.

ii *Curzon's Decision*

With Margot and Juliet safely in London living with Mrs. Kennedy in her flat at Shelley Court in Chelsea, Elinor was free to go back to the Ritz. Her feelings for Curzon were just as strong as they had ever been: she needed to have her own independent establishment, so that she could go on seeing him in private. This, of course, also suited her preference for living alone in two or three rooms, looked after by servants. She could see her family whenever she, or they, wished, but treasured her privacy – as she always would.

A letter to her daughters, whom she now treated as equals – almost as competitive sisters, a repetition of her relationship with Lucy – illustrates her mood at this point towards Curzon and their possible future together:

> For myself I must give my message, and then God will dispose of me as he thinks best. If what my sweet baby [Juliet] wrote about comes my way, I will take it, but I cannot scheme for it. I *believe* that strong enemies have given him the impression that a certain section of the public would be violently anti.

Who were these enemies? Not Curzon's daughters, for they had become friendly with Elinor, Margot and Juliet. Cynthia, in particular was much attached to her unofficial stepmother. The finger must point again at the Souls who had never changed their view of Elinor as a woman of little breeding who had written a shocking novel.

Curzon, moreover, still nurtured political ambitions, and a notorious novelist, who would have to get a divorce before he could marry her, did not constitute the perfect match for a man with justifiable aspirations to the highest political office in the land. But during 1915 and most of 1916 they were, it would seem, closer than ever. Elinor had started a new novel, *The Career of Katherine Bush*, and 'Milor' lent her his house at Broadstairs in June 1915 to provide her with the necessary seclusion for her writing.

Elinor nevertheless picked up the threads of her old acquaintanceship with Milner by re-opening the correspondence, which had virtually ceased in 1911 at the time of her reconciliation with Curzon. Milner was quick to respond.

The necessary permits for a journalistic visit to the front were not forthcoming and Elinor grew increasingly restless at the Ritz in London. Finally, early in 1915, she decided to go back to Paris and find whatever relief work was available. Her house in the Avenue Victor Hugo was too far from the centre of things, so she moved into the Ritz in Paris and attached herself to the British Hospital in the Trianon Palace Hotel at Versailles, where she helped by talking to the wounded and giving them cigarettes and flowers. It was all she could do at the time for the war effort.

Clayton was still living in retirement at Twickenham, buying and drinking quantities of brandy. He was ill and in debt again. Elinor had become disillusioned with Paris and with the French whose lack of enthusiasm for the war horrified her. And she wanted to see Curzon again. So in the summer of 1915 she returned to London.

On May 27 Curzon was asked to join the Coalition Government as Lord Privy Seal. His long years in the wilderness were over. It was not yet apparent to Elinor that her days were numbered for, being excluded from the company of his friends, she had no means of knowing that, apart from the fulfillment of his political ambitions, a dangerous new interest had entered Curzon's life.

Curzon first met Grace Duggan at a lunch party given by one of his Soul friends, the Duchess of Rutland. Grace was a beautiful, intelligent and rich American, married to an ailing Anglo-Argentinian, Alfred Duggan. She went out and about in London society on her own, and while not a true member of the Souls she was popular with them. Curzon was attracted to her. At the end of 1915, her husband died suddenly, and she was left a very rich widow indeed, with two young sons.

In November 1915, Curzon made what appeared to be the most positive move yet towards establishing Elinor as a permanent part of his life – or so it seemed to her, ignorant of his growing relationship with Mrs. Duggan. He leased Montacute in Somerset, one of the finest Jacobean mansions in the country, a grand, remote and beautiful house and he asked Elinor if she would like to live there temporarily and decorate it for him.

Curzon was fascinated by architecture, restoration and decoration. Much in the same way that he had lovely women painted for posterity, so he collected houses and restored them to beauty. Elinor, too, loved decorating but her motives were less to do with posterity than with providing a setting within which she could shine. This new move on Curzon's part must have given her renewed hope for the future. It was not Kedleston, but it was something. But Montacute was also a long way from London and from Mrs. Duggan, and this may have had something to do with Curzon's offer.

In the same month, while Elinor was in Paris again trying to obtain permission to visit the battlefields, the chief obstacle in the way of her possible marriage with Curzon was removed. After a short illness, Clayton died. Very suddenly but not unexpectedly. He had lived quietly for the past three years, and had undergone that distinct personality change which is the classic symptom of the advanced alcoholic. To the bitter end, he ordered his one remaining comfort from his brandy merchant – and Elinor paid.

Margot, always devoted to her father and by now an extremely capable young woman, took in hand the organisation of his cremation and the disposition of his estate. Elinor arrived the day after his death. It is a measure of how highly Clayton's family had come to regard her heroic efforts to keep him out of debt, and Margot and Juliet decently educated and started in life, that his sisters and cousins were unanimous in their sympathy toward her – and that even Dick Richards, the cousin who had not spoken to Clayton since the incident of the unpaid wine bill some fifteen years previously, wrote her a sympathetic letter.

To another cousin, Elinor wrote in response to his letter of condolence: '. . . it is always sad and pathetic, death, but I am only so glad he never knew of the fresh grief and worry I was feeling at his bunch of fresh debts, which I now have to pay.'

To Clayton's sister Milly she wrote: 'The tragedy of these last years is too sad to talk about, is it not? Poor, poor dear Clayton, I *know* it was the disease and not his kind generous soul. I always feel the real soul went about five years ago after one of his bad illnesses, and that some queer entity got into his body. I have never really felt any resentment against him although it has often been very cruel, the things which happened . . . life is a strange tragedy altogether.'

Of Clayton's great expectations, Elinor, Margot and Juliet were left with about £500 a year among them – and the debts. All that remained from the estate was £200.

For the rest of 1915 and the early part of 1916 Elinor divided her time between a small flat she had taken above her mother's in London, and decorating the huge stone rooms of Montacute. To a woman who had always preferred to curl up like a cat in front of a fire, a life spent up stepladders in an unheated country house must have been purgatory, but it was all for Curzon, and she approached her work eagerly. All that now remains of her schemes is a small bathroom she had installed in a powder-closet.

She was photographed at Montacute wearing deepest black widow's weeds, looking almost ethereally beautiful, as if she was living on a diet of hope and love – which indeed she was.

Curzon's youngest daughter, Lady Alexandra Metcalfe, who was a child at the time, can still remember Elinor at Montacute 'pasting parrots on to my nursery walls'. It is a yardstick of Curzon's attitude toward her at that time that he, who liked to have the ordering of even the minutest housekeeping details himself and had done so even when Mary Curzon was alive, was now content to let Elinor have her way.

While at Montacute, Elinor found the time to write a fascinating appreciation of Curzon's character, his ambitions and his motivations. It is a clear though obviously subjective look at the one man above all others she considered to epitomise all the qualities of a Great Man.

In reading this assessment of Curzon's character, it should be remembered that Elinor was writing from the vantage-point of a long-standing mistress, rather than that of a wife. Curzon had treated his first wife very much more as a confidante and ally, rather than a possession and was to adopt the same attitude with his second wife. It is, therefore, unlikely that either of his wives or close woman friends would have agreed with all of Elinor's strictures.

She wrote it carefully (there are no deletions, and the spelling is painstaking) in a small leather book which locked with a tiny gold Bramah key attached to a fine gold bracelet that she wore ever afterwards. In a sense, although she perhaps did not realise this herself, this essay can be seen as a valediction. She was unconsciously preparing herself for a final parting, after eight years.

> I wish to leave on record for posterity to read a pen portrait of this great man. . . . Historians will not be able to do him justice because they will inevitably be prejudiced by the impression left by those who did not know him well enough to discover the magnificent nobility of his true self and only chronicled his public achievements, being also biassed by that strange hostility he evokes . . .

She is obviously writing to be read, for she then warns that 'the section dealing with his point of view about women, and his estimate of them, may shock those who are not accustomed to analyse things for themselves, but accept regulation standards without asking why – such as that if a man is courageous and noble, he must also be chivalrous to woman! Perfect fallacies!'

He has always been loved by women, but he has never allowed any individual woman to have the slightest influence on his life; it is only collectively that they influence him. He likes their society for entirely leisure moments – they are of no real importance in his scheme of things. He likes them rather in the spirit in which other men like fine horses or good wine, or beautiful things to embellish a man's leisure – but not as equal souls worthy of being seriously considered or treated with that scrupulous sense of honour with which he would deal with a man.

They are on another plane altogether and so to be viewed and judged by a totally different code of moral laws – He has a fond gentle contempt for the sex and accepts their adoration with complacent amusement – this adoration is largely composed of sexual emotion and not really worship of his character because he is never entirely frank with them, and he often under estimates their intuition, which takes the place of logic and intelligence in the majority – so he will attempt to give them a false impression as to his doings, likings for people, interests and motives, in a way he would never do to men.

Elinor concluded that

however a woman might adore him, if her soul was not great enough, and her breadth of judgement not expanded enough to realise the cause of his ways towards her, she would always have to blink at some fraction of his methods with her, to keep herself from despising them and him. But if she had a great soul, she would understand that he was merely expressing his personality in his own way, and that if this is his attitude towards women, it is because women in this life, or his former ones *have caused him to take this view of them.*

She developed the theme further:

His leisure is always spent more with women than with men. They are more his natural companions. But his leisure is so rare that this does not amount to anything great in his life. With his general view of the sex he is not necessarily attracted to women who have fine characters. He is perfectly indifferent as to their moral worth so long as they are ladies outwardly and amuse him. His most frequent companions are nearly all drawn from a group who however clever and sought after they may be do not call forth in the general opinion respect and esteem for possessing noble characters of quite untarnished reputations and who are not really looked up to but rather are regarded as worldly successes to be envied for their social positions.

Elinor could not resist having the last word on the Souls. She gave a glimpse of what it must have been like to have been in love with Curzon:

> He never gives a woman a single command and yet each one must be perfectly conscious that she must obey his slightest indication. He rules entirely – and when a woman belongs to him, he seems to prefer to give her even the raiment which touches her skin, and in every tangible way show absolute possession. While in words avoiding all suggestion of ownership, all ties and all obligations upon either side.

This surely is a description of Curzon's attitude toward a mistress, rather than to a future wife.

That summer of 1916 another rival entered the lists against Elinor: Kedleston. The most perfect eighteenth-century house in England finally became Curzon's on the death of his father, the parsimonious Lord Scarsdale. Curzon loved Kedleston more than any of his other houses, and it was in a parlous state. He wished to restore it to its former greatness but his father had left insufficient funds to do this. Curzon needed money – a great deal of money. He would have to marry it.

He proposed to Mrs. Duggan in the church at Winchilsea that summer, having taken her to see another acquisition – the dreamlike Bodiam Castle. Mrs. Duggan accepted him but, having been recently widowed, decided that the engagement should be kept secret until the end of the year, after she had visited Duggan's parents in Buenos Aires and attended to financial matters there.

Curzon now found himself in a difficult position. Consuelo Vanderbilt, then the enchantingly pretty Duchess of Marlborough, went to see him at his request at Carlton House Terrace in the late summer of 1916; she found him in bed, answering queries from his chef, his chauffeur and his butler. 'There was,' she wrote in her memoirs, 'something rather ridiculous and altogether pathetic in the manner in which, interruping our talk, he was answering the most trivial questions in a gradiloquent language and a strong North Country accent while all the while tears were pouring down his cheeks.' He was, she remembered, 'discussing certain difficulties that loomed in the way of his second marriage'.

The 'certain difficulties' probably amounted to how he was going to tell Elinor.

By October 1916 he had said nothing to her but she was writing to Margot:

> It is my karma this strange withholding by fate of *honour* from those I love most, and who have most reason to hold me in reverence. So if I have not yet paid the price, this one the baby [Juliet] spoke of, will be withheld, or only offered in some manner which degrades the spirit. But I am completely unrebellious – I will accept whatever is given to me by God.

On December 16, 1916, Curzon finally took to the centre of the political stage again: he was appointed to Lloyd George's War Cabinet. On looking in *The Times* on the following day to read about the appointment, Elinor saw the notice of Curzon's engagement.

She never saw or spoke to him again.

The news came as a tremendous shock to Elinor's friends and family. Even Lucy, despite her antagonism towards her sister, was indignant, writing to Esmé:

> How is Aunty Nellie? We are in our ignorance infuriated at the matrimonial news in the papers here. But if she is happy, that's all that matters. But to us – well, we won't believe it true – what did she do the country house for!!!!!, we boil when we think of the ungrateful sneaking cad, but of course that's how it looks to our ignorant eyes!

To her mother, Lucy wrote:

> What faith can one have in 'noblesse oblige' any more? Not that I've ever thought anything of them – I think the English aristocrats unless you are really one of them, are in their set or you are an American millionaire, are a vile set of cruel snobs . . . of course I have been wondering just how you and the girls would look upon the widow's garb. Just how would you feel about the *moral* and spiritual side of it? I always detested the creature – and that is why I was so mad over the decorations of Montacute and the waste of time and the bondage – but God is good and her Karma is thro' on that score. There has been a most ridiculous 'announcement of a marriage' here in all the papers, of a widow in her weeds and a noble statesman, but I pay no heed. Imagine the class of woman she must be to use her crape and its meaning as a pathetic appeal in a photo!!

iii *The War Correspondent*

The first months of 1917 were for Elinor like a period in limbo, during which she turned to *Katherine Bush* for distraction.

When it came out (under the title *The Career of Katherine Bush*) it was held to be the best book she had written and was particularly well reviewed by the *Times Literary Supplement*. Imbued – for obvious reasons – with a sense of the cynical side of Elinor's nature, it tells the story of a girl from a lower-middle-class family from Brixton who decides to make her way into society. As the book opens, Katherine is working in a moneylender's (shades of Clayton) and overhears a young nobleman borrowing money against future expectations.

Her first step up the slippery social slope is with the same young nobleman, Lord Algy FitzRufus (modelled on Innes Ker), who takes her to Paris for a weekend and from whom she learns such useful things as the way to eat oysters. After telling Lord Algy that they must never meet again, even though she realises she is in love with him, she leaves her job with the moneylender and becomes the private secretary of a leading member of society. Lady Garribardine (the model for whom was the redoubtable Lady Londonderry) is a penetrating portrait of a woman wise in the ways of the social world; she is one of the most realistic women Elinor ever created and for once she managed to give a female character three dimensions.

Katherine sets herself to become a lady by observation and by deliberately attracting Lady Garribardine's nephew Gerard, so that he can teach her the finer points of Renaissance art. Her cultural and social education virtually completed, this relentless character chances to hear a debate in the Lords, where her eye alights on the recently widowed Duke of Mordryn (whose pro-consular style and attention to minute detail, such as the choice of books for guests' bedrooms, are obviously modelled on Curzon).

Katherine finally gets her Duke and, unlike Elinor and Curzon, they live happily ever after. Unusually for Elinor, the book contains some very funny, if cruel, observations on the life and manners of the lower-middle classes, and it also tells much about her attitude towards Curzon before he made the final break.

The idea behind this cynical book was a favourite aphorism of Elinor's: 'It is wiser to marry the life you like, because, after a little, the man doesn't matter.' Ten years after it was published, Elinor wrote on the flyleaf of her own copy:

> At the time this book was written, to be an English Duchess was the height of any young woman's ambition. Now, of course all that has passed away. But the great lesson which the book still teaches is to make yourself the round peg before you aspire to the round hole – never try and force yourself into a position you are not fitted for. Make yourself fitted for it; then in justice you can shout and complain if you cannot obtain it. It is the shouting of the square pegs for the round holes which makes all the difficulty in life.

In April 1917, limbo disappeared in the wake of permission to visit the battlefields. Elinor had become accredited to Lord Riddell's *News of the World*, and also wrote for the Hearst newspapers. She returned to Paris and took a suite on the rue Cambon side of the Ritz.

Olivier made sure she had her favourite corner table, but the Ritz was full of expensively dressed women in silver foxes from both the beau- and the demi-monde. In the evening it was deserted, for everyone went to the Café de Paris or the Folies Bergère.

Pausing only long enough to have a smart khaki ensemble tailor-made for her (worn with a black and white chiffon veil), Elinor went to the battlefields in the Front line, and narrowly escaped death on several occasions. She was bombed on the road, and caught in artillery fire. But far worse was being made to shelter one night in a deep dug-out which brought on a very severe attack of claustrophobia. Afterwards she insisted on sleeping in the car or in a ditch.

In spite of her permits (she was there officially as a journalist), she was arrested at one point as a spy by the French, but her most moving experience was watching the bombardment of St. Quentin from the first floor of a deserted house, where she had bivouacked for the night. After one such tour, she wrote in her diary:

> As I returned to the car I passed once more the heaps of stones that marked the site of the shattered village and I noticed the pathetic evidences of family life protruding from the ruins – a poor old bedstead of iron, a sodden mattress and in one place the head of a child's toy horse. A curious feeling of stupefaction came over me and I looked up into the blue sky for relief. Then suddenly the air was rent with the distant thunder of battle beginning again towards the south.

The country for miles around and beyond Bailly was one vast desolation rendered the more piteous to look at by the contrast of the tender spring green of any bush and sapling which had chanced to escape the blast of shells. And not merely of shells. One of the things which enrage me the most was the wanton destruction of all the young fruit trees by the Germans before their retreat. For miles and miles the smiling innocent trees, their early bloom still on them, lay prone, hacked down out of pure malice and brutality.

The curious alternate depths and shallowness of Elinor's character are never more evident than in the concluding lines of this impassioned diary entry – in which she described her rage at discovering that a new Reboux hat had been dented.

When she was not touring the battlefields or trying to discover whether there was any truth in the many stories she had heard of German atrocities (there was), Elinor worked very hard at a war job, becoming Vice President of a society called the Secours Franco-Americain. This had been formed to re-settle refugees as soon as possible in the recaptured battle areas and enable them to start growing food again.

Elinor soon found herself in charge of building temporary huts in the district round Noyon. What with incessant travelling to and from the district, writing stories for the American press (which irritated Lucy profoundly) and entertaining such war leaders as Colonel Le Roy Lewis, the military attaché, and his assistant, Colonel Spears, to dinner at the Ritz, Elinor appeared happy and busy. But she had thrown herself into activity in order to forget the void left by Curzon. None of this was, in the end, enough and once more she escaped into a world where she was in control and so nothing bad could ever happen – the world of fiction. She started a new book, calling it *The Price of Things*.

It was now that Milner, a member of the War Cabinet and thus obliged to spend time in Paris, found in Elinor a sympathetic, sagacious and discreet ear. He became a regular at her corner table, and wrote ever more frequently when he was away.

There are no extant letters in 1918, but early in 1919 Milner was back in England writing to his 'dear Elinor'. A hint of jealousy and possessiveness crept into his letters, prompted by a letter from Elinor in which she mentioned an American millionaire and the newspaper proprietor Lord Riddell, to whom she had been introduced by the painter Sir William Orpen, who writes of Elinor in his memoirs:

. . . we had some very amusing out-of-door dinners at Laurent's. During dinner and afterwards, Mrs. Glyn would teach us many things about life, Nature and love: why women lost their loves; why men did not keep their wives; the correct way to make love; the stupid ordinary methods of the male; what the female expected; what she ought to expect, and what she mostly got. It was all very pleasant, the modulated voice of Elinor under the trees and twinkling stars. Her elocution was certainly remarkable and Lord Riddell's dinners excellent.

By April 1919, Milner had gone far further in revealing his feelings but they came as a great disappointment to Elinor, as she discussed in a letter to Margot and Juliet of April 12. It is an extraordinary letter for a woman to write to her young daughters.

Darling Pets – I am not coming until the 25th, if then – because Captain Milly [the family code-name for Milner] telephoned to Evangeline [Elinor] and asked her to wait until then, as he would have to be constantly out of London, and might even be sent for here.

He wants to take her into the country to see the Spring green – he wrote again this morning *exquisitely* sweet. He is the *queerest* creature living. I think he is determined not to tie himself up, but wants to have all he can get without. . . How will it end no one *could* tell. It looks like settling down into a tender friendship. Evangeline at all events is indifferent thank God, and is out now only to make her fortune . . . He personally loves Evangeline so passionately physically that he is afraid that at his age it would absorb his vitality, and that he *would* not be able to do his work, and would turn into a decrepit old man in a year!!! So that even if he could remove the barrier he still *fears* . . . So he wishes now to have only a tender friendship with her, principally by letter and *out of doors* so that temptation may be less . . . if you could have heard him telling Evangeline all this!!!! Very difficult to say, as you can think, and yet all the time clasping her in his arms!!

He said that the emotion a man felt for Evangeline must always be of such wildly physical nature, that it would be *impossible* for him to be moderate and balanced if she *belonged* to him he could never let her be away from him, and so would come disaster . . . is it not ironic? Afraid of what is his supreme joy, because of the physical reaction!

What do you say about it? Is not it a pity, since they could be *so* happy and he is such a *darling* to Evangeline, and pets and kisses her, and does all the Alastair [Innes Ker] silly divine tricks, and is passionately loving.

What a pity to be a fool!

By the end of August, 1919 Milner appeared to have come to a decision about the future:

> . . . My last letter was not '*camouflage*' but a genuine attempt to fit in thoughts and desires with what is attainable. Fate . . . but as long as I am there I can't neglect things. It is all for the country, and having given all the best of myself to that cause for two-thirds of my life, I am not going to relax my efforts in the last lap.
>
> As soon as I can possibly get through here, there is Egypt [Milner had been appointed Head of Mission to Egypt – by Curzon] . . . a more interesting job but a difficult one. If I could bring it off, it would be a good finish to my life's work for the Empire – and I should like to finish at that point, but one never knows. In this turmoil of the world, other calls may come, quite as imperative, and one may die in harness after all. All of which does not mean that we shall not see one another, and probably quite soon.
>
> When you and I meet, anything may happen . . . as far as I have a plan, and can shape things, I should like to steer our boat into the calmer waters of a friendship which need not suffer from the lapse of time, and let the more glowing past be quite a glorious memory . . . I think we have both at various times been of this view and come away from it.

Poor Milner. He had always been second-best . . . held in reserve by Elinor through the years of her affair with Curzon and only brought back into play after Curzon's final defection. Elinor was fond of him, but he was never a grand passion. Marriage to Milner, however, would have put Elinor back inside the pale and also might have 'shown' Curzon.

In spite of her preoccupation with her relationship with Milner, Elinor neglected neither her writing nor her war work. She was thrilled when America came into the war and it was suggested that she should visit the American base camp at St. Nazaire. Milner urged her to accept in order to try and make the Americans feel how much their help was appreciated by the Allies. So Elinor became an unofficial ambassador. She toured the base camps and also gave recitals from her books to the men in drill sheds and canteen huts, sometimes declaiming her piece *Destruction*, a dramatic and moving performance with Elinor standing alone on the platform dressed in black, in front of the American flag, one blinding white spotlight falling on her red hair.

Thus the country house recitatives which had been an entrée into society in the early days of her married life now came to be useful on a more important stage.

After a short visit to London to see Mrs. Kennedy, Margot and Juliet in July 1918, Elinor came back to Paris and continued to write her articles for the British and American press, and to finish her novel *The Price of Things*. She started a new work immediately, returning to an old vein: letters. This time from Elizabeth's daughter. It was so pro-American that Duckworth decided its publication in England would detract from the sales of *The Price of Things*. It was therefore serialised in Newnes' *Novel Magazine* and by the Hearst press in America, but never published in book form. The chief interest in the story lies in the acid comments Elinor puts into the mouth of Lady Ermyntrude (the daughter of the original *Elizabeth*) on the subject of the fading, middle-aged beauty of her companion, a red-haired, green-eyed authoress who had written a shocking novel called *Nine Months*. Elinor dramatised every slighest emotion but she could laugh at herself, too.

After the Armistice Elinor decided to move out of the Ritz and away from the distractions provided by the flood of friends now in Paris to celebrate. She needed seclusion to write commissioned articles on such subjects as *If I Were Queen* and *Is Chivalry Dead?* for the *Grand Magazine*, and accordingly she rented a flat at No. 23 rue du Peintre Lebrun at Versailles. Having spent many happy weeks completely re-decorating the new flat, she nonetheless still kept on her suite at the Ritz, so that she could see Milner whenever pressures of state business allowed. For the moment the future seemed propitious and serene. She was now in funds, Duckworths having brought out a cheap edition of her novels in the autumn of 1917; this million-copy edition, selling for 1s. 1d. provided a large new public for Elinor.

Her equanimity, now that the war was over and she was living near her beloved Versailles, may best be judged from a letter she wrote in March 1919 to Cynthia (Cimmie), Curzon's middle daughter, who was confused about the role she would be playing in the world. Elinor's reply embodied the philosophy she had developed, and the serenity which she thought was her portion, now that at last she had reached the calm waters of middle age.

Your letter touches me – it is sad – or to me it seems so. You know my theory of life is that we have had countless lives on this earth already, and that the soul of each one of us is evolving from just the life principle to a conscious being, aware of good and evil, and that until we become conscious beings, we only belong to the group-soul, and are not individual.

We are entirely responsible for every little single thing which happens to us. We have drawn it to ourselves by some previous action or strong desire of our own, so we can blame no one for any misfortune but ourselves.

The whole of life is a lesson, and until we have sense enough to learn the obvious one, which our intelligence could tell us – if we searched – is being taught us by the particular circumstances, fate will go on knocking our heads against the wall until we do grasp it.

As an instance of what I mean, I had to learn the lesson of humility and self-reliance in this life, so that I should not go on being arrogant as I must have been in my former lives. I had also to learn to stand alone, so fate has dealt me every blow to accomplish those two things, and all my young life I rebelled and thought I had 'bad luck' and so I never improved. But at last, after having to weep tears of *blood* I have learned the meaning of all that ever happened to me, and I reap the lesson from it, and lay up for myself *no further limitations*.

You are, to me, at the stage when you are first coming through into a conscious being – you are restless, you have aspirations for higher things and yet you have not yet evolved a scheme of action. So first we have to examine what is for good, that if we have been entrusted by God with a high position, we must not commit any action which could give a bad example.

That we should examine our own souls, and without glamour in the eyes, dissect our failings, weakness – want of justice – selfishness – whatever they may be, and keeping in mind that to hand back to God this loan of a responsible soul, elevated and not degraded by this life passage, must be our aim. We should then use all our will to curb and contrast everything which common-sense tells one could militate against this end. In this I am not suggesting all the old 'ticketed' virtues, half of which are now obsolete, but those qualities which common sense convinces us are necessary for the lifting of our own souls, and for the good of the community.

Thus to come to the concrete case of *you*. You were born with great beauty, great position, charm, riches, a certain amount of talent, a strong will – what huge gifts! What are you going to do with them? Drift on, doing no particular harm, but certainly no good?

The true socialism should be to help conditions so that every child has an equal chance until it comes to fifteen, say, and then sift the chaff from the corn and only admit the round peg to the round hole and not permit the square peg to force itself into the round hole.

Conventions were made to keep decencies together. No sensible person need observe silly ones, or ones out of date, but all *sensible* people *should* observe them enough not to outrage the sensibilities of refinement.

Your letter gives me the uncomfortable fear that an indifferent and inexperienced dressmaker is going to pick up a divine bit of silk, and reduce it to a dowdy rag instead of making it into a Queen's garment and I want to help to make the Royal dress!!

All that Elinor had hoped for herself, married to Curzon is, revealed ironically, to Curzon's daughter in this letter. For probably the only time in her life, she became 'Pallas Athene' in advising a woman (most of her advice had been lavished on younger men). She herself had finally learnt, in a very hard school, the value of detachment, if not of resignation.

iv *The Aristocracy of Dress*

If Elinor was trying to evolve a philosophy of life that would create a calm acceptance of the fate into which her temperament had led her, Lucy was in an entirely different mood during her independent years in America. Having always refused to listen to her husband or her partners and curb her expenditure, she became more intransigent than ever. In spite of her constant reiterations that she was there to make and save money, she insisted on living in a style which—even then—belonged to a more sumptuous age. Houses, rented for a brief summer season, had to be completely re-decorated before she would live in them. The silk flowers, the jewelled jade trees, the emerald lacquered walls, the antique furniture had to be perfect. To finance these schemes she leeched Lucile of capital. There would, she assumed, always be more.

The story of how Lucy squandered the business she had built up and the fame she had acquired is a sad one: it began with her estrangement from Cosmo over Bobbie which effectively removed Cosmo as a restraining influence in her life. Cosmo had kept Lucy on a personal allowance of two hundred dollars a week during her early days in America. In return, she was contractually bound to the company to create Lucile models. However Lucy had spotted a loophole. If she worked as 'Lady Duff Gordon' rather than 'Lucile' she could pocket the money. She also discovered sponsorship and began to lend her name to anything from a motor car to the products of a velveteen manufacturer. Her work for the *Follies* also brought her a supplementary income, for which she was paid in cash which she spent as soon as she had earned it mainly on household expenses that included seven indoor servants, five dogs, keeping Bobbie and three of his friends (including the music teacher), and throwing houseparties. She also had a full-time chauffeur and a sailor to look after her motor boat on the sound.

Naturally Cosmo and Miles, living in war-time London, trying to keep the business going, lectured her constantly on her selfishness. Tempers became even shorter when it was learned that Bobbie had been made Manager of the Flatiron model-making room. Lucy hired a devious American lawyer, by the name of Sullivan, and sent him to London to see what was going on. While he was there, he turned his coat and told Cosmo and Miles about the increasing (and expensive) influence on the business of Bobbie. Cosmo was very angry indeed.

In 1917, Lucy scored a tremendous success with a new venture, which seemed as if it would further her ambition to clothe the masses. As Lady Duff Gordon, she entered into a contract with Sears Roebuck to design mail-order dresses. Lucy rose to the occasion with a flower-and-fairy-covered catalogue with a 'message' to the women of America. She called it *Spring and Summer and the Well Dressed Woman*. 'I believe most of my inspiration comes from nature . . . and that is how I feel that women should dress – in harmony with nature.' So Lucy admonished her readers: 'When spring comes dancing over the little hills with its joyous promise of things to be, then it is time for us to put little, glad notes of colour into our clothes and make ourselves harmonious parts of the joyous theme of Spring.' This must have come as a revelation to the sturdy farmers' wives of the mid-West who were the backbone of the Sears Roebuck's customers. Lucy ended her whimsy on a more realistic note: 'If you choose the simple things, you may be sure you will never go far astray.'

The loss to Lucile of the income from this contract infuriated Cosmo and Miles. Worse, from their point of view, was to come. Late in 1917 Lucy began what was to become an extended business flirtation with a New York clothing manufacturer called John Lang Shuloff, who offered to buy into the business – and buy Cosmo and Miles out. In order to be able to do this, Lucy had to have proxies from enough directors to form a majority. This meant ranging her mother, Elinor and Esmé on her side (as she saw it) against Cosmo and Miles. Mrs. Kennedy and Esmé agreed, probably because they shared a fervent desire for a quiet life. Elinor acquiesced too, but then reneged, causing yet another row between the sisters. As a result, they did not speak again until 1919.

Lucy wanted to form a completely new company. Cosmo and Miles became threatening: they stopped dividend payments to Mrs. Kennedy and Esmé, made the lawyer Sullivan a director and sent him back to America to close down the Chicago house. This naturally incensed Lucy and led her to write fifteen-page letters to her mother and Esmé on the repetitious theme of the iniquity of Cosmo and Miles. So long were some of these letters (and so illegible) that the censor enclosed a note in one forwarded to Mrs. Kennedy asking her to tell Lucy to keep her letters short and to the point as it was a waste of time reading them. There was, the censor pointed out, a war on.

When America entered the war in 1917, the initial success of the Chicago house and the well-established prosperity of the New York establishment were not proof against the new mood of austerity in America at war and Lucile started to show the strain. Trade in Paris was virtually non-existent and London was faring no better. The one bright spot in an otherwise extremely gloomy picture was Toni Molyneux, now a Captain; when he was on infrequent leave from the Front, he continued to devote his time to Hanover Square, keeping the house going with his neat, unassuming designs using the only fabrics, such as serge and barathea, that were available. These deceptively simple designs were 'modern', the antithesis of the Lucile look, and they began to attract a new younger clientele.

Lucy was oblivious of the forces ranging against her as is shown in a letter she wrote to Esmé in early 1918:

> . . . I'm so sick of the way Miles and Cosmo have managed Lucile since I left. Toni's letter of fury about them has determined an action on my part that I've had in mind for some time. He says that their entire mis-management, everything, is ruining Lucile. Nicely have they broken my trust while I am away here making the models, working and fighting for them . . . their vile croaking of economy is ruining the fine business I left in their hands and trusted to them. . . . Toni says the dilapidation is awful there and in Paris, and he, poor tired wound-worn soldier is now fighting for me on his leave, the darling. The noble hero.

The row rumbled on, but eventually (at the end of 1918) Lucy had virtually run out of money, and Shuloff gained control. Together they bought Cosmo and Miles out of Paris, New York and Chicago, leaving them the London business. The name Lucile belonged to Shuloff and the London business was 'allowed' to use it. Lucy no longer owned the name she had made so famous. Thus Shuloff was effectively in control of Lucile – and of Lucy. Under this new contract she stayed on as a director on a fixed salary. She expected everything to remain the same, but within weeks she discovered that Shuloff and his colleagues were not to be bullied as easily as Cosmo and Miles.

Her extravagant design studio in the Flatiron building, always sacrosanct to her whims and fancies, was suddenly invaded by designers hired from wholesale houses. Their assignment was to create much cheaper dresses which could be sold in greater quantities. The pink satin underslips, the hand-made dresses, the boxes of flowers, the bolts of delicate silver and gold lace, the glimmering brocades were, almost overnight, things of the past. So were the happy hours spent draping and fitting and trimming a dress. Shuloff soon found there were snags in reproducing exquisite hand-made fantasy clothes on a large scale for 'the people', as Lucy had always referred to wholesale or mail order customers. In 1918 'the people' were not in the mood for cheap copies of Lucile dresses. The American business began to decline rapidly.

Lucy still had one outlet for her fantasies in the latest production of *The Follies*. There was a craze in New York at the time for 'Dearest' bracelets, and Lucy busied herself recreating 'Dearest' in what she called her 'Jewel Pageant'. The dresses she designed were embroidered with imitation diamonds, emeralds, amethysts and rubies. The show-girls also wore real jewellery. This and her flower pageant (in which the girls appeared in costumes inspired by marguerites and lilies) were triumphant theatrical successes, but they could not, in themselves, revive the flagging fortunes of Lucile.

Lucy now began to complain in letters home that she was lonely. The reason (though she never specified) was not hard to find: Bobbie had been called up when America entered the war and had eventually been commissioned in the 5th Engineers, in which regiment he was, appropriately, given the job of running the choir.

The terrible blow came in 1919. It ended Lucy's hopes and dreams about the future. Bobbie, now stationed in Washington, died very suddenly of influenza complicated by pneumonia. 'My heart is broken – my Bobbie died this morning,' Lucy wrote to her mother. 'The loss of his loving care and sympathy and his kindness and gentleness to me, and his complete understanding of my character is irreparable. I wonder what I have done to earn this supreme unhappiness . . . he was with me two weeks ago in all the brilliant beauty of his young manhood . . . oh, it is all incomprehensible to me . . . I can't write more . . .'

In her memoirs she wrote: 'He was only ill a few hours and died before I could reach him . . . when I got out of the train in Washington the entire platform appeared to be covered with coffins . . . there was only just space to walk between them.'

This was the end as far as Lucy was concerned. All she now wanted was to go back to Europe, a desire Shuloff encouraged, for obvious reasons. Free from her 'meddling' in the design studio, he could try and make the business work. The plan was for her to work on her designs either in London or in Paris. So, after four years, Lucy finally set sail for Europe at the beginning of 1919. She longed for the old days in Hanover Square, picturing the 'cars drawn up outside "Lucile" and everybody choosing gowns for Ascot'.

Looking upon her return as a triumph, she believed that she would be received as a queen might be welcomed back to her country, having concluded an advantageous treaty abroad.

It was not until she stepped off the boat, accompanied by Hebe and some of the other mannequins, that she began to consider, for the first time, how much things might have changed during the years of her absence.

Sir Cosmo, Esmé, Tiverton, her grand-children and her nieces had endured over four years of war. They had lost many of their friends and life would never be the same again. There would be other Ascots and other Drawing Rooms, but the old world she had known had indeed vanished for ever, as if it had been a dream.

Lucy spent a few weeks in England trying to pick up the threads, resting and paying a round of visits to friends and family, with the exception of Elinor, who was incommunicado in France. It did not take long for Lucy to realise that there was no obvious niche for her in post-war England. Cosmo was leading his own life; Esmé was living in the country and rarely came to town. By going to America in 1914, Lucy had virtually cut herself off from her sources of information and inspiration – the women who lived in the tiny fashionable world that moved from London, to Paris, and thence to the smart European resorts. These same women had now run war canteens, driven ambulances or worked in hospitals and they had become liberated from the tyranny of the corset and the yards and yards of clinging chiffon and lace that had been the outward expression of what has been described as a 'seductive servitude'. While Lucy concentrated on the 'aristocracy of dress', her erstwhile clients were doing men's jobs. She was still catering for an elitist way of life that had vanished forever in the trenches of Flanders.

Her age, too, told against her. Now fifty-six, her tastes and attitudes had been formed by late Victorian and Edwardian manners and modes. She failed to appreciate that, as the war drew to a close, women wanted to look forward, not back to the past. Lucy's dresses had been designed to complement the soft chiaroscuro of the Edwardian boudoir; the grandeur of a Belle Epoque Ballroom; the exaggeration of the music hall stage. They could not withstand the harsher, plainer ambience of the cocktail bar and the nightclub. As the lights of peace were lit, her world of opulence and seduction faded into a past that women were now keen to forget.

On her first visit to Hanover Square, the commissionaire did not know who she was. The old house was shabby after five years of war. The business was doing even worse than she had been led to believe. 'Everyone was in the midst of a wave of economy and people were buying as few clothes as possible. It was difficult to get silks, for half the looms in Lyons were idle and others had just re-started. The colours were very bad, and it took weeks to get orders executed.' Typically, Lucy completely failed to appreciate the dire consequences of the most devastating of all wars the world had yet seen.

She decided to go to Paris and run Lucile from the rue des Penthièvre. She was 'sure that Paris would still be interested in clothes. . . . I
told myself so many times on the train. The Parisian temperament,
always more volatile than the Saxon would, I thought, recover from
the after-effects of the war far sooner.'

But Paris too had changed. It was now that Lucy revealed how
distanced she had become from fashion development, for she attributed the new success of simple, elegant 'little' dresses, designed by
Chanel and other new couturiers such as Patou and Lanvin, to a
conspiracy to make these 'nothing' clothes in order to cut the cost of
production to the lowest possible limit.

'There must be no more "picture" dresses with trailing yards of
lovely satins and brocades . . . Every yard of material saved must be
looked upon as a yard to the good. It was,' Lucy imagined them
agreeing, 'the only plan to work on . . . the rue de la Paix is nothing if
not resourceful. It brought in the ideal of the "boyish woman". Here
was the perfect solution to the problem. Slight figures covered with
three yards of material, skirts ending just below the knees, tiny cloche
hats trimmed with a band of ribbon. No woman,' said a horrorstruck
Lucy, 'at least no woman in civilization, could cost less to clothe!'

Establishing herself, inevitably, at the Ritz while the little Pavillon
Mars was being redecorated by Elsie de Wolfe, Lucy at first refused to
go out into this new Paris. She stayed in her suite sulking and
complaining to her maid, Rachel. And then, fortuitously, Howard
Greer, her erstwhile design assistant, now demobilised and eking out a
living writing squibs for *The Theatre Magazine*, read of her arrival in
the Paris edition of the New York *Herald*. Losing no time in presenting
himself, he found Her Ladyship unchanged.

> There, in her usual patrician and languid manner, she lay upon a
> chaise-longue. Above a cool linen suit her flaming hair stood out
> like an aura. Horn-rimmed spectacles were tilted low upon her
> small nose and she peered over them in astonishment at me. Three
> pekingese and a chow thrashed across the carpet and threatened to
> annihilate me.

He also realised that she had no intention of changing.

> Like so many successful and creative artists, she believed that her
> own peculiar talent was everlasting. From frumps she had turned
> women into Marie Antoinettes at a bal masqué, and she saw no
> reason why they shouldn't go on that way.

'Do women think that their upper knees are attractive?' Lucy asked
Greer. 'This emaciated masculine look they're flaunting! Are they

trying to be men? Well, don't worry my poor Greer! We'll soon have them looking like ladies once again! They need me here!'

And so, complaining bitterly about how old-fashioned her pre-war town car was in comparison to the grand new Cadillacs she saw everywhere, Lucy, with Greer in tow, went once again to the rue de Penthièvre where, after admonishing her staff for their neglect of her business, she plunged into making her first post-war collection.

She decided, however, first to eliminate competition uncomfortably close to home. Toni Molyneux, who only a year before had been her hero, was still working at Hanover Square, where he had been achieving some success with his modern, sleek designs, so much so that the London business was looking – if not as prosperous as before the war – at least a little healthier. Summoning the unsuspecting Molyneux to Paris, Lucy gave him an ultimatum: either he design in the approved Lucile mode, or he would, she thought, find it happier working for someone else. He chose to leave and soon found backers, whereupon his spare simple clothes, of a ladylike simplicity and refinement, became extremely successful.

His dismissal was the coup-de-grâce for Hanover Square and the London business was wound up late in 1919, leaving Mrs. Kennedy – the original investor – with virtually nothing to live on. Had Lucy allowed Molyneux to continue, the name of Lucile might have become as relevant to the style of the jazz age as it had been to the Belle Epoque. It was possibly the most disastrous decision she ever made. Molyneux, however, bore no grudge and was extremely kind to his former patroness, up to her death.

Early in 1919, Lucy showed her new collection in Paris and *Vogue* reported it in minute detail as befitted the work of a couturier who still enjoyed pre-war réclame. The salon was crowded with polite English and French society. Elinor was there, as was Elsie de Wolfe (who had already partly defected to Chanel), and the French actress Cécile Sorel, whom Lucy had dressed before the war. *Vogue* reported that there were an 'extraordinary number of men present', eager no doubt to see Lucy's famous mannequins.

Outside, women were striding around in jersey suits and military greatcoats in navy serge. In the salon, in an atmosphere heady with tuberoses and winter violets, mannequins were mincing along on the purple carpet in hobble or panniered skirts.

v   *Versailles and After*

Thanks to her friend Lord Riddell, who gave her an accreditation as Special Correspondent in his newspaper *The News of the World*, Elinor was one of only two women present at the signing of the Peace in the Hall of Mirrors at Versailles in 1919.

> As I stood there upon the tottering bench, feeling that I must take care to be able to keep my balance, a sadness fell upon me. I did not want to see any more. It seemed as if the peace of the world must be as insecure as my own footing upon the bench had been.

Elinor managed to file a front-page background story for *The News of the World*.

WHERE BISMARK STOOD
Brilliant Scene as the Envoys Assemble
Contrast With Gathering of Fifty Years Ago
Hall of Mirrors, Versailles, June 28

Elinor's journalism was of a piece with her novels: careful observation coupled with a heightened sense of the dramatic. In this short feature piece she displays a care and attention to detail and a well-informed interest in the history behind the event that does her credit.

Paris in 1919 must have thrilled her for, with peace, social life had come back with a vengeance. If Congress danced the gavotte in 1815 in Vienna, the Peace delegation in Paris in 1919 danced to the new jazz and drank cocktails while they gossiped at the Ritz bar. Elinor was in her element that summer.

For Lucy, the Lady Muff Boredom years were over and she retreated more and more to the house she loved above all others – the Pavillon Mars – where she re-decorated in the pale Fragonard colours she now loved. Lucy spent many hours there dreaming of other days and happier times. She still enjoyed entertaining on a small scale and preferred to do it here in this environment which she felt suited her best. Her newest acolyte, Howard Greer, followed her to Versailles, moving into an apartment over a small garage not more than half a mile away.

They spent many happy days walking through the gardens of Versailles while Lucy told the attentive Greer anecdotes about the courtiers who had once walked, powdered and patched, on the tapis vert. 'They were not the stories one finds in the guidebook,' Greer remembered. 'They had nothing whatsoever to do with the statistics of marble or bronze or crystal used in the construction of the buildings. They had to do with intimate and sometimes shocking little tales about the personalities who moved through the crazy maze of the eighteenth and nineteenth centuries.'

Lucy had by now come to share her sister's belief in re-incarnation. In the supposition that she had in a previous existence been Rose Bertin, Marie-Antoinette's dressmaker and the first true couturière, she wafted around Versailles tapping along the corridors with her 'Tosca' stick. Pausing before a large painting of the queen, for instance, she would tell the adoring Greer how well she remembered the day she 'finished that dress for her Majesty! She was in such a sweet mood! How we laughed over the dogs that morning. What a divine dress! Do look at it closely. See how well I've blended the colours on the bodice! People don't appreciate beautiful things these days,' she would say, sighing.

Sometimes, though, the present intruded into these happy hours of make-believe. One rainy afternoon, the ill-assorted couple wandered into the Hall of Mirrors. In a far corner, a little man was working upon an enormous canvas. Lucy, never one to pass up an opportunity to give advice to a struggling artist, went up to him to look. 'Dear me,' she said to Greer in English. 'Why is he being so ambitious . . . some day he might do a little canvas and be quite good at it.' Then, to the painter, who had paused to blow on his red fingers she said, 'C'est exquis, Monsieur! Quelle beauté, vraiment!'

'Merci, madame,' he replied.

'Poor thing,' said Lucy. 'He probably hasn't enough to eat. Why don't we ask him to come home and have lunch with us?' Greer, playing his supporting role to perfection, nodded his head. Responding with thanks to the invitation (couched in Lucy's perfect French) and to the information that he was talking to Lady Duff Gordon of whom he had probably heard, the little man introduced himself in English . . . as Sir William Orpen.

Unlike Elinor, who still spent several days a week at the Ritz socialising and gossiping with the tidal wave of foreigners now pouring into Paris to discover the charms of a more exciting and civilised life, Lucy preferred the past. Wandering around Versailles as if in a dream, she found the eighteenth century a great deal easier to deal with than the problems of the present. She had, however, a ready-made social circle in her self-imposed isolation, for Elsie de Wolfe had moved back into the Petit Trianon and had re-established the salon that she had made famous before the war.

Lucy never turned down Cécile Sorel's Sunday afternoon salons in her apartment on the Ile Saint Louis. Here Lucy could indulge her taste for High Bohemia and intellectual discussions; she could also meet again the remains of the circle she had known and been fêted by in Paris before the war.

Another old friend, Isadora Duncan, re-entered her life. Meeting her at Sorel's, Lucy immediately invited Isadora to the Pavillon Mars the following Friday night, suggesting she should dance by moonlight in the garden, under the shadows of the great oaks painted by Le Notre. 'We'll give a big party . . . just as we did before the war . . . we'll ask lots of people,' Lucy told Greer who was, as usual, trailing along several moves behind her.

A hundred guests were invited; Japanese lanterns were suspended in the noble trees, trellises were re-painted. But Isadora omitted to turn up. The last guest left, and just as Greer was about to retire, Lucy having already done so, a motor-car drew up outside, put its brakes on too late and crashed into the garden wall.

Isadora had arrived.

'The entire Pavillon Mars rocked on its foundation,' wrote Greer. Running to the front door, he found Isadora (with an escort) reeling in a purple velvet cloak. Letting the cloak fall to the floor to reveal a Greek tunic of crimson chiffon, she demanded brandy. Lucy, re-appearing in a pink negligée, took in at a glance Isadora's condition. The impressionable Greer recounted what happened next: 'When Isadora finished her drink, she rose and walked toward the drawing-room doors that led into the garden. With both arms held high above her head and her eyes raised to the full moon, she said "I'm going to dance – alone – in your garden".' Pausing only to discard her chiffon tunic, Isadora stepped into the garden, nude, as her escort struck the first chords of a Schubert waltz on the piano. 'An unreal Isadora moved with unerring grace and skill. Her smooth white arms were lifted towards the yellow moon, a beatific expression took the place of the weary, slightly vague look which had stamped her face in the hard light of the dining-room. It wasn't alone the witchery of the night that laid its spell upon us . . . people might say that Isadora was getting fat; that she drank too much, that she was lazy; but upon this memorable night she transported us from an earthly house and garden to an imaginary Greek terrace of two thousand years before.'

Lucy's reaction was typical: 'I'm glad she didn't come when she was expected,' she told Greer. 'I'd have hated sharing that experience with a lot of people.'

By her Spring 1920 Collection, even Lucy was beginning to realise that she must change and she began to design sportsclothes. A tan leather aviatrix suit was exhibited at the Paris Air show of that year, 'an impudent and dainty mockery of masculine apparel'. Lucy was trying to acclimatise to this new world.

But the stage at the rue de Penthièvre was still hung with chiffon. The chandeliers still shone and their blue lights made a soft twilight in the crowded salon. 'Through it,' said *Vogue*, 'walked a procession of beautiful girls . . . all arrayed in clothes which were the epitome of the feminine, of lovely woman perfumed, powdered and adorned, artistic creations that are the products of aesthetic imagination combined with perfect handicraft.' In other words, nothing to do with fashion.

Vogue reduced the coverage they had traditionally accorded Lucile, headlining a meagre half page with the news that 'Lucile Finds Inspiration in Epochs of Romance'. In early June 1921, *Vogue* told its readers that 'Lucile is still Loyal to her Sprays of Softly Tinted Silken Flowers'. It was the last time they accorded her a major article. By the end of 1923 even faithful *Vogue* had consigned Lucile to footnotes and to small photographs of oriental evening dresses.

Lucy's eclipse was completed. She had gone out of fashion.

However, this exile was for a long time imperceptible, for Lucy and two powerful allies in her self-imposed mission to reconvert garçonnes into ladies. One was Elinor who – dining with statesmen and duchesses, moving from salon to musicale to ball – invariably wore Lucile clothes. She still chose to great effect, wearing black, emerald or purple, and she still possessed presence and elegance even though, in contrast to the neat spindly little new woman, Elinor must have looked somewhat like a stately ship in full sail. The other was Cécile Sorel, one of the most elegant women of her epoch. The star in the Comédie Française firmament, her interpretations of the classic roles in French literature were world famous. It was said of her in Paris that she had in her time played the part of so many queens that her manner in private life was as regal. Married to Elinor's old acquaintance from her debutante days, the Comte de Ségur, Sorel had the reputation for being careful . . . to the point of meanness. She and Lucy shared a consuming passion for grand decoration.

Even Elinor approved of Sorel, as she explained in a letter to her mother:

Sorel has a divine house and entertains all sorts of people – literary, artistic, actresses and people of the world – just the Bohemian milieu suited to L's tastes. She is impossible in the Grand Monde because she does not know how to behave, but in that one she will be received as a *great artist* not just as a dressmaker and have all the flattery she wants; her own Bohemian artist's milieu – only for the *first time* of the *best* class and not the people of the caste of troisième sexe and spies . . .

Sorel lived in a sumptuous apartment in the Quai Voltaire filled with eighteenth century furniture and bedizened with leopardskins – in its lushness it could have been described by Elinor in her *Three Weeks* mood. Lucy now began to dress her again, privately and on the stage, as she had done before the war.

Lucy, by now even more reclusive, was nevertheless persuaded to go to a first night to see Sorel as Célimene. Taking Greer as her cicisbeo, Lucy went to a great deal of trouble, unusual for her, to create a dramatic impression, dressing in trailing black chiffon with a black hat on her red hair which bristled with Bird of Paradise plumes.

Elinor's apartment in the rue Peintre Lebrun near Versailles was on the second floor of an old house situated halfway between the chic Hôtel de Réservoirs and the entrance to the palace grounds. Attended by her maid, Maria, Elinor wrote without interruption, surrounded by bibelots from the still-rented house in the Avenue Victor Hugo. Once a week she dined with Lucy at the nearby Pavillon Mars. The sisters still did not get on. They wrote constantly to their mother complaining about each other.

Greer recorded one terrible scene:

One morning . . . when Mrs. Glyn was up to her ear lobes in a new plot for her waiting public, her sister stopped by on her way to Paris. 'I can't take Fleurette into town with me,' she explained. 'The poor little thing is so unhappy when I'm working on a collection. Do you mind terribly if I leave her here?' Mrs. Glyn nodded absent-mindedly and replied 'Leave her with Maria'. Maria took Fleurette who was the tiniest whiniest Pekingese I ever gazed upon, placed her in the drawing room and promptly dismissed her from the mind. Her Ladyship went off to Paris, Mrs. Glyn went on with her romancing, and Maria went about her morning's work.

Unnoticed, Mrs. Glyn's chow, a vicious, enormous animal wandered into the drawing-room. Hours later Her Ladyship returned from Paris and when they began looking for little Fleurette, they found her in pieces and in many places. A bit of her tail had been tossed upon the mantel. A portion of one foot was on a divan. Odds and ends of her anatomy decorated footstools, rugs and window ledges. Her Ladyship exploded and Mrs. Glyn said she was sorry, most dreadfully sorry, but after all she wasn't the one who'd destroyed poor Fleurette.

Even this contretemps faded in time and the sisters declared a final armistice in the rivalry that had been going on for the last thirty years. Both lonelier now and facing futures that held less promise than they had done ten years ago, they turned to one another again as they had so many years before when neglected adolescents in Jersey.

Lucy was so preoccupied with the Paris house that she had little time for small grandchildren, a daughter now living quietly in the country and an estranged husband.

Elinor, too, had grown further away from her children during the years of war. She had virtually abandoned them to Mrs. Kennedy's care after the death of Clayton while she pursued Curzon and then a career as a war journalist in Paris. They had been brought up by their strong-minded grandmother and had developed into very serious girls, both interested in the new mood of feminism that had arisen during the war.

Margot had distinguished herself as a VAD, then as a clerk at the Woolwich Arsenal, then in the War Office. In 1918 she had become briefly engaged to General Groves, a man much older than herself, who then broke off the engagement. Mrs. Kennedy was, as ever, the conduit through which family news was channelled. 'I love to hear the chat of the girls,' Elinor wrote to her mother, 'and to know that they meet interesting people . . . do they make friends "on" as I used to do? I mean so that the people they meet at the places ask them on again.' In a letter dated December 1919, Elinor wrote about Margot:

Thornton [an American admirer] said she was the most beautiful creature he had ever seen in his life at the Victory Ball, but he thought that perhaps the world's problems bothered her brain a little too much. I asked him exactly what that meant and he said 'Well for anything as beautiful as that I am not sure that she is not just on the side of being too darned intellectual' . . . I hope she will let her beauty speak and not her brain on this visit, don't you?

That may have been Elinor's way; it was certainly not Margot's.

Juliet too had worked long and hard as a VAD during the war, and had met her future husband while nursing him. But Elinor knew nothing of this attachment and started matchmaking:

> Tell me darling Gran (I can't get either to answer) did Lord Woodhouse deliver the letter & how did J. like him? If he could screw up his courage to take it, he was going with the deliberate intention of seeing if they would suit in marriage – he had heard of her wonderful works and brain and wants a girl who will help him in his political career . . . He is awfully nice looking and a dear character with 'it' but a common voice – but one can't have everything . . .

Both girls were living with their grandmother in Shelley Court and saw their mother when she made brief visits to London. They were at the stage when they found Elinor and her attitudes highly embarrassing, and moreover she was very competitive when it came to their young men.

The rapprochement between Lucy and Elinor did not mean that the habits of their lifetimes had changed. Despite her publicly professed contempt for Elinor's grand friends, Lucy harboured some vestiges of well-concealed jealousy. When Elinor let slip that her 'friend' the Queen of Rumania would be having tea with her in her flat, Lucy angled for an invitation . . . telling her sister that she, too, had known the Queen as a pre-war client of Lucile.

The tea party went well. So well indeed that Lucy asked the Queen to tea with her at the Pavillon Mars the following Sunday. The intervening week was one of much preparation, particularly on the part of the hapless Greer who was pressed into action to paint all the wickerwork garden furniture in different colours to enable Lucy to arrange them in harmonious groups. Wicker chairs, stools and tables were painted in the Lucile colours of lemon yellow, dusty pink, periwinkle, jade green and mauve. Despite much bickering between the sisters about the correct way to receive the Queen, this party was a great success, marred only by Elsie de Wolfe's unexpected arrival with her house-guest, the ubiquitous sapphist Elsa Maxwell, who immediately asked the Queen to take pot-luck with them at the Petit Trianon. United for once, the sisters were relieved when Marie of Rumania told the insistent Elsa that she was already engaged for that evening.

And so the spring and summer of 1920 passed. Lucy went to the rue de Penthièvre two or three times a week but the business was doing badly. She wandered aimlessly – a ghost among ghosts – through the vast empty grounds and rooms of Versailles, re-tracing the footsteps of those mythical eighteenth century aristocrats whom she had learned about so long ago from her hated grandmother in 'dirty little Guelph'.

Elinor, on the other hand was full of the future. She had not entirely abandoned the idea that she might marry Milner, and they still wrote regularly. This hope had been encouraged by an invitation from Milner to visit Egypt, where he was then heading what proved to be the abortive 'Milner mission'. Elinor had many friends in Egypt at that time, one of whom was Lady Congreve whose husband was G.O.C. Possibly in the hopes of reviving Milner's old passion for her amidst the inflammatory surroundings of the pyramids and her favourite Sphinx, she accepted.

But, as with so much in those immediate post-war times, Egypt failed to live up to her expectation. The mysterious Sphinx, brooding alone in the limitless desert of her memory, was alone no longer. It was surrounded by little shacks and hoardings. Milner was preoccupied with his mission reporting back to Curzon who was now Foreign Secretary in London, and had little time and possibly little inclination for flirtatious meetings with Elinor. She was growing older and she knew it, although Milner retained enough gallantry to say that she shared, in common with the Sphinx, the apparent secret of eternal youth.

A month of this sufficed. Disappointed, Elinor returned to Versailles and the routine of writing, bickering with Lucy and occasional sorties to Paris. Money had, yet again, become a problem and Egypt had proved expensive. But in April 1920, she was invited to visit Spain by Queen Ena. Keen as ever to see a new country, she spent a month with the royal family. Easter Week was passed in Seville. Had she but realised it, she was a witness to the last days of the only court in Europe that, in its formality, even approximated to Versailles in its heyday.

She wrote a travel book (which was eventually published in 1924) about her visit and also started to work on a novel which would be set in the romantic gardens of the Alcazar in Seville, but this never came to fruition, for on her return to Paris in 1920 she was swept up in another adventure.

A letter from her agent, Hughes Massie, awaited her, telling her that Miss Mayo, a representative of the film company Famous-Players-Lasky, was in Europe. She was interested in recruiting Elinor to the stable of well-known European authors then being brought to Hollywood at the bidding of Jesse Lasky, to write original scenarios, or to adapt their books for this still-new medium.

Lasky had been prompted in this idea by the example of the visionary producer Samuel Goldwyn, who had set up what he endearingly called *Eminent Authors Inc.* Goldwyn having cornered the market with native American talent, Lasky determined to go one better and scour Europe. Accordingly Maurice Maeterlinck, Somerset Maugham, the playwright Edward Knoblock and Elinor's old friend Gilbert Parker had already signed.

The prospect of going back to America to work in this unknown medium intrigued Elinor. She had a brief acquaintance with film. *The Reason Why* had been filmed as a silent two-reeler in 1915 and she herself had been filmed by George Eastman while de Laszlo was painting her in 1912.

In spite of her snobbery, Elinor had an inquiring mind. Besides, what was there left for her in Europe? Both her daughters were living their own lives in England. She herself was living, if not in penury, at least in reduced circumstances in a small apartment. Her romance with Milner was fading. Though she was still invited to grand houseparties or to travel abroad, she was realist enough to admit to herself that these invitations would operate under the law of diminishing returns, as old friends died off.

A fresh start in a new world seemed to offer the brightest prospect. One evening at dinner with Lucy she revealed the plan in a typically off-hand manner to the stage-struck Greer. 'I'm so fatigued after a day in town,' she told him. 'I've been hours with one of those extraordinary Americans. A man from the far end of the world, mind you. California! It would seem they make motion pictures there . . . isn't it amusing? they want me to go to Hollywood to help them make films.' 'Who is going to star in them?' asked Greer, extremely inpressed. 'They have a girl whose name, I believe is Gloria Swanson . . . they want me to teach her how to act like a lady. Of course it would be amusing,' said Elinor. 'And the money – I may be tempted . . .'

Finally, at the end of 1920, the protracted and complex negotiations were complete and Lasky invited Elinor to go to Hollywood and study the technical and other problems of moving pictures in the studios. She was then to write a scenario to be made into a film and herself to supervise its production. For this she was to receive ten thousand dollars, plus travelling expenses, plus the prospect of the renewal of the contract on better terms if the picture should succeed.

At fifty-six, Elinor had lost none of her zest and she accepted. She packed up her apartment and left for a new world and a new medium in which she would have to compete with experienced professionals half her age. She wrote to her mother the night before she left:

> I want to think of you as perfectly happy darling and surrounded by warmth and love while I am out fighting for riches in this glorious adventure. I am looking forward to it more than I can say, and am going full of hope and confidence with the spirit free and strong.

FANTASY

(1920–1929)

'This was a new Queen to worship
and die for, if necessary.'

Three Weeks

i 'Madame Glyn'

'If Hollywood hadn't existed, Elinor Glyn would have had to invent it,' wrote Anita Loos, already established as a writer in the film colony when Elinor arrived there at the end of 1920.

Elinor tackled Hollywood as if she were a queen come to re-claim a barbarous province that had got out of hand. Somewhere between New York and Los Angeles, 'Elinor Glyn' became 'Madame Glyn', and the tired middle-aged woman – with precarious finances, an interesting 'past' and an uncertain future – became a self-confident haughty aristocrat, with a thousand years of 'race' and civilisation in the crook of her little finger. 'Madame Glyn' was Elinor's finest part, and it ran and ran.

Elinor arrived in Hollywood at exactly the right time. Having recently recovered from the Fatty Arbuckle scandal, the film colony was in the process of mending its ways, minding its manners (in public at least) and generally cleaning up its act. So the advent of a 'real' English aristocrat seemed to endorse the new high tone of tinsel town. What Elinor found, when she descended from the train at Pasadena, was a small provincial town of one and two-storey pepper-pot Spanish houses surrounded by orange groves. Being Elinor, she lost no time at all in checking into the best hotel the town had to offer.

This, to a woman accustomed to staying at the Ritz as if by divine right, must have come as a shock. It was a 'fifth-rate, rambling barn-like establishment known as the Hollywood Hotel,' recalled Charlie Chaplin in his autobiography. 'It had bounced into prominence like a bewildered country maiden bequeathed a fortune. Rooms were at a premium, only because the road from Los Angeles to Hollywood was almost impassable and these literary celebrities [Elinor and her fellow authors] wanted to live in the vicinity of the studios. But everyone looked lost, as if they had come to the wrong address . . .'

Elinor wasted no time in getting on the right side of Miss Hershey, the eighty-year-old owner of this former boarding house. Anita Loos remembered that Elinor's first move in Hollywood, after decorating

her two rooms with purple pillows, pagodas and tiger skins – was
to

> establish a salon . . . on Sunday afternoons she invited us all to her
> suite in the hotel for tea (tea!) during which she lay on a tiger-skin
> rug, wearing Persian pyjamas in the pastel shades made famous by
> her sister Lucile, and recited poems of Shelley and Swinburne to
> which, for good measure, she added Ella Wheeler Wilcox. A
> favourite line from the latter was 'Smile and the world smiles with
> you, weep and you weep alone' recited in lugubrious tones that
> precluded any attempt at smiling.

Having made a start on refining Hollywood, Elinor then turned her
attention to the Famous-Players-Lasky studio, where work was
beginning on her scenario, *The Great Moment*. At first she was
disappointed. For Lasky, having copied Goldwyn's idea of importing
authors to Hollywood as what Sheridan Morley has described as
'literary window dressing', really did not have the first idea as to
how to employ their talent.

At first, the writers spent their time being lionised, starring at
dinner parties rather than writing scenarios. Sam Goldwyn met Elinor
at a party given by Douglas Fairbanks and Mary Pickford. He was
impressed:

> One evening before dining at the Fairbanks home Douglas took
> me out for a walk through his beautiful grounds. As we came to
> the famous swimming pool I caught sight of a woman seated on
> one of the stone benches and gazing pensively into the water. The
> evening sun caught in reddish hair – whether these tresses are a
> gift or an acquirement is often a theme of speculation – and in
> girlish folds of sea-green chiffon. And as the woman lifted her eyes
> I saw that these, too, were sea-green.
> 'That's Elinor Glyn,' whispered Fairbanks; 'she's dining with us
> tonight.'
> In a spirit of great curiosity I began my conversation with the
> Circe-looking woman to whom sun and pool and sea-green chiffon
> lent an atmosphere of which she herself was perhaps not altogether
> unconscious. She was exceedingly gracious and cordial, but as she
> talked, I could not help making a few inward observations on her
> manner of speaking. She has the trick, so I found, of convincing
> you that her voice is some far-away mysterious visitant of which
> she herself supplies only a humble and temporary instrument of
> escape.
> For example, when she remarked, 'Isn't this pool beautiful?' It

sounded like some lonely Buddha's prayer echoing down through the ages from the far heights of Tibet.

Goldwyn invited her to a very exclusive dinner party to celebrate the completion of Charlie Chaplin's film, *The Kid*. Elinor, who was to become a close friend of Chaplin's, put her foot in it on this occasion. When the film finished, she announced in her grandest manner that it was 'the finest film I have ever seen in my life!'
'Have you seen many?' Chaplin asked.
'Well . . . no. This is my first.'

Elinor worked very hard indeed on her first script, *The Great Moment*, and gave the studio a strong story. Passion, romance, danger, unmarried love and rattlesnake bites all contributed to the drama and there were plenty of vivid scenes based on her own observations culled from her trip long ago to the mining town in Nevada.

The commotion she created when she found that Valentino, whom she had been promised for the lead, was not available was as nothing to her reaction to the treatment she got when she went to the studio to help make the film.

All they required was the use of my name to act as a shield against the critics. Every person connected with the production studios, although few had travelled as far as New York, and many were all but illiterate, was absolutely convinced that he or she knew much better how to depict the manners and customs of whatever society or country they were attempting to show on the screen, than any denizen of that country or society . . . when I arrived, spittoons were still being placed in rows down the centre of a set which was supposed to be the Baronial hall of an old English castle, while an actress taking the part of an early eighteenth century French marquise [Gloria Swanson] was encouraged to wear her hair in the exaggerated golliwog style then prevalent in Hollywood.

The director, Sam Wood (a man who divided his time equally between fairly pedestrian film directing and his deals in real-estate), despised the work of this interloper who, he felt, was not part of the close-knit film community. This encouraged his continuity writer, who enjoyed himself cutting Elinor's script into pieces. They next decided to treat the film as a knock-about farce in order, rather curiously, to increase the suspense.

Elinor stayed in her rooms at the Hollywood Hotel sulking and writing long letters to her mother while the film was shot without her. But one day toward the end of production, chancing to be on set, she heard Sam Wood audibly despair of finding the right dénouement, while pointedly ignoring Elinor.

As it happened, Cecil B. de Mille was walking by and overheard the conversation. Catching his eye, Elinor pounced. 'I felt that he had seen the joke, and greatly encouraged I ventured to propose that – perhaps – the author might be able to help a little by suggesting the end!' de Mille laughed, and became one of Elinor's most fervent supporters in and out of the studio. She was allowed to re-write the ending and put back some of the characterisation lost in the comedy.

The Great Moment was completed in August 1921 but Elinor had reservations about its final form, as she revealed in a letter to her mother:

> . . . know that I am not responsible for the set of the boudoir scene in Washington (vile bad taste and muddled) nor for Miss Swanson's awful hair in that scene, with the two Chinese fans in it!!!! . . . Nor am I responsible for the fearfully vulgar get up when she looks like a cook as she becomes engaged to Hopper . . . All common and awful and the vulgar plush curtains!!!!

Elinor did not confine her reservations to her mother's attention. At a screening of *The Great Moment* Goldwyn said:

> I can truthfully say that never in my life have I enjoyed any film so heartily. This was due, not to the character of the performance, but to the remarks which garnished its entire unfoldment.
>
> 'See that frock,' whispered the author eagerly, as sitting beside me, she pointed to one of Gloria's creations; 'I designed that gown.'
>
> Another second and she was calling attention to the finish of a certain setting. 'Do you see that? An exact copy of my rooms in London. Do you suppose they would have known how to arrange a gentlewoman's rooms if it hadn't been for me?'

But there were other times, Goldwyn remembered, 'when this robust mood of self-congratulation shifted to a minor chord. 'Ah, how terrible, how shocking!' I heard her moan several times. '"All wrong, all wrong – they've ruined that scene. I might have known it. I was away that day, you see."'

Most of Elinor's fellow-authors, brought to Hollywood to elevate its 'tone', could not stand the indifference of the directors towards their work. Somerset Maugham lasted nine days. Maeterlinck, having written an unsuitable story about small boys and fairies at the bottom of the garden, little more. But Elinor, happy in this new environment and shrewdly realising that in many ways the Hollywood experts were right to discount the established writers if they refused to adapt themselves to the new medium, began to watch and to learn. Unlike many of her fellow-authors, Elinor could view her material from what came to be known later as the 'screen angle'.

She told Gloria Swanson, who had now become a close friend:

> You children don't realise yet what has happened, I know. But you will. Motion pictures are going to change everything. They are the most important thing that's come along since the printing press. What woman can dream about a prince anymore when she's seen one up close in a newsreel? She'd much rather dream about Wallace Reid [a top star of the time]. People don't care about royalty any more. They're much more interested in queens of the screen, like you dear.

Gloria Swanson took up Elinor.

> Her British dignity was devastating. She was the first woman I'd ever seen wearing false eyelashes and although she was old enough to be my grandmother, she got away with it. She had small, squinty eyes and took tiny steps when she walked. Her teeth were too even and white to be real; she smelled like a cathedral full of incense, and she talked a blue streak. Her hair was the colour of red ink and she wore it wrapped around her head like an elaborate turban. She was something from another world.

Anita Loos was less impressionable:

> . . . for all her pretensions to a Mayfair background she belonged, heart, body and soul, to Hollywood . . . her appearance was bizarre; the make-up she wore might have been scraped off the white cliffs of Dover, and it provided a startling contrast to her dyed red hair, green eyes and mouth of vivid crimson. She jangled with long earrings, economically set with second-rate gems.

The film set worked hard, but they played hard too, especially at weekends when there were no early calls. Elinor began to join in. She had always loved dancing and often made a foursome with Gloria Swanson and two young men to visit such popular haunts as the Patent Leather Room in the Ambassador Hotel, or the rowdier Vernon Country Club which, run by gangsters, was the centre of drug-dealing in Hollywood. Elinor would sweep in, trailing chiffon and refinement, smiling at the ever-present newspaper cameras.

Once *The Great Moment* became successful, Elinor claimed her crown. Not that of queen, for it already belonged to Mary Pickford, but of dowager-empress. 'She took over Hollywood,' said Gloria Swanson:

> She went everywhere and passed her fearsome verdicts on every-thing. 'This is glamorous' she would say. 'That is hideous' she would say, as she baby-stepped through this or that dining room or garden party. People moved aside for her as if she were a sorceress on fire or a giant sting ray.
>
> After Herbert [Swanson's second husband] moved out of my life, Elinor got in the habit of taking me with her on her social rounds . . . going places with Elinor was never dull.

1921 was an eventful year for Elinor in a personal as well as pro-fessional sense, for both Margot and Juliet married, Margot to Sir Edward Davson and Juliet to Sir Rhys Rhys-Williams. Both men were much older than the girls. Rhys-Williams was over thirty years older than Juliet. It is a matter of family rumour that Elinor refused to attend either wedding, thoroughly disapproving of the disparity in ages. Milner, in a letter to Elinor of February 10, 1921, took the charitable view:

> I fancy you have decided not to come for the wedding [Juliet's] and though this is hard for you, I dare say you are right, for having faced so much boredom and discomfort to get your American show properly started, it would have been too great a sacrifice to risk its being spoiled owing to your absence at a critical time . . . I only hope your American enterprise will in the end free you from all further need for amassing money . . . living where you like in your dear Versailles or some spot of your own choosing . . .

This was one of the last letters Milner wrote to Elinor. Later that February, he retired from the government and, two days later, wrote to her of his plans:

> . . . I am about to make another great change in my life, which will perhaps lead you to say that I have only gained my freedom one day in order to surrender it the next! I am going very shortly to be married, which is, I know, an absurd thing to do at my age . . . I hope the Tiger may not look upon the Elephant as now so domesticated as to be quite uninteresting, but that we may still have many opportunities of exchanging ideas about books and men in that free spirit and with that mutual understanding which always made us such good company to one another . . .

These blows were softened for Elinor by the fact that she had made a group of new friends in Hollywood led by Douglas Fairbanks and Mary Pickford. Their 'gracious' life at Pickfair and their status of uncrowned king and queen of Hollywood appealed to Elinor, who had always collected royalty – whether of the silver screen or of a real country made little difference.

Charlie Chaplin became a friend, too, and, being English and working class, was fascinated by Elinor's airs and graces. But, being Chaplin, he also regarded her with some dispassion. One day, for instance, he observed her watching a scene being played. Films in the early silent days were lit by Cooper-Hewitt mercury vapour lamps; these banks of purple lights cast a weird glow over the set and they also turned Elinor, powdered with thick white paint, green and her teeth (which were false) mauve. When Elinor opened her lips to smile, Chaplin shrieked with laughter.

Elinor loved going to parties in Hollywood – relishing both the rather stuffy, selected groups at Pickfair and the rowdier crowd she found at Marion Davies' beach house. Amateur theatricals and charades were then popular and Elinor joined in with alacrity.

> Charlie [Chaplin] drew me as his partner and from the bowl I picked our subject, which was 'Hate'. Our turn was last and as all the rest had treated their themes in a comic vein, Charlie decided that we would be serious. By some magic, he got himself up into an alcove behind which the supports of the window appeared like a cross. He wore nothing but a cloth twisted round him and spread out his hands as if crucified. I knelt, draped in a white sheet, at the foot of the alcove to represent the Mourning World, while Charlie's Japanese servant lit up the whole scene with a single candle, held low from the side, where he could not be seen. The room was otherwise in darkness and the effect was extraordinarily moving. I remember the sudden reverent hush as the audience first saw his face, so wonderfully filled with agony and resignation.

William Randolph Hearst's mistress, the witty, pretty, blonde, ex-Follies girl Marion Davies (who had known Lucy well during her New York days), was the means by which Elinor met Hearst, the most important friend she would have in Hollywood. He had, over the years, published serialisations of her novels, but the two had never met before. Marion was fond of Elinor – in *Show People*, Marion's funniest film, directed by King Vidor, Elinor made a superbly regal walk-on appearance. W. R. Hearst also seems to have appreciated her and (what was more important to Elinor) took her at her own valuation. She was frequently asked to San Simeon for the weekend, sometimes accompanied by Chaplin.

San Simeon must indeed have seemed like a parody of the country houseparties of Elinor's youth, containing as it did furniture, panelling, painted ceilings, complete Tudor rooms looted from Europe and now lying about in packing cases. While San Simeon did not have the refinement of an Easton or a Hackwood, Hearst's guests were drawn from the ruling elite of Hollywood and Elinor felt herself to be in her element. She was a great admirer of her host who was, like most of the men to whom she had been attracted, powerful and decisive. He advised her on business matters – sometimes she listened and sometimes she did not.

Even though Elinor played hard, she worked long hours in the film studio. She would often retire early to work on next day's scenes or to read Plato or Herodotus in order to keep a distance between herself and what she called 'The Californian Curse' which she diagnosed as

> . . . nothing less than that of the Evil Fairy . . . able to banish the real personality of those whom she bewitched, forcing them against their wills to carry out her commands, to forget the land of their birth, the purpose of their journey and many of the principles which they had hitherto held most dear.

Elinor was not sufficiently inoculated by Plato, however, to escape the curse entirely; '. . . a sense of exaggerated self-importance . . . a great desire for and belief in the importance of money . . . a loss of the normal sense of humour and proportion and finally, in extreme cases the abandonment of all previous standards of moral value'.

The Great Moment finished and the scenario for her second film for Lasky, *Beyond The Rocks*, accepted, Elinor felt able to return to Europe for a holiday. She sailed to France on board the *Olympic* in September 1921 with her new friends Douglas Fairbanks and Mary Pickford who were accompanied by Mary's 'kind-hearted vulgar mother'.

Lucy and Esmé were at the station in Paris to meet Elinor but in spite of this warm welcome from part of her family, she was still estranged from her daughters and wrote to Mrs. Kennedy, asking where Margot was. 'If she is still in France, I hope she will come to see me . . . fondest love to Juliet if she is in London . . . I dare say the thought of my coming fusses [her] so I am not going to bother the darling unless she wants me. We are not sentimental and love makes us understand.'

By the middle of December, Elinor was back in Hollywood and
Beyond The Rocks was already shooting. Elinor had the same director,
Sam Wood, and wrote to Mrs. Kennedy that she 'found it touching
to see the joy of everyone in the studio to see me . . . quite touching!
Now that their wounded vanity at a stranger coming in with new
ideas has quietened down, they feel that I am their chief and one of
the family who is going to win their game for them.'

Beyond The Rocks starred Gloria Swanson and Rudolf Valentino
'. . . he is an Italian, extremely dark so they are putting in that his
mother was "French" to account for it!!'

Gloria Swanson remembered:

> Everyone wanted *Beyond The Rocks* to be every luscious thing
> Hollywood could serve up in a single picture; the sultry glamour
> of Gloria Swanson, the steamy Latin magic of Rudolph Valentino,
> a rapturous love story by Elinor Glyn and the tango as it was
> meant to be danced by the master himself . . . Elinor introduced
> historical flashbacks so that Rudy and I could wear costumes of
> some of the most romantic periods of European history . . . For
> the tango sequence, the wardrobe department made me a gold-
> beaded and embroidered lace evening gown so shimmering and
> beautiful that moviegoers talked about it for the next year. I also
> wore a king's ransom in velvet, silk ruffles, sable, and chinchilla
> all dripping from shoulders to floor with over a million dollars'
> worth of jewels.

Elinor was not as enthusiastic.

> Ye gods! The clothes. Full evening dress, bare arms, feathers and
> jewels in the hair of the ladies and feather fans! For a simple evening
> in a Swiss Inn up the high mountains amidst snow!!

Of course, Elinor and Valentino got on well. Each day Elinor, Sam
Wood and sometimes her maid, Maria, would lunch at a restaurant
called Armstrong's to discuss the psychology and action for the
afternoon shooting and often Valentino would take Elinor dancing
in the evening – a curious duo.

Beyond The Rocks takes place in France and England; Elinor was in
her element correcting the naivety of the director and designers.
Appalling rows broke out, but Elinor usually got her way down to
the minutest detail:

> They had never heard of powdered footmen, and I had to argue
> with the head property man about it . . . he wanted them to wear
> wigs!!! Then I had to paint their hair myself with wet stuff . . . It
> is a pity Miss Swanson is such a marionette and so common but

the public adore her. She has a 'sex charm' which attracts the men – you will loathe her in the part.

Beyond The Rocks was finished at the beginning of February 1922 and (perhaps because Elinor showed Swanson and Valentino how to make love 'in the European manner' – by kissing palms, rather than backs of hands) the film was a huge commercial success, to the point where the distributors were advised to 'boom the author'.

Elinor's contract with Famous-Players-Lasky was now completed and she was finding it less easy than she had thought to start a third film. She had finished a new book *Man and Maid* – by March she was reading the proofs. 'Then I am to see if Lasky will buy the picture rights . . . I am getting so fed up with everything here,' she told her mother. 'The uncertainty, the delay about everything, the cheating and lying that I am going to just write stories and not bother to supervise any more.' The real problem in negotiations for a new contract was Elinor's inflated idea of her own value. Fairbanks and Pickford had wanted her to write a picture for them, but she asked for too much money. Lasky turned down *Man and Maid* for the same reason. Just when she was planning a strategic retreat to New York, Metro-Goldwyn-Mayer offered her a contract to supervise the filming of *Three Weeks*. Elinor was triumphant. She had always hoped that, some day, someone would make a film of her bestseller and she accepted this tempting new offer without consulting her advisers . . . and, as she had done so often in the past, negotiated a very bad deal for herself.

Three Weeks was not scheduled to begin shooting until the end of March 1923, and she therefore decided to make a short trip to England, being reconciled to her daughters, both of whom had presented her with grandsons – Geoffrey Davson and Glyn Rhys-Williams. She stayed with her mother in Shelley Court and also found time to flit over to Europe, where she re-occupied her house in the Avenue Victor Hugo and went to Cannes with Margot for a short holiday. She also went to Scandinavia, at the invitation of the Anglo-Swedish Literary Society, to give a series of lectures on such subjects as 'Woman's Place in Modern Civilisation', 'Discipline' and 'Marriage Customs' – on all of which Elinor was, as ever, eager to give advice.

Elinor found time to give a great many interviews. She even won over the young journalist and leading Bright Young Thing, Beverly Nichols, himself a sceptical member of the jazz age.

I liked her enormously. If there was ever any occasion on which I found myself forced to use that nauseating word 'Queenly' it would be now. She is 'Queenly'. She ought to have been born on some dark evening when Balkan thrones were tottering like scenes on the backcloths of our less draughty London theatres. She ought to have been hustled over the waters of the Ishky-Repoka by faithful nurses, while grizzled prime ministers faced bloody men who demanded a new regime. She ought to have grown up among surroundings of crepe and asphodels. And then, one day, she ought to have returned in a golden chariot, driven toward a beflagged palace, walked slowly down immense corridors, stood on a throne and started a world-war in a girlish caprice.

'It seems a great pity,' Nichols summed up, 'that such a fiery personality should have caused only ink, and not blood to flow.' What he did not realise was that Elinor was going back to a country over which she reigned as dowager empress. It was a shadow-play country, lit by Cooper-Hewitt lights, where life only ran to three reels — but there, for the time being, she had a make-believe throne and could find contentment.

Lucy, left behind at Versailles, was growing restless again. Lucile demanded less and less of her time as the business slowly descended in almost exact ratio to the ascent of her erstwhile protégé Molyneux. She was beginning to be forgotten and very often she had only the sycophantic Greer for company in her exquisite little house.

Her old friend Elsie de Wolfe was busy adjusting to the jazz age, going out every night in knee-length diaphanous dance frocks from Chanel, shingling her hair, and bustling about decorating apartments and châteaux for the Americans coming to Paris. Lucy refused to admit there was any virtue at all in this new world of jazz music, chemise dresses and cocktails – and she drifted, becalmed on a sea of regrets and envy.

Lucy wearied of the Pavillon Mars and rented a small villa in Ville d'Avray, overlooking the lake where Corot had painted so many of his landscapes. The villa was in a very dilapidated state, for it had not been lived in since before the war. Leaving Greer as the unpaid caretaker and dog-minder, Lucy went to England for the Christmas holidays, intending to start work on it in the spring.

On her arrival back after Christmas, she found Greer living in the local hotel, whence he had decamped, with flu, from the damp unheated villa, and the dogs dead or dying, having perforce been abandoned by him. They never spoke again.

In 1923, Lucile finally went bankrupt, and Lucy fled to England. She was sixty years old. On arrival in London, Lucy drove straight to the Ritz. Cosmo came to see her the next day. 'Unfailingly kind as he always was, he had to confirm my fears. Nearly all my capital had been swallowed up.'

Lucy of course blamed her partners. 'It was only when the hard-headed "business men" came into it that it all collapsed.'

She could not afford the Ritz and took a temporary furnished flat in Park Place. It was here that she received a potential acolyte in the Molyneux mould. His name was Norman Hartnell and he appeared with some of his sketches. In his memoirs he professed himself unimpressed:

> . . . on entering a stuffy, dimly-lit room I found this celebrated lady to be rather advanced in years. A green and silver tissue turban surmounted a wealth of bright red hair which drooped down on either side of her face 'like a couple of fire escapes' I thought to myself. She pulled down the rather ugly lampshade of stretched green silk until it was only a few inches away from the beetroot-red chenille cloth that covered a small circular table. Then she whipped out horn rimmed lorgnettes and closely examined my dress designs under the glaring light.

Hartnell waited some time to hear from Lucy who had warned him that she would first have to reach a decision about his salary. She retained his designs, and he was at first excited to see one of them published in *The Sketch*, illustrating a weekly piece (her 'Dorothy' column) written by Lucy.

He wrote to her telling her how glad he was that she liked his work and 'when exactly did she propose that we start our business association. No answer came. I waited and wrote again; still no answer.'

Then another sketch appeared, and another. Hartnell sued and settled, on the advice of his solicitor, for £50 and costs.

Perhaps he might not have been so censorious if he had known the desperate state of Lucy's finances. Her weekly 'Dorothy' columns provided her only income. Her granddaughter, Lady Flavia Anderson, remembers her:

> sitting up in bed when I arrived on a Saturday struggling with her attempts at journalism in her 'Letters to Dorothy.' The newspaper for which she wrote had to have delivery of her article by a certain time each week. Sometimes my grandmother was at a loss as to what was new to write about. Anyway, the discipline of having to produce an article was hard on an aging woman.

Lucy used to take her granddaughter on expeditions to Pontings and Barkers to research her articles, written to advise the working girl how to dress better and to be more attractive. 'Together Gaga (as her grandchildren always called her) and I would gaze through the windows,' Lady Flavia remembers, 'and she would say "We must get Dorothy into Russian boots, they keep the legs so warm in winter".'

But the longing to design still remained: 'I used to read of the new fashions that Paris was launching,' Lucy wrote, 'and attend other designers' mannequin parades with an absolute longing to be back in the studio once more. I felt my life incomplete with my one special gift lying idle . . . I could never walk through the big stores and see yards of materials, silks, chiffons and velvets without a feeling of homesickness for the studio. I was like an artist shut away from his colours, or a violinist deprived of his violin.'

Elinor's success in Hollywood did little to help matters. Lucy admitted in her memoirs that she was 'almost envious of my sister Elinor Glyn who was making cinema history in Hollywood. She was perfectly happy finding self-expression in the work she loved. Her letters to me were full of enthusiasm.' Sometimes this subterranean envy, so much a feature of both the sisters' lives, bubbled to the surface. Lady Flavia remembers that when she was

> about twelve or thirteen, Gaga had just come over from New York and Elinor from Paris to their mother's flat near the Chelsea Embankment. Her two daughters began to quarrel because Gaga, noticing Elinor's short skirts up to the knee and almost above said 'Oh! Those were given up a year ago. They are only worn by negresses in New York today!' Elinor took tremendous umbrage and Great Gran – a very forcible and very lovable character – had a face of thunder at the bickering of the two sisters.

It was her longing to design again that led Lucy to start making a few models for private clients in her flat at Rossetti Studios, in Chelsea. 'I had no mannequins and no showroom, only one or two girls to sew for me. The fitting was done in my drawing-room, which was terribly inconvenient.' The private clients were few . . . and became fewer.

Lucy was lonely in her flat, no longer surrounded by agreeable young men, although her old spirit was not entirely dead. She looked forward to Lady Flavia's Saturday visits and took her to 'thé dansants in some strange High Street Kensington Hotel,' Lady Flavia remembers. 'Thé dansants were the rage when I was about fourteen, and we would be accompanied by her latest hanger-on – a Russian emigré but a queer. Gaga decreed that he should dance with her granddaughter and the poor man had to oblige – we were neither of us very happy.'

From time to time, Elinor told Mrs. Kennedy that she was bestirring herself on Lucy's behalf . . . but not to get her a designing job on any film of hers, for Elinor was still envious of Lucy. She repeatedly told her mother that she would ask whether Hearst (who had known Lucy before the war) would let her write in his papers, for she could then 'live without Lucile', but nothing came of this idea

– probably because Elinor, then in great favour with Hearst, never asked.

The deep-rooted jealousy between the two was as central to their relationship as ever. But after the final failure of Lucile, Lucy never again managed to get the upper hand.

In 1928, Elinor wrote a sad postscript to her mother on Lucy's outstanding career:

Tell Lucy that by the most extraordinary coincidence I came across the rose room pink silk curtains and flowers and the blue gauze stage curtains at a sale. They had been bought and sold and thrown back again. They were, of course, dirty and finished, but I *could not* bear to see them lying there in the auctioneers' cellar (I came on them going down there to see some chairs I wanted) so I bought them and will try to put them somewhere, just to keep them as a souvenir of how beautiful that room was . . . I thought she might like to know they were cared for – the blue gauze did not look so torn and ruined – would she like them for her house? Ask her and I will send them.

Elinor was never at her best when victorious. Lucy behaved in a courageous manner. Though she never succeeded in having her own couture business again, she began to find compensations in the company of her grandchildren and in the other necessarily small pleasures her retirement brought.

iii   Scene 137: Interior The Lady's Suite

The M.G.M. version of *Three Weeks* was not the first film to be made from Elinor's novel. In 1915 the Reliable Feature Film Corporation had adapted the story. There had also been a satirical film called *Pimple's Three Weeks (Without the Option)* made in the same year. Elinor sued the makers, Western Feature Film Co., on the grounds of travesty. Curiously, she lost her case because her original work was termed 'salacious' – an interesting legal precedent which has never been challenged.

On her return to Hollywood Elinor found that attitudes had changed towards her. Metro Goldwyn Mayer were taking the *Three Weeks* project very seriously indeed. As Sam Goldwyn said at the time, 'Elinor Glyn was the first person to put sex appeal into the cinema.' M.G.M. were taking no chances with the mercurial temperament of their writer and unofficial director. Red carpet was figuratively laid out for her when she arrived in Hollywood and everyone from the studio, from Louis B. Mayer and Sam Goldwyn down, met her at the station. A suite was provided for her at the new Ambassador Hotel, a Hispano-Mauresque palace some way out of Hollywood. A pseudonymous author of the time, writing under the revolting soubriquet *Alice in Movieland*, breathlessly reported on Elinor's new setting in a book of the same name:

> She has four or five rooms, including a sleeping porch. Her sitting room has lovely blues and greens which harmonize as those colours do in flowers and their leaves. Besides there are touches of a peculiar orchid shade which is neither pink nor mauve. And an extremely clever cabinet maker who has come from China has made for this room chairs and desks and tables of this green and this orchid shade in admirable Chinese lacquer.

No sooner settled in, than Elinor started to meddle in the casting for *Three Weeks*. With the film already three months behind its initial schedule, she now endeavoured to promote a protegé of hers, as she wrote to her mother at the end of July: 'The boy we hope to get for Paul will delight you – a perfect gentleman of our class and ideas. Oh! So different to those dear good people! And very good looking!'

Eric Glynne Percy was an English stage actor who had come to Hollywood to make his fortune. Elinor's sharp green eyes spotted him as he was walking his dog in the grounds of her hotel and she swooped down on him. On her instructions he dyed his dark curls blonde, and she persuaded Goldwyn to give him a screen test.

But Goldwyn had other ideas – chief among them being the fact that the German matinée idol, Conrad Nagel, was better box office than an unknown British juvenile lead. Elinor was furious. Added to her rage at having her own 'discovery' rejected, was her deep antipathy toward all Germans, dating from Margot's near-fatal illness years before. Goldwyn was made of stuff every bit as stern as was Elinor. After epic storms on the M.G.M. lot, including a notable scene in the studio cafeteria when Elinor burst into hysterical tears at the sight of Nagel, Goldwyn got his way in round one.

This left round two: the even bigger problem of casting The Lady. While not on the epic scale of Selznick's later search for Scarlett O'Hara in *Gone With The Wind*, Goldwyn shrewdly extracted the maximum publicity out of the rejection of the hundreds of candidates for the role. It became the talk of Hollywood. Anita Loos was at the Vernon country club one evening accompanied by Joe Frisco, a successful vaudeville comic who spent most of his time at the race track and was known for his quick wit. The twosome ran into Elinor Glyn who was, remembered Anita Loos, 'as usual talking of the problem it was a find a "lady" to play her Balkan Queen'.

'Leave me get this straight,' said Frisco. 'You want to find some tramp that don't look like a tramp, to play that English tramp in your picture. But take it from me, that kind of tramps don't hang out in Hollywood.'

At length the search ended, to the satisfaction of both Goldwyn and Elinor, with the casting of Aileen Pringle. 'A beauty and a lady!' Elinor wrote thankfully to her mother. 'Quite remarkable . . . she is the daughter-in-law of Sir John Pringle, Governor of Jamaica.'

M.G.M.'s publicists tore the covers off their typewriters and the race for superlatives was on. Aileen Pringle lived a life filled with teas, polo, dancing . . . sleek servants anticipated her every wish . . . every meal was a banquet . . . she was buried in Parisian frocks . . . trips to the great capitals of Europe broke the monotony. . . . Anita Loos confirmed that Aileen had culture: 'I shall never forget the night she trapped us in her parlour and put us on the rack by declaiming sections of that grand old cornball called *The Spoon River Anthology*.'

The film began shooting on August 1. In October, Elinor gave her mother a progress report:

The picture is going splendidly now (touch wood) after endless fights on all sides to get what I want, especially as the director thinks he knows the ways of ladies and gentlemen, Kings and Queens better than I do. (He did not wish Lady Henrietta to rise to welcome guests!!!) The Lady is too beautiful – exactly as she should be . . .

This favourable comment (Elinor was never – for obvious reasons – enthusiastic about her leading ladies) was not surprising: Aileen Pringle bore a marked resemblance to Elinor herself at around the time she had written *Three Weeks*.

Three Weeks was directed by Alan Crosland, a run-of-the-reel M.G.M. director, whose subsequent claim to fame would be that he directed the first talkie. Elinor, concerned that her novel should be transferred to the screen faithfully, was lucky in having, as her art director, Cedric Gibbons – a man ever ready to add another pair of orchid chiffon curtains or a barrelful of real rose petals in the interests of authenticity.

But *Three Weeks*, as written, proved very difficult indeed to transfer to the screen. The central part of the book, being virtually a continuous love-scene, imposed tremendous problems for Elinor's recently-acquired skills in the art of the silent movie and the avoidance of the censor's scissors.

No dialogue meant that action was all-important. But how to get action without alerting the Hays Office, Hollywood's self-regulating censor? Eventually, she solved the problems by inter-cutting the love scene with Balkan backgrounds and, to add spice, introducing a fight on the edge of a Venetian canal.

M.G.M.'s experienced continuity writer had difficulties with Elinor's work. When the queen lies on the tiger skin, quivering with emotion and passion, writhing around and caressing the fur, he wrote:

SCENE 137, CLOSEUP INTERIOR THE LADY'S SUITE
Better than describe this scene, I will simply mention that Mrs. Glyn will enact it for Mr. Crosland on the set. The Lady makes her decision to accept Paul as her lover. She hears Paul coming and indicates for him to come in.

Released in March 1924, *Three Weeks* was enormously successful at the box office in America. It appeared later that year in England under the title *The Romance of a Queen*. The Lord Chamberlain's office, having made a large number of cuts, also disallowed the original title, even as a sub-title.

Elinor's stock in the film colony was now very high . . . and it started to go to her head. Goldwyn – obviously fascinated by the strange paradoxes of her character – had this to say of her:

> I myself believe she plans her personality quite as carefully as she does her stories. When, for instance, arrayed in the most superb evening attire and accompanied by the handsomest man she has been able to find in the assemblage, Mrs. Glyn sweeps slowly through a ball-room; When she murmurs soulfully 'Orange, orange, how I love it! Often I sit in a room by myself and think orange. I fill my whole soul with its beautiful warm rays – I drink them down into my heart – ah, orange!' – then she is showing her supreme ability, not only as the writer who can tell a popular tale, but as the writer who knows how to get herself constantly before the popular mind. I once said of her that she was a great showman, and when she heard my comment she was exceedingly gratified.

But Goldwyn saw beneath this cultivated pose:

> . . . underneath all this pageantry of manner is a heart overflowing with the warmest interest in her fellow beings. One of the waitresses at the Hollywood Hotel . . . once said to me, 'Of all the people I ever waited on Mrs. Glyn was the nicest and kindest and most considerate. I never knew her to be cross – not even at breakfast.' And, after all, the only trustworthy epitaph is composed by the person who serves us our breakfast.

Adulation always produced an adverse effect on Elinor. She now began to believe herself the authority on everything, including business. Alone among people whom she often despised, gullible to flattery especially where attractive and not particularly scrupulous young men were concerned, buoyed up by her huge film earnings, she easily became potential prey for every sort of adventurer then descending on Hollywood. Shares in gold mines and other highly questionable ventures paled into insignificance beside the fifty per cent of all her earnings she had contracted to give to one particular agent.

At the end of 1923, Elinor went back to her house in the Avenue Victor Hugo for a holiday. Juliet and her husband joned her there with the express purpose of forming a company which would take care of her business dealings. Rhys was made chairman of the company which was eventually incorporated on March 1, 1924 to: 'Acquire the copyright in all or any of the existing and future original literary dramatic and artistic works of Mrs. Elinor Glyn and to deal with same as expedient.' The formation of this company did not, however, automatically cancel previously-signed contracts, and it was to deal with Elinor's agent and his outrageous fifty per cent contract that Juliet and Rhys accompanied Elinor back to Hollywood. When Rhys Williams threatened to publish the contract if he insisted on holding Elinor to it, the agent tore it up. Then began the infinitely more complicated business of renegotiating the M.G.M. contract. Fortunately, Louis B. Mayer was the latest in a long line of reasonably hard-headed men to be entranced by Elinor; he even placed enormous faith in her claim to occult powers. Although negotiations were tough, in the end Rhys Williams won.

Rhys Williams then incorporated the company, with various members of the family becoming directors and Juliet as secretary (Elinor did not have a seat on the board). He obviously hoped that this would reduce the number of commitments that Elinor might rashly enter into. His success was limited.

His Hour, her second film, proved a happier experience. The director, King Vidor, having once been a journalist, well understood the problems of continuity. Aileen Pringle played Tamara and a new-comer, John Gilbert (discovered by Elinor working as an assistant director on the M.G.M. lot), played Gritzko with so much passion and conviction that the film made him a major romantic star.

King Vidor had mixed feelings about Elinor. 'Madame Glyn's contract provided that she be allowed to "help" with the production. I was beginning to fear that my abilities as a diplomat, rather than my capabilities as a director, had earned me this assignment.'

As usual, Elinor meddled, as King Vidor recorded in his autobiography *A Tree is a Tree*:

> One Sunday afternoon Madame Glyn telephoned to say that she had a wonderful idea that I could use in a love scene . . . have Count Gritzko caress the cheek of Tamara, enacted by Aileen Pringle, with the tips of his eyelashes.
>
> In this scene Gilbert and Pringle were borne through the streets of St. Petersburg in a troika, reclining only a few degrees above a completely horizontal position . . . I had Jack start kissing Aileen at her fingertips and slowly work his way upward . . . after three or four hundred feet of film he found himself in the vicinity of Aileen's cheeks which he stroked with the recently suggested eyelash caress.

Months later, Vidor was called into the projection room to be shown a group of scenes that had been eliminated from recent pictures at the behest of the Hays Office. 'Second on the reel was the greater part of our troika love scene . . . I was happy that much of the footage had been eliminated, including Madame Glyn's inspiration.'

Juliet now came into her own as far as Elinor (who had always preferred Margot) was concerned. She too started meddling, by 'helping' to write continuity for *His Hour*. Elinor wrote to her mother: 'I am still overcome at the brain of Juliet! She has mastered all the technique which it takes ordinary mortals years to learn.' What Elinor refused to acknowledge was the solid back-up of Hollywood professionals in every area of film-making, including continuity, which meant that her worst excesses could be eliminated along the production line.

Towards the end of the picture, Elinor felt she had been accorded the supreme accolade:

> We had to do the snow night scenes – and one night I had my triumph. It was worth sitting up all night for! The director was ill and asked me to direct the sequence of the Wedding evening myself – a proof at last of what I can unaided do!

Unfortunately, Elinor was now convinced that she could do everything herself.

His Hour was finished at the beginning of August 1924 and Elinor immediately tried it out on a select audience of her new friends, including Douglas Fairbanks, Mary Pickford and 'two experts from New York. They were unanimous in declaring that it is the best picture of its kind (that is of romantic princely modern society) that has ever been made,' she told her mother, adding that the experts told her, 'my value after this as a maker of pictures – not only the author, would go up to top notch in the trade . . .' Elinor had fallen victim to that very Californian Curse she had described two years earlier. By the beginning of 1925, she was enmeshed in its toils, as a letter to her mother of February that year indicated:

> How I loathe Common Things, don't you? One of my chief happinesses here is that everyone tells me I am an uplift. The people don't drink at the parties I honour – they drop their coarse swearing and language – the community calls me 'Madame' and I am treated with the respect of a Queen by everyone. This is worth having waded through misunderstanding and insolence and four years is it not? . . . now that I am great I am going to make pictures which will be a light to humanity. ·

Elinor, however, did not manage to avoid an involvement, albeit an unwitting one, in one of the nastiest scandals of the era. Hearst, by

now a close and powerful friend, invited some friends for a short
cruise on board his yacht Oneida in November 1924.

What happened on the *Oneida* has been a matter of controversy for
the lasty sixty years. Marion Davies recalled later that dinner had been
uneventful – and that everyone had drunk water, to which Elinor had
objected, saying it brought bad luck. One thing only is certain: some-
time during the night one of Hearst's guests, Thomas Ince the producer, died. What the cause was, or even whether the tragedy took
place on board the yacht, is not clear. The Hearst papers said that he
had been taken ill on his ranch . . . but rumours started circulating
around Hollywood almost immediately that Hearst had shot him in a
fit of jealousy over Marion Davies and that he had died on board.

The day after, Elinor wrote a callous letter to her mother:

> . . . I have had such a riotous evening time lately!!! Working all
> day – then at night there have been a series of banquets for Mr.
> Marcus Loew [the owner of the biggest cinema chain in America]
> given by Hearst and Mr. Grauman and then returned by the Inces
> and Mr. Loew. But the last thing has ended tragically – we all
> went off on Mr. Hearst's magnificent yacht on Saturday after
> dinner and on Monday after coming ashore Mr. Ince dropped dead
> of heart failure. He was perfectly well on Sunday. This will put a
> stop to all gaiety for a time.

Even allowing for Elinor's vagueness about dates, this letter is curious.
The yacht set sail on Tuesday, not Saturday, and Ince was dead on the
morning of the 19th – the day Elinor wrote to her mother. She never
mentioned the incident again, but it is worth recording that Hearst
remained a devoted and interested friend until Elinor's death.

Elinor's next picture was *Man and Maid*, one of her favourites.

> I like the new director very much and I think we'll get on, but this
> farce of forcing a director on me at all is the laugh of everybody,
> since he only has to give my orders down the megaphone and is
> not allowed to do a thing on his own. They do it to put up the
> value of the director there (M.G.M.) as they have them on contract
> and doing a picture with me just polishes and makes them (Thalberg
> told me!) so now all the directors are only too glad to work with
> me; not as it was when they insulted me.

Elinor relished her role as a power behind the director's chair.

> I would rather do it than anything else – it is like living thrilling
> love stories instead of writing them – seeing the scenes grow under

your eyes . . . of course, if I had no director and could direct entirely alone I would get the characterisation much finer and the grouping better and the 'tempo' faster . . . the papers have said 'If Elinor Glyn can make the dumb beauty [Harriet Hammond, the star of *Man and Maid*] act, she certainly is a wizard.'

Once again, Elinor not only meddled behind the scenes, but also appeared on screen, as part of the opening title:

What we call coincidence is nothing but the weaving of Destiny's threads for a given end which we cannot see.

Elinor's hand is seen writing these words; then the scene dissolves to show Elinor at her desk signing her name.

Elinor's last two films for M.G.M. were not very successful at the box office, and the percipient Goldwyn sensed that the vogue for lushly romantic pictures of the Glyn genre had had their day.

Her last M.G.M. film, *The Only Thing*, was a 'quickie' designed to wind up her contract as soon as possible. Her meddling on set was costing money, her interference in studio politics off set was causing trouble, too. Elinor, however, was full of enthusiasm for her new film, originally intended as a starring vehicle for John Gilbert. He however was unable to participate (or perhaps did not want to). The excuse given was that he had had his head shaved for his role in Von Stroheim's *The Merry Widow* and the tightness of the filming schedule did not permit him the time to grow a full head of hair again.

The Only Thing was the last of Elinor's Ruritanian romances to be put on screen. Set once more in a mythical Balkan kingdom, the heroine being, yet again, a beautiful young queen, it must have seemed passé even as it was being made. But to Elinor it was perfect:

You can't believe the immense interest the work is for me, now that I am allowed an absolutely free hand in everything. It is like writing a book with living people or painting a picture with human beings instead of colours. And now that I have 'delivered the goods' every department is so eager to serve me and 'obey me blind' as they say here . . . once I had to persuade and plead . . . but that spirit of creation is so strong in both Lucy and me that we just get things as we mean in the end . . . I have invented a new system of backgrounds against black velvet with only suggestions of windows and things – weirdly quaint . . . Gibbons is crazy with joy to do something new . . .

When not occupied with her sets and her leading men, Elinor was beginning to chafe at the restrictions imposed upon her by the structure of Elinor Glyn Ltd. The first note of complaint comes in a letter to her mother in March 1925, when she grumbles of the 'misunderstandings' and 'impossibilities' contained in cables from her directors. The truth was that she had found another unscrupulous hanger-on, a young Englishman called John Wynn. An old Etonian, a good dancer and very attentive to Elinor, Wynn bore a marked resemblance to her old love, Alastair Innes Ker. He started to give her business advice and Elinor mentioned him in her letters home with increasing frequency. 'Mr. Wynn's brains are a great comfort.' 'Mr. Wynn is in New York investigating new contracts.' 'The Duchess [of Sutherland] and I and Mr. Crocker and Mr. Wynn go out, just the four of us, and dine and dance. It seems so entertaining,' she wrote. 'Two grandmothers, both really rather attractive, with two of the very best-looking young men you ever saw, too enchanted to be with us and in years young enough to be our sons!!!' The disquiet of Mrs. Kennedy and Rhys-Williams may be imagined on receipt of the following: '. . . JW's intense intelligence and knowledge of business saves me all trouble, he supervises all the "fan" letters which now come in hundreds – and he watches for the tricks of Thalberg and Mayer.' In July 1925, Elinor made formal approach to the directors of Elinor Glyn Ltd., to hire Wynn as official business representative, after which she maintained she would have '. . . no bothers in the world'.

Wynn's blandishments succeeded: in November Elinor hired him at the enormous salary of £5,000 a year, to the horror of her family who, upon receiving the news, cabled her that this was more than an English cabinet minister's salary. Elinor replied she thought the figure entirely reasonable for the work he was doing. But to her mother, she wrote defensively:

> I am working hard to become free, by that I mean to go where I want and do what I want and give those I love what they want. 'Elinor Glyn' was only meant to help me, but is impossible to operate from England. So as soon as they dissolve the company and leave me free, all will be well. They are going to do this, I hope and believe – I am just going to make this one more picture with Metro Goldwyn Mayer and then go to United Artists.

Elinor was convinced that Europe was finished and that her future lay in America, which was the only place that rewarded her talents. In this, she exhibited many of the same symptoms as had contributed to Lucy's folie de grandeur during her most successful New York days. However, Elinor had not entirely turned her back on Europe, being always ready to welcome distinguished visitors to the film capital. In 1925, for instance, she entertained a brace of Spanish duchesses, Alba and Penaranda, in addition to Millicent, Duchess of Sutherland, and (a reminder of very different days) Lady Ravensdale, Curzon's eldest daughter. Bizarrely, they attended Valentino's funeral together and then Elinor gave a party for her.

Her last days with M.G.M. were probably the happiest of Elinor's long stay in Hollywood. Surrounded by admirers, visited by distinguished European aristocrats, enthroned as social arbiter and guardian of manners and morals she felt herself to be the personification of aristocracy and 'race' in a kingdom she had made her own.

iv 'It'

Elinor's last three Hollywood films were made for her old studio, Famous-Players-Lasky, now called Paramount. It had been the only studio willing to offer her the creative control and the money she demanded. Elinor's first film with Paramount, *Ritzy*, did not do well. It starred two unknowns and was an attempt on Elinor's part to write something more modern. But just when it would seem that 'Madame' had lost her touch, Elinor came up with something that made her more money and attracted more notoriety to her than even the publication of *Three Weeks* had done twenty years earlier.

'It' began as a novella-length story, serialised in Hearst's *Cosmopolitan* in 1926 and then published in book form in America and England in 1927.

'It' was the fruit of Elinor's frequent musings on the nature of who had sex appeal – and why. She developed these musings into the story of John Gaunt, who had 'It', and who through personal magnetism had become the head of a prosperous New York business from an unpromising start in the Bowery. The heroine, whom Elinor called Ava Cleveland, also had 'It', and was well-born and impoverished.

Whether you had 'It' or not became the burning question of the day – and one which Elinor was only too pleased to answer. In an interview in *Photoplay* in February 1926, Elinor defined her term:

> 'It' is the peculiar fascination possessed by men much oftener than women which makes them immensely attractive to all women and even men. . . . 'It' is largely to do with animal magnetism . . . the person who possesses 'It' is always utterly unselfconscious and perfectly indifferent and unaware of anyone's interest in him . . . 'It' is one of the rarest gifts in the world.

The interviewer then canvassed experts. '"It" cannot be explained briefly any more than radio can,' Cecil B. de Mille said portentously. John Gilbert on the other hand waxed poetic: '"It" is like a lamp that glows and glows.' Confused, the interviewer finally concluded that '"It" was . . . well, "It".'

'It' was not something Elinor dreamt up overnight: she had first used the expression in her 1915 novel, *The Man and the Moment*:

I know one particular case of it in a friend of mine. No matter what he does, one always forgives him. 'It' does not depend upon looks either, although this actual person is abominably good-looking – it does not depend upon intelligence or character or – anything – as you say, it is just 'It'. Now you have 'It' and the Princess, perfectly charming though she is, does not.

'It' may not even have been an original idea of Elinor's, it may have been Victorian or Edwardian slang. Kipling certainly used the expression in Elinor's sense in 1904 in *Traffics and Discoveries*:

It isn't great beauty, so to speak, nor good talk necessarily. It's just IT. Some women'll stay in a man's memory if they once walked down a street.

The publication of *'It'* re-established Elinor: suddenly she found herself in great demand as a lecturer and pundit on sex appeal. But it was Dorothy Parker who saw in Elinor's *'It'* a fertile field in which to exercise her own wit, which she duly did in *The Constant Reader*.

. . . in her foreword, Madame Glyn goes into the real meaning of 'It'. 'To have "It"' she says – and is she the girl that knows? – 'The fortunate possessor must have that strange magnetism which attracts both sexes'. (Pul-ease Madame Glyn, pul-ease!).

Having defined Elinor's term, Dorothy Parker then went on to précis the story – in her own fashion:

. . . Ava was worried. Indeed at the end of the very first chapter we get a sharp flash of her terrible state of mind 'What the H--- are we to do?' she said to herself in not very polite English. Madame Glyn, as you see, does not flinch from plain talk. When she presents a street-Arab to us she has him cry 'Well, I'll be d-----d!' It looks to me as if, out in Hollywood, she must have been on the adjoining lot to that on which *What Price Glory?* was being filmed. . . . 'It' goes on for nearly three hundred pages with both of them vibrating away like steam launches . . . and then what do you think? She finds out it isn't the money; it isn't the principle of the thing, either. It is because she Loves. And what else do you think? He was going to marry her all the time . . . do you wonder that I am never going to read anything else?

B. P. Schulberg, a power at Paramount and Associate Producer on the unfortunate *Ritzy*, had a protegée – a former typist from Brooklyn called Clara Bow. He was busy trying to make her into a star and he lost no time persuading Elinor that this pert little red-head was just the person to star in *'It'*.

Apart from the title, the resulting film bore no resemblance to the book whatsoever. Elinor was persuaded by Schulberg to change the emphasis from the man who has 'It' to the woman, and this change enabled her to produce the best scenario she ever wrote: a light, frothy modern comedy not starring a stately Balkan queen but a thoroughly contemporary working girl seen in realistic surroundings, such as the department store which employed her. There is more contemporary truth in 'It' than in any other of Elinor's films and much of this influence can be attributed to the effect Clara Bow herself had on Elinor.

For Clara Bow was very sexy in a 'snappy' modern way – a world away from tiger-skins and trailing purple chiffons. Unlike Lucy who had ruined her career by failing to recognise this new 'type', Elinor was intrigued by her. She had a saucy, mobile face, a mop of bright red hair and a quick line in repartee, delivered in a nasal Brooklyn accent. This of course was of no consequence as 'It' was a silent movie. Nor did it matter to Elinor who (though she thought Clara was common 'just like a shopgirl') had the wit to recognise her comic potential.

Elinor pronounced: 'Of all the lovely young ladies I've met in Hollywood, Clara Bow has "It".' That did it. Clara Bow transcended stardom and became a national institution, the 'It' Girl. Millions of representatives of America's 'flaming youth' danced and smoked and laughed and necked like the 'It' Girl. She reigned supreme as the wayward careless spirit of the last moments of a wayward and careless decade. By 1929 her salary was five thousand dollars a week and Clara, accompanied by her pack of red chow dogs, tore around Hollywood in her red Packard roadster, often accompanied by Elinor, the éminence grise behind this thoroughly modern phenomenon.

'It' remains an enchanting film in which Clara plays a shopgirl who falls in love with the owner of the department store in which she works. The film is very well made – because Clarence Badger, the somewhat pedestrian director, was ill and Josef von Sternberg shot many of the important scenes.

Elinor was once more in her element: coaching Clara as she had coached Gloria Swanson; going on location; meddling with the myriad details of the film; and also making a personal appearance in it, descending a long staircase in her Balkan queen persona, and explaining 'It' by means of sub-titles.

'It' made more than a million dollars for Paramount – an enormous profit at the time. For Elinor herself it was a great financial success and she enjoyed a resurgence of popularity that would not have seemed possible even a year before. Not all, however, were enthralled. *The Bioscope* commented:—

Few authors have boomed themselves so relentlessly as Elinor Glyn. Her latest effort is as astute as it is likely to be effective. Having written a book called 'It' she proceeds to get a picture produced explaining what 'It' is and incidentally appears in the picture and tells the hero what 'It' is. Then for the past year she has been lecturing on 'It' and the new cult has spread across the continent to the east coast.

Taking a short holiday in mid 1927, Elinor went back to Paris. She stayed at the Ritz, the house on the Avenue Victor Hugo having again been let on a long lease. She took her great-niece Lady Flavia Giffard, now being 'finished' in Paris, out and about with her and showed that she had lost none of her zest, as Lady Flavia remembers:

> . . . She brought with her two escorts. A young man suitable in age to dance with me and one older man for herself. As an example of the circles she liked to move in, she took me to dinner at Saint-Germain to a wonderful hotel run by Americans where I sat next to a Danish Prince and was presented to the Grand Duke Alexandre Mikaelovitch the brother-in-law and cousin of the Czar. . . . I shall never forget that weekend in Paris. There was I, a dumpy little seventeen year old with no self-confidence, and I was taken out and given the most wonderful frocks by Elinor and taken everywhere and made to feel at last that I was grown up. She showed me how to put on lipstick, but she over-did the make-up which I had later to reduce. She was used to bringing out Hollywood tarts such as Clara Bow, for whom the phrase 'It' had been invented. Anyway, she imbued in me that I had more 'It' than I was hitherto aware of and I was extremely grateful to her.

Back in Hollywood at the end of July 1927 to make *Red Hair*, the final film under her Paramount contract, Elinor found she missed her family. Hollywood had changed and she longed once more for home.

Red Hair was written to provide a showcase for Clara Bow and to illustrate the passion inherent in the possessors of red hair – a topic dear to Elinor's heart. It was a light, amusing comedy with a final very daring scene in which Clara Bow, recipient of presents from three male admirers, undressed as far as the censor would let her and returned them their presents of clothes in each other's presence, before skipping off into the sunset with the right man.

On this high note, Elinor decided that her days in Hollywood were over. She had made her fortune, she was as famous and courted as she had ever been and she could now, she thought, afford to retire and lead a more leisurely and cultivated existence. But, homesick as she believed she was, she could not yet bear to abandon her splendid life in America so she compromised by going to New York, taking an apartment in the newly completed Ritz Tower and decorating it in the Chinese manner.

In addition she bought a charming 1790 house in Georgetown in Washington which she referred to as 'the garage'. She lost no time in completely redecorating this little house as well; perhaps in the back of her mind she entertained the notion of running a political salon, rather as she had done in Paris during the First World War. She told her mother, in a statement worthy of Lorelei Lee:

> There are lots of gentlemen in the State Department . . . the older I grow, the more I loathe common or bohemian people . . . actresses and dancers and common new rich and artists and musicians! I really only get on with the aristocrats in all countries, and dear quiet low classes who work . . . it is the half and halfs who are awful.

Elinor spent the next year writing magazine articles for Hearst with titles such as *It Isn't Sex – It's Good Pictures* and *How to get A Man and How to Hold Him.* She also wrote longer magazine stories, one of which – *Such Men Are Dangerous* – she sold to Twentieth Century Fox for six thousand pounds. It was the first of her stories to be produced as a talking picture.

Paramount offered her a talkie test in which she lectured on what she now called 'that interminable "It". I was made up as dark as a red Indian,' she told her mother. 'I wore the magenta Lucile teagown, the model Lucy made for Hebe years ago and I am telling everyone she has just designed it for me now.' Elinor found her talkie test rather trying. The studio had been so efficiently sound-proofed it had become air-tight and halfway through she began to run out of oxygen.

1928 and the first part of 1929 went by quickly and pleasantly. There were many parties in New York and Washington, a return visit to Hollywood during which she stayed with Marion Davies at her beach house and saw old friends and colleagues again, and a constant stream of visitors from Europe.

Late in the summer of 1929 Elinor went back to England to see Mrs. Kennedy and the rest of her family on what was intended to be a brief visit. She was never to return to America.

The reason for this is, unfortunately, a simple one. Elinor had been increasingly improvident with the money she had earned in Holly-wood; bad investments and bad advice had dissipated a great proportion of it and there were sudden large demands for American Income Tax.

EPILOGUE

(1929–1943)

'And Loveliest sight of all, in front of the fire,
stretched at full length was his tiger –
and on him – also at full length, reclined the lady
garbed in some strange clinging garment of heavy purple
crêpe, its hem embroidered with gold, one white arm
resting on the beast's head, her back supported
by a pile of the velvet cushions
and a heap of rarely bound books at her side.'

Three Weeks

i *The Price of Things*

Elinor's head was filled with grandiose notions: England in 1929 was a backwater, an unsuitable small stage for her personality.

Unpleasant reality, however, soon intruded. Rhys Williams and Edward Davson told her that she would face tremendous problems if she returned to America for (like Lucy) she had regarded Income Tax demands as being beneath her notice and she now would have to pay enormous sums out of inadequate funds. Perhaps they overstated the gravity of the case . . . but at least if she remained in England they would have a better chance of saving what funds she had left for her old age.

Elinor gave in with (for her) good grace. Her mother had had a slight stroke and this worried her. She had also become closer to Lord Ilchester during their periodic meetings in America and the prospect of a devoted, rich and very grand admirer appealed. Margot and Juliet took Wolsey Spring, a house near Kingston, for her and decorated it to please her in rich rose colours. It was a large house, needing a great many servants and Elinor found this new regime oppressive for, hitherto, she had always preferred to emerge into society from more modest and private accommodation, needing only one or two maids. It had not been her habit to entertain at home, but rather to lunch or dine in hotels and now she felt encumbered with a big establishment to run.

Once settled in Wolsey Spring with Mrs. Kennedy, Elinor, finding time on her hands, had the idea of directing her own film in her own country, bringing to the depressed British film industry all the craft and experience she felt she had accumulated from her Hollywood years.

Another spur for such a venture was the realisation that her name was now virtually forgotten in England. Other romantic novelists were now in the forefront of public attention. Like Lucy, Elinor was left over from a past, remote age. As Beverly Nichols put it:

> . . . after she had been served with a huge portion of smoked salmon, she 'drew herself up' and fixed me with a glistening eye and said 'Tell your readers that *sex has never touched the hem of my*

garment!' It was the most wonderful sentence and it made my luncheon. There was something agonizingly nostalgic about it; it made me think of rich interiors in the nineteen hundreds and sofas and tiger-skins and joss-sticks burning in brasspots, and a gentleman with a moustache – from a Guards regiment of course – fumbling about in the hopes of reaching the hem, but never quite succeeding.

In October 1929, announcing that Elinor would herself direct her first film in England, *Knowing Men*, *Film Weekly* asked its readers 'Can Women Direct Films?' Elinor replied:

> I have almost always had a hand in the making of my pictures, but I have never been proclaimed as a director . . . I have never asked for the credit of production. After all, it only belonged partially to myself and I didn't want the additional publicity.

Knowing Men was shot at the British International Studios at Elstree, directed by Elinor, with a script by her old Hollywood friend, Edward Knoblock. Carl Brisson and Elissa Landi played the leading roles, and Elinor's latest discovery, The Hon. David Herbert, the younger son of the Earl of Pembroke, was the second male lead, as he remembered in his memoirs:

> . . . I don't know why she singled me out for this quite important part, but she pronounced that I had great vitality and an extraordinary magnetism in my eyes which 'came across' in my tests. I wasn't particularly good-looking, and my great fault was that I hadn't got enough chin. Undaunted, Mrs. Glyn gave me facial exercises . . .

After two months of torture, David Herbert was woken in the night by

> a tremendous click. My jaw had come forward nearly an inch . . . and it has never gone back since.

Lucy designed the clothes for the film and Juliet (who had learnt how to cut when she was in Hollywood) cut the film at home in the evening. Even Margot got bitten by the film-bug and persuaded her husband to join Rhys Williams in investing money in the production, to supplement the money Elinor herself had put up.

After a month's rehearsal, filming began in November 1929 and things began to go wrong almost immediately. From the start Elinor had, through the publicity she had engineered, offended other directors who became jealous and obstructive.

Knowing Men was based on a story Elinor had written for Clara Bow which had never been filmed. It concerned an heiress who pretended to be a poor companion to her aunt so as to discover the real characters of her male admirers. The film opened with Elinor, dressed in Ruritanian black velvet, pearls and a plaited hair-do twenty years out of date, analysing the various shortcomings of the male sex. This list was illustrated by vignettes so amateurish in conception and execution as to be laughable. The pace was slow; the actresses appeared ridiculous, clad as they were in Lucy's dresses which looked as if they had just survived a touring company of the *Follies* circa 1915. *Knowing Men* was a deplorable film.

Edward Knoblock took fright at the appalling notices and took out a temporary injunction to prevent the picture being shown in its final form ever again. Pending the hearing, it had to be taken off after one performance. Knoblock lost, but the damage had been done as the film missed its release date and, except for the advance which had been guaranteed by United Artists on delivery of the negative, the film was a complete financial loss.

Joseph Schenck, a Hollywood friend of Elinor's and now head of United Artists, told her he disagreed with the critics' verdict and, unfortunately, he persuaded her to make further films, which he would then distribute for her. So furious was Elinor at the treatment *Knowing Men* had received that she decided to make another film immediately, against the advice of her friends and her family.

This second film, *The Price of Things*, taken from the novel Elinor had written just before she went to Hollywood in 1920, went into production early in 1930. The story concerned identical twins. Instead of having a well-known 'draw' in the lead (and using trick photography about which she understood little) she cast the unknown Tennyson d'Eyncourt twins in two roles. Elissa Landi again took the female lead as the bewildered bride. To raise the money, Elinor borrowed from the bank, from friends such as Lord Ilchester and again from the family.

In spite of Joe Schenck's promise, *The Price of Things* was never released and it was a total financial loss. This caused a great deal of acrimony within the family particularly between Margot and Juliet, for Margot, who felt that Juliet had persuaded her to invest, was now forced to sell her house in St. James's and remove to Eaton Square, then a less smart address.

Why did these two films fail? Apart from the meandering stories and the old-fashioned style, the main reason was that Elinor, in her Hollywood-engendered self-confidence, had not taken into account the fact that she had previously worked with the support of some of the best professionals in their field. Her directors, notably King Vidor, had paid lip-service to her notions; but the camera-work, the continuity, the cutting, the costuming, even the hairdressing were all of the highest standard. Elinor was no Josef von Sternberg and the sheer amateurishness of *Knowing Men* and *The Price of Things* demonstrated that she had absorbed but little of the essential craft of film making.

Their failure left her with virtually no money at all.

Wolsey Spring had to go (much to her relief, for she had never really liked it, nor the decorations supervised by Margot) and she took a small service flat in Hertford Street, Mayfair. Much of her furniture had to be sold, a few of the best pieces going to Hertford Street, and what remained to furnish Mrs. Kennedy's rooms at Miskin where, late in 1930, she had to retire, to live on the charity of her son-in-law.

Although she now had to live on the tiny annuity which had been invested for her by the Rhys Williamses from the savings of her first four American films, Elinor, far from being cast down, immediately turned once more to novels and journalism. She wrote many cheerful letters to Mrs. Kennedy, telling her how convenient her flat was:

> Oh! so comfortable and handy and no responsibilities of servants more than in an hotel! . . . I like solitude and peace and no responsibilities . . . Fate evidently did not mean us to have a settled home – Fate has never allowed me one anywhere or anyhow if one looks back . . . each one I am rooted out from by *circumstances* never any direct action on my part.

ii Red Queen

The late 1920s and early 1930s were a time of gradually diminishing resources for Lucy. Her little dressmaking business run from her flat in Rossetti Studios had evaporated. Juliet had tried for a time to help her, and Elinor had renounced her interest, amounting to a thousand pounds (money she could ill afford at this time).

Sir Cosmo died in 1931, having first made a Will to try to protect Lucy. He left her the income from his estate for life. His trustees were his brother Henry and his nephew Newton Streatfeild. Administration of the trust proved a recurrent problem, as Lucy did not understand that she could not touch the capital.

In 1932 she published her biography, *Discretions and Indiscretions*, which had many of the qualities of observation and wit that hallmarked the best of Elinor's output. It was deservedly popular and brought Lucy a measure, small though it was, of the attention and réclame she still felt to be her due. However, in being discreet rather than indiscreet, she painted a picture of a genius who had been misunderstood by the people who surrounded her; Lucy never changed.

In 1933 Lucy moved to a charming small house on Hampstead Heath, bought by the trust. For the time being, she was very happy. She had a car and could meet her friends frequently. The sisters saw a good deal of each other in the early 1930s. They lunched at the Bath Club; Lucy gave lunches and once a cocktail party for three hundred people at Jack Straw's Castle.

But by early 1934, financial matters were desperate. On January 25 Tweedie, the solicitor, received a long letter from Lucy:

> This is S.O.S. in deadly earnest. I cannot go on somehow until I can get a job. The trustees must do something for me . . . The trustees must hold a meeting as to what can be done about me.

Various suggestions were put forward, among which was that the house in Hampstead should be sold to give Lucy money to live on and that she should live in 'a handier part of London, where she could see her friends more easily' as Henry Duff Gordon suggested to his fellow trustee Newton Streatfeild, but he did not 'look forward to an easy solution'.

Streatfeild wrote to Margot and Juliet asking for help. And what of Esmé? She was ill, she had been ill for many years, she was living in the country. She had never really been well since the early 1920s and was, according to her son, suffering from an undiagnosed hypoglycaemic condition, and was incapable of helping her mother. Lucy's granddaughter, Flavia, was living in Scotland and expecting a child, but her grandson visited her regularly every Sunday.

By July 1934, Tweedie reported to Henry Duff Gordon that he had had a visit 'by request, after office hours' from a Miss Ruby Sutton:

> She informed me that Lucy Lady Duff Gordon was without money in the house, overdrawn considerably at the bank, heavily in debt, and as Miss Sutton feared, in very indifferent health indeed.

An immediate cash advance of five pounds was sent, and from then on cash was provided from time to time for current expenses. But Lucy had to promise to give up her motor. This effectively isolated her from her few remaining friends, and she was terribly lonely. 'She had to learn, over the age of seventy, to get on buses, perhaps in the rain and go to cocktail parties,' says her granddaughter.

Lucy had none of Elinor's capacity for self-entertainment. She had always needed to be surrounded by people to amuse her and divert her from her frequent rages. Now she had but one or two friends who visited, and the loyalty of Ruby Sutton, last in a long line of lady companions. But Miss Sutton had to support herself and could only see Lucy in the evenings and at weekends.

Toward the end of 1934, Lucy started to complain of sciatica, but she proved to have cancer. On March 10, 1935, she went into a nursing home in Putney, thanks to the good offices of a friend, a Mrs. Cunliffe, who paid the bill. On March 25, Elinor told her mother:

> I go out to Putney to see Lucy every other day, so it takes up a great deal of my time and I can't work so steadily as I did. She seems so much better on some days than others, according to the rheumatism in her leg with the weather. But she is much better at the home . . . her friends send her such wonderful flowers – like Molyneux, he sends her roses and lilac. Her room is a bower and all nice books and everything one could dream of.

Lucy died in the nursing home at the end of April. Elinor and her grandson were with her at the end and she died peacefully. Her spirit – turbulent, wayward, chafing always at the restrictions of domesticity and convention – was finally at rest. In her biography she said of herself:

> When I was young I always turned to the last pages of a book before deciding whether I wanted to read it or not, for I held the view that no story which had not a satisfactory ending could possibly be worth bothering about.
>
> I should not like anyone to apply this test to the story of my life as I have lived it and as I have tried to set it down here, for the climax is neither a very romantic nor a very thrilling one. I have had more, perhaps, than my fair share of romance and adventure, but I have crowded both into the earlier years of my life. I am content now to be a spectator. Yet there is something eternally adventurous in us all and I can still look forward to the unknown, the blank page at the end of the book, which has yet to be filled in.

Lucy always did look forward. She once told her mother 'I love changing homes . . . perpetual change . . . moving on always pleases me – never going back.'

The Red Queen never did go back. At the very end she still believed she could, once again, become 'Lucile'.

iii *White Queen*

Lucy's death went unrecorded in Elinor's letters to her mother. Possibly the family had decided to keep the news from Mrs. Kennedy, who was now ninety-four and whose mind, affected by her stroke, wandered far away to the memories of her distant youth and Douglas Sutherland. On April 28, for instance, two weeks after Lucy's death, Elinor told her mother that Lucy could not write just at present, for her hand was very bad, but sent her love. 'She knows you will understand,' Elinor wrote.

Since Elinor's letters to Mrs. Kennedy are the main record of her thoughts and her doings at this time, there is no way of ascertaining how much of a gap Lucy's death left in Elinor's life. The sister, with whom she had fought, whom she had consoled, envied and looked down on, had gone. One Queen, the fiery Red Queen, had been removed from the board, leaving Elinor in sole possession.

There is little sign that Elinor helped her sister when she was verging on destitution. But Lucy's death must have left Elinor feeling lonely, insofar as this essentially solitary woman ever felt lonely, when she still had the world of her imagination for company and the energy to play a lesser, but nonetheless visible, role in society.

By the end of 1934, Elinor was more confident. She had earned enough money to move from her small Hertford Street flat into a much larger flat in Connaught Place, Bayswater, which she filled with the remains of her collection of French furniture and pictures, her silks and brocades, and of course the five tiger-skins. She also had two cats, tigerish creatures – 'Candide' and 'Zadig', so called as a tribute to Voltaire. She had become a legend in her own time and thoroughly enjoyed being interviewed by reporters in search of good copy on the subject of Men, Life and 'It'.

The publication of several new novels provided her with a comfortable income. In 1936, her autobiography, *Romantic Adventure*, appeared and was well received. She drew on her diaries and quoted them and, while the conventions of the time and Elinor's own natural reticence forbade enlarging on such important events in her life as her relationship with Curzon and the desperate straits into which

Clayton's extravagance put her, the book does convey something, at least, of the unique qualities she possessed.

She turned her powers of observation on herself and her experiences. Her shrewd assessment of her fellow human-beings – in particular of the powerful men to whom she had always been attracted – gave her readers insight into the real world of Elinor Glyn – not the legendary world of a queen lolling on tiger-skins, but one of hard work, of courage and of daring.

She went on writing. How could she stop? Two novels came out in 1932, following an inspirational visit to Hungary in 1931. These were in the high romance vein and were *Love's Hour* and *Glorious Flames*. In June 1933, Duckworth brought out a volume of short stories, which included *Such Men Are Dangerous*.

Duckworth offered her extremely disappointing terms for her next novel *Sooner or Later*, and it was brought out in 1933 by Rich and Cowan who also published the penultimate novel *Did She?* in 1934. This, it may be remembered, was the story of the poor but well-born girl who, to save her father from bankruptcy, agrees to be paid to sit for a portrait by the rich financier Adrian Vandene. She then agrees to be kept by him for a period of three months, and in spite of herself falls in love with him. For *Did She?* drew on long-ago memories of her early relationship with Curzon.

Elinor's last book, *The Third Eye*, was her only attempt at a thriller and it was based on stories of the secret service, related to her by a close friend. It came out in 1940 when she was seventy-six.

During the last decade of her life, Elinor finally came into her own socially. Her close friendship with Lord Ilchester opened doors to many grand houses that had been shut in the past, and she delighted in describing to her mother weekends at Wilton with the Pembrokes, at Kelmarsh with the Trees and at Melbury with the Ilchesters. On one such Saturday to Monday she met her old enemy Lady Desborough and told her mother: 'She is still odious.' Elinor never lost her enthusiasm for society or for titles.

She was extremely popular with the younger generation, who often tried to shock her but invariably failed. Through her 'discovery', Lord David Herbert, she had met his close friend Sir Michael Duff, and both young men became devoted to her, Michael Duff often inviting her to weekend parties at Vaynol, his house in the north of Wales. As David Herbert remembers in his memoirs:

Mrs. Glyn had psychic powers. She was a great clairvoyant and we had many sessions of table-turning at Vaynol. One evening when Prince George, later the Duke of Kent, was present, Mrs Glyn went into one of her trances during which she said 'I see the Prince of Wales's feathers dragging in the mud'. Prince George was so angry that he refused to speak to her again for the rest of his visit.

Elinor maintained the traditions of a lifetime in disliking the society of literary people. However, in 1939 she went to a literary lunch at the Dorchester Hotel as the guest speaker and caused a sensation by wearing Candide the cat round her neck as a stole. The cat behaved impeccably. 'Great success,' she wrote in her diary.

On April 20, 1937 her mother, the most important person in Elinor's life, died. She was ninety-seven. Mrs. Kennedy had spent her last years at Miskin, looked after by Frances, her devoted maid. Elinor saw her mother infrequently but as always, when apart from her, wrote to her at least once a week.

Mrs. Kennedy had always been the keeper of Elinor's conscience; the final arbiter in rows between Elinor and Lucy; the mother who had guarded and protected not only Elinor, but her children as well. Apart from the emotional bereavement, Elinor had lost an absent but important part of her life – a confidante to whom she could recount her triumphs and her disasters. She now assigned this role to her younger daughter.

In the summer of 1938 she took a small cottage at Taplow and quite often went over to take Geoffrey Davson (now Sir Anthony Glyn) and his brother Christopher out from Eton. Christopher Davson can remember her asking him, in a loud voice, 'What do you think of LOVE?' as they were having tea, and the embarrassment this caused him.

In 1939 she took a modern flat at Saltdean, Brighton (ironically the building was called 'Curzon House'). She decorated it, as she had decorated so many other homes, in Louis XV style, impervious to the fact that the flat was modern, with low ceilings. She was at Saltdean when the Second World War broke out and she wrote a perceptive entry in her diary on September 5, 1939:

> War was declared on Sunday last with Germany – that pagan doomed country ruled by a mad upstart, evidently under the strong influence of very evil forces. So that it is not like an ordinary war waged between greedy human-beings. This seems to be the first war since the inspired Crusades, which on our side is for purely altruistic reasons. So that we shall certainly win it presently, if we learn the lesson of it in time.

She moved back to London, taking a much smaller flat in Carrington House, Shepherd Market. When invasion became a threat in

May 1940, Margot and Juliet insisted she go to Miskin to live. She hated its isolation and the reminders all about her of her mother's extreme old age which now, at last, seemed to be threatening her too. In September, she went back to London, this time for good.

She found the raids 'truly too interesting! One has to keep saying "I am not dreaming, this is really England and not a wild west show of incessant shooting". . . . I am,' she wrote to Margot, 'enjoying it all.'

Of course Elinor wanted to 'do her bit' as she had done in the First World War, but she was too old and she became discouraged. By 1941 she had begun to weaken physically, though her mind was as clear as ever. In July 1941, Hearst brought back happier, more active times by asking her to write some war articles for America. She went to Downing Street to interview Lord Beaverbrook, then Minister of Aircraft Production. She wrote to Juliet:

> . . . I have been so excited and keyed up by the turn of events in my career and so busy and rushing up here I'll try and be coherent. . . . I was summoned to an interview with Beaverbrook in Downing Street!!!! I was praying that I might be given an *ear* as I had in the last war, to be of use. . . . I got to Downing Street on the tick of 4. I was shown into his room at once . . . he seemed to be very pleased to see me and remembered our former meeting 30 years ago, dining with Blumenfeld at the Savoy . . . he said he thought I was the most wonderful personality of my day and like Cecil Rhodes represented 'Energy'.

Beaverbrook was, according to Elinor, delighted with the resulting interview and passed it for publication immediately, sending her a message that they must meet again soon. 'So there it is darling!' Elinor told Juliet. 'I found my brain came back quite clearly as I was at my old work. I felt young and sprightly and walked jauntily without a stick!'

So enlivened was she by being in demand that she started to write film scenarios again and sent one story, *Destiny or Luck*, to one of her former agents in Hollywood. He was quite enthusiastic about it, but nothing ever came of it.

For the last two years of her life, Elinor failed slowly but surely. She had always seemed to possess an almost supernatural capacity for keeping time at bay – with her self-discipline, when it came to the care of her own body; with her lifelong habit of alternating periods of intense activity and sociability with solitude and rest. But now time slowly overtook her. She was cast down by the news of the death in action of her eldest grandson Glyn Davson and in the summer of 1942 she fell ill, but recovered.

A year later, in the summer of 1943, she fell ill again and was taken to a nursing home, where she died peacefully on September 23, 1943. She was seventy-nine years old.

She had created a durable legend and she lived it to the end. Some weeks before she died Michael Duff and David Herbert went to see her in her flat. Her hair was now pure white, and she was virtually blind. 'She made us sit, one each side of her, in an alcove lined with leopardskin,' David Herbert remembers. 'She put her hands on our two heads and soothed us by saying "I shall die within the next six months, but don't you two worry. The war will be over in under two years and both of you will come through it.'"

Elinor had come 'through it' – triumphantly, for she lived her life the way she had wanted to live it, as a queen. As someone, somehow, above ordinary mortals. She was the queen of romance, and her own definition of it is a fitting epitaph to this extraordinary woman:

> Romance is a spiritual disguise created by the
> imagination to envelop material happenings
> and desires, so that they may be in greater
> harmony with the soul.

APPENDIX A

'Lucile's' Theatre Designs

This is, of necessity, a selected list including only those productions where all the costumes were by the Maison Lucile, as opposed to those of the leading lady.

THE LIARS, 1897
Director: Sir Charles Wyndham
Leading Ladies: Irene Vanbrugh, Mary Moore

WHEN A MAN'S IN LOVE, 1898
Director: Arthur Chudleigh
Leading Ladies: Irene Vanbrugh, Marion Terry

MY DAUGHTER IN LAW, 1899
Director: Charles Frohman
Leading Lady: Ellaline Terriss

ENGLISH NELL, 1900
Director: Frank Curzon
Leading Lady: Marie Tempest

PEG WOFFINGTON, 1901
Director: Frank Curzon
Leading Lady: Marie Tempest

A MAN OF HIS WORD, 1901
Director: Fred Mouillot
Leading Lady and Manager: Lillie Langtry

THE LITTLE FRENCH MILLINER, 1902
Director: Eille Norwood
Leading Lady: Fannie Ward

THE CATCH OF THE SEASON, 1904
Director: Charles Frohman
Leading Ladies: Zena Dare, Maie Ash, Ellaline Terriss

ALICE SIT-BY-THE-FIRE
   A PAGE FROM A DAUGHTER'S DIARY 1905
Director: Charles Frohman
Leading Ladies: Ellen Terry, Irene Vanbrugh

THE MERRY WIDOW, 1907
Director: George Edwardes
Leading Lady: Lily Elsie

THE ARCADIANS, 1909
Director: Robert Courtneidge
Leading Ladies: Irene Vanbrugh, Mary Moore

THE COUNT OF LUXEMBURG, 1907
Director: George Edwardes
Leading Lady: Lily Elsie

THE DOLLAR PRINCESS, 1909
Director: George Edwardes
Leading Ladies: Gabrielle Ray, Gladys Cooper, Lily Elsie

THE FOLLIES

The Follies of 1915 with Mae Murray

The Follies of 1916 with Ina Claire, Marion Davies

The Follies of 1917 with Fannie Brice, Lilyan Tashman, Dolores, Peggy Hopkins

The Follies of 1918 with Marilyn Miller, Dolores

The Follies of 1919 with Marilyn Miller

The Follies of 1920 with Fanny Brice

APPENDIX B

Books by Elinor Glyn

The Visits of Elizabeth	Duckworth 1900
The Reflections of Ambrosine	Duckworth 1902
The Damsel and the Sage	Duckworth 1903
The Vicissitudes of Evangeline	Duckworth 1905
Beyond the Rocks	Duckworth 1906
Three Weeks	Duckworth 1907
Sayings of Grandmamma	Duckworth 1908
Elizabeth Visits America	Duckworth 1909
His Hour	Duckworth 1910
The Reason Why	Duckworth 1911
Halcyone	Duckworth 1912
The Contrast and Other Stories	Duckworth 1913
The Sequence (1905–1912)	Duckworth 1913
Letters to Caroline	Duckworth 1914
The Man and the Moment	Duckworth 1915
Three Things	Duckworth 1915
The Career of Katherine Bush	Duckworth 1917
Destruction	Duckworth 1918
The Price of Things	Duckworth 1919
Points of View	Duckworth 1920
The Philosophy of Love	Newnes 1920
Man and Maid	Duckworth 1922
The Great Moment	Duckworth 1923
Six Days	Duckworth 1924
Letters from Spain	Duckworth 1924
This Passion Called Love	Duckworth 1925
Love's Blindness	Duckworth 1926
The Wrinkle Book	Duckworth 1927
'It' and Other Stories	Duckworth 1927
Love – What I Think of It	Readers Library 1928
The Flirt and the Flapper	Duckworth 1930
Love's Hour	Duckworth 1932
Glorious Flames	Benn 1932
Saint or Satyr? and Other Stories	Duckworth 1933
Sooner or Later	Rich & Cowan 1933
Did She?	Rich & Cowan 1933
Romantic Adventure (autobiography)	Nicholson & Watson 1936
The Third Eye	John Long 1940

We are indebted to Anthony Glyn who first published this list in his biography of his grandmother 'Elinor Glyn' and who notes that in many cases her books were given different titles in the American editions and in some instances in the English cheap editions; thus the same book was simultaneously available under two titles.

APPENDIX C

Elinor Glyn: A Filmography

1915   THE REASON WHY
Adapted from her book
Starred: Clara Kimball Young
Costumes: Lucile

THREE WEEKS
The Reliable Feature Film Corporation
Directed by: Perry N. Vekroff

PIMPLE'S THREE WEEKS
Western Feature Film Co.
No Details

The Famous-Player Lasky Films
1920   THE GREAT MOMENT
Screenplay: Elinor Glyn
Directed by: Sam Woods
Starred: Gloria Swanson, Murray Stills

1921   BEYOND THE ROCKS
Original Screenplay: Elinor Glyn
Directed by: Sam Woods
Starred: Gloria Swanson, Rudolph Valentino

The Metro-Goldwyn-Mayer Films
1923   SIX HOURS
Original Screenplay: Elinor Glyn
Directed by: Charles Rabin
No Details

1923   THREE WEEKS
Screenplay: Elinor Glyn
Directed by: Alan Crosland
Starred: Aileen Pringle, Conrad Nagel
Art Direction: Cedric Gibbons

1924   HIS HOUR
Screenplay: Elinor Glyn
Directed by: King Vidor
Continuity: Juliet Rhys-Williams
Starred: Aileen Pringle, John Gilbert

1925　MAN AND MAID
　　　　Original Screenplay: Elinor Glyn
　　　　Starred: Lew Cody, Harriet Hammond, Renee Adoree

　　　　LOVE'S BLINDNESS
　　　　Original Screenplay: Elinor Glyn
　　　　Starred: Pauline Stark, Tony Moreno

1926　THE ONLY THING
　　　　Original Screenplay: Elinor Glyn
　　　　No further Details

　　　　The Paramount Films

1927　RITZY
　　　　Original Screenplay: Elinor Glyn
　　　　No further Details

1928　'IT'
　　　　Screenplay: Elinor Glyn
　　　　Directed by: Clarence Badger (with additional scenes by Joseph von Sternberg)
　　　　Starred: Clara Bow, Tony Moreno, Introduced Gary Cooper

　　　　RED HAIR
　　　　Original Screenplay: Elinor Glyn
　　　　Directed by: Clarence Badger
　　　　Starred: Clara Bow

　　　　The 'English' Films

1930　KNOWING MEN
　　　　Screenplay: Edward Knoblock
　　　　Directed by: Elinor Glyn
　　　　Starred: Carl Brisson, Elissa Landi
　　　　Costumes: Lucy, Lady Duff Gordon

1930　THE PRICE OF THINGS
　　　　Screenplay: Elinor Glyn
　　　　Directed by: Elinor Glyn
　　　　Starred: The Tennyson d'Eyncourt twins, Elissa Landi

Select Bibliography

ABDY, Jane, Lady, and GERE, Charlotte: *The Souls*, Sidgwick & Jackson, 1984

AMORY, Mark (Ed): *The Letters of Evelyn Waugh*, Weidenfeld & Nicolson, 1980

ANTOINE: *Antoine by Antoine*, Prentice Hall, 1945

ASQUITH, Margot: *Autobiography* (2 vols), Thornton Butterworth, 1920 and 1922

BALSAN, Consuelo Vanderbilt: *The Glitter and the Gold*, Heinemann, 1953

BEATON, Cecil: *Glass of Fashion*, Weidenfeld & Nicolson, 1954

BENCKENDORFF, Count Constantine: *Half a Life: Reminiscences of a Russian Gentleman*, Richards Press, 1954

BLANCHE, Jacques Emile: *Portraits of a Lifetime*, J. M. Dent, 1937

BLUMENFELD, R. D.: *Blumenfeld's Diary*, Heinemann, 1930
   All in a Lifetime, Ernest Benn, 1931

BUCHAN, Susan (Lady Tweedsmuir): *An Edwardian Lady*, Duckworth, 1966

CARTER, Randolph: *The World of Flo Ziegfeld*, Paul Elek, 1974

CHAPLIN, Charles: *My Autobiography*, The Bodley Head, 1964

CHISHOLM, Anne: *Nancy Cunard*, Sidgwick & Jackson, 1979

COMYNS CARR, Mrs. J.: *Reminiscences*, Hutchinson, 1925

COOPER, Lady Diana: *The Light of Common Day*, Rupert Hart-Davis, 1959

CORNWALLIS-WEST, G. F. M.: *Edwardian Hey-Days*, Putnam, 1930

COTES, Peter and NICLAUS, Thelma: *The Little Fellow, The Life and Work of Charles Spencer Chaplin*, Paul Elek, 1951

CURZON OF KEDLESTON, Marchioness: *Reminiscences*, Hutchinson, 1955

DAVIES, Marion: *The Times We had – Life with W. R. Hearst*, Bobbs Merill, 1975

DE STOECKEL, Baroness: *Not All Vanity*, Hamish Hamilton, 1950

DE WOLFE, Elsie (Lady Mendl): *After All*, Heinemann, 1935

DUFF GORDON, Lady (Lucy): *Discretions and Indiscretions*, Jarrold, 1932

FORBES, Lady Angela (St Clair Erskine): *Memories and Base Details*, Hutchinson, 1922

GLYN, Sir Anthony: *Elinor Glyn – A Biography*, Hutchinson, 1955

GLYN, Elinor: *See Appendix B for full list*

GOLDWYN, Samuel: *Behind the Screen*, George H. Doran, 1923

GRACIE, Colonel Archibald: *TITANIC*, Allan Sutton, 1985 (first publ. New York 1913 as *The Truth About The Titanic*)

GREER, Howard: *Designing Male*, Hale, 1953

HARTNELL, Norman: *Silver and Gold*, Evans Brothers, 1953

HERBERT, David: *Second Son*, Peter Owen, 1972

HIGHAM, Charles: *Ziegfeld*, H. Regency Co., 1972

JONES, L. E. (Sir Lawrence): *An Edwardian Youth*, Macmillan, 1955

LESLIE, Anita: *Edwardians in Love*, Hutchinson, 1972

LESLIE, Shane: *Studies in Sublime Failure*, Ernest Benn, 1932

LOOS, Anita: *A Girl Like I*, The Viking Press, 1966
   Cast of Thousands, Grosset & Dunlap, 1977

LORD, Walter: *A Night to Remember*, Longmans, 1956

MACKENZIE, Compton: *Extraordinary Women*, Theme and Variations, Martin Secker, 1929

MARCUS, Geoffrey, J.: *Maiden Voyage*, Allen & Unwin, 1969

MARX, Samuel: Mayer & Thalberg, *The Make Believe Saints*, W. H. Allen, 1976

MORLEY, Sheridan: *Hollywood Raj*, Weidenfeld & Nicolson, 1983

MOSLEY, Nicholas: *Rules of the Game, Sir Oswald and Lady Cynthia Mosley*, Secker & Warburg, 1982

NICHOLS, Beverly: *The Sweet and Twenties*, Weidenfeld & Nicolson, 1954

NICOLSON, Sir Harold: *Curzon*, Constable, 1934

PARKER, Dorothy: *The Constant Reader*, Duckworth

PICKFORD, Mary: *Sunshine and Shadow* (autobiography), Heinemann, 1956

PONSONBY, Sir Frederick: *Recollections of Three Reigns*, Eyre & Spottiswoode, 1957

ROBINSON, David: *Hollywood in the Twenties*, The Tantivy Press, 1968

ROSE, Kenneth: *Superior Person, A Portrait of Curzon and His Circle*, Weidenfeld & Nicolson, 1969

RUTTER, Owen: *Portrait of a Painter The Authorized Life of Philip De Laszlo*, Hodder & Stoughton, 1939.

SCHULBERG, Budd: *Moving Pictures, Memoirs of a Hollywood Prince*, Stein & Day, New York, 1981

STUART, Denis: *Dear Duchess – Millicent, Duchess of Sutherland 1867–1955*, Gollancz, 1982

SWANSON, Gloria: *Swanson on Swanson*, Michael Joseph, 1981

VIDOR, King: *A Tree is a Tree*, Longmans, Green & Co., 1954

WARWICK, Francis, Countess of: *Life's Ebb and Flow*, Hutchinson, 1929

WILLIAMSON, Alice M: *Alice in Movieland*, A. M. Philpot, 1927

WOOLMAN CHASE, Edna, with CHASE, Ilka: *Always in Vogue*, Victor Gollancz, 1954

NEWSPAPERS
Daily Graphic
Daily Telegraph
News of the World
New York American
The Sketch
The Times
The Times Literary Supplement
MAGAZINES
L'Art et La Mode
Bioscope
Film Weekly
Ladies' Field
Picturegoer
Tatler
Vogue

Index